D1596591

CHRISTIAN DOCTRINE
and the OLD TESTAMENT

THEOLOGY in the
SERVICE of BIBLICAL EXEGESIS

GARY A. ANDERSON

Baker Academic
a division of Baker Publishing Group
Grand Rapids, Michigan

Published by Baker Academic
a division of Baker Publishing Group
P.O. Box 6287, Grand Rapids, MI 49516-6287
www.bakeracademic.com

Printed in the United States of America

Library of Congress Cataloging-in-Publication Data
Names: Anderson, Gary A., 1955– author.
Title: Christian doctrine and the Old Testament : theology in the service of biblical exegesis / Gary A. Anderson.
Description: Grand Rapids : Baker Academic, 2017. | Includes index.
Identifiers: LCCN 2016044521 | ISBN 9780801098253 (cloth)
Subjects: LCSH: Theology, Doctrinal. | Bible. Old Testament—Criticism, interpretation, etc. | Christianity and other religions.
Classification: LCC BS543 .A53 2017 | DDC 230/.0411—dc23
LC record available at https://lccn.loc.gov/2016044521

In keeping with biblical principles of creation stewardship, Baker Publishing Group advocates the responsible use of our natural resources. As a member of the Green Press Initiative, our company uses recycled paper when possible. The text paper of this book is composed in part of post-consumer waste.

17   18   19   20   21   22   23   7   6   5   4   3   2   1

CONTENTS

ACKNOWLEDGMENTS

The publisher and the author wish to thank the following sources for permission to reuse previously published material:

Chapter 1: "Apophatic Theology: The Transcendence of God and the Story of Nadab and Abihu," originally appeared as "'Through Those Who Are Near to Me, I Will Show Myself Holy': Nadab and Abihu and Apophatic Theology," in *Catholic Biblical Quarterly* 77, no. 1 (2015): 1–19. Used by permission of the Catholic Biblical Association of America.

Chapter 2: "The Impassibility of God: Moses, Jonah, and the Theo-Drama of Intercessory Prayer," originally appeared as "Moses and Jonah in Gethsemane," in *Seeking the Identity of Jesus: A Pilgrimage*, edited by Beverly Roberts Gaventa and Richard B. Hays (Grand Rapids: Eerdmans, 2008), 215–31. Reprinted by permission of the publisher; all rights reserved.

Chapter 4: "Original Sin: The Fall of Humanity and the Golden Calf," originally appeared as "Biblical Origins and the Problem of the Fall," in *Pro Ecclesia* 10 (2001): 17–30. Used by permission.

Chapter 5: "Election: The Beloved Son in Genesis and the Gospels," originally appeared as "Joseph and the Passion of Our Lord," in *The Art of Reading Scripture*, edited by Ellen F. Davis and Richard B. Hays (Grand Rapids: Eerdmans, 2003), 198–215. Reprinted by permission of the publisher; all rights reserved.

Chapter 6: "Christology: The Incarnation and the Temple," originally appeared as "To See Where God Dwells," in *Letter & Spirit* 4 (2008): 13–45. Used by permission.

Chapter 7: "Mariology: The Mother of God and the Temple," originally appeared as "Mary in the Old Testament," in *Pro Ecclesia* 16 (2007): 33–55. Used by permission.

Chapter 8: "Christology: Tobit as Righteous Sufferer," originally appeared as "Tobit as Righteous Sufferer," in *A Teacher for All Generations: Essays in Honor of James C. VanderKam*, edited by Eric Mason et al., 2 vols. (Leiden: Brill, 2012), 2:493–508. Used by permission of Koninklijke Brill NV.

Chapter 9: "The Treasury of Merits: Faith and Works in the Biblical Tradition," originally appeared as "Redeem Your Sins," in *Letter & Spirit* 3 (2007): 39–69. Used by permission.

Chapter 10: "Purgatory: Sanctification in This Life and the Next," originally appeared as "Deliverance from Purgatory," in *Charity: The Place of the Poor in the Biblical Tradition* (New Haven: Yale University Press, 2013), 162–81. Used by permission of Yale University Press.

ABBREVIATIONS

General and Bibliographic

AB	Anchor Bible / Anchor Yale Bible
ABD	*Anchor Bible Dictionary*, ed. D. N. Freedman et al., 6 vols. (New York: Doubleday, 1992)
ACW	Ancient Christian Writers
AJSR	*Association for Jewish Studies Review*
alt.	altered translation
ANF	*The Ante-Nicene Fathers*, ed. A. Roberts and J. Donaldson, 10 vols. (New York: Christian Literature, 1885–96; repr., Grand Rapids: Eerdmans, 1950–51)
AT	author's translation
b.	born
BEATAJ	Beiträge zur Erforschung des Alten Testaments und des antiken Judentum
BKAT	Biblischer Kommentar, Altes Testament
ca.	*circa*, about
CAD	*The Assyrian Dictionary of the Oriental Institute of the University of Chicago* (Chicago: The Oriental Institute of the University of Chicago, 1956–2006)
CAT	Commentaire de l'Ancien Testament
CBQMS	Catholic Biblical Quarterly Monograph Series
CEJL	Commentaries on Early Jewish Literature
CF	Cistercian Fathers Series
chap(s).	chapter(s)
CSCO	Corpus Scriptorum Christianorum Orientalium
CWS	Classics of Western Spirituality
d.	died
DJD	Discoveries in the Judaean Desert
ed.	edited by, edition
ed(s).	editor(s)
Eng.	English translation / version(s)
esp.	especially
FAT	Forschungen zum Alten Testament
Gr.	Greek
HBS	History of Biblical Studies
HCOT	Historical Commentary on the Old Testament

Heb.	Hebrew	NICOT	New International Commentary on the Old Testament
HSS	Harvard Semitic Studies		
HThKAT	Herders Theologischer Kommentar zum Alten Testament	NIV	New International Version
		NJPS	*Tanakh: The Holy Scriptures; The New JPS Translation according to the Traditional Hebrew Text*
HUCA	*Hebrew Union College Annual*		
ICC	International Critical Commentary		
		NPNF²	*A Select Library of Nicene and Post-Nicene Fathers of the Christian Church*, ed. P. Schaff and H. Wace, 2nd series, 14 vols. (New York: Christian Literature, 1890–1900; repr., Grand Rapids: Eerdmans, 1952)
JAOS	*Journal of the American Oriental Society*		
JBL	*Journal of Biblical Literature*		
JQR	*Jewish Quarterly Review*		
JSJSup	Supplements to the Journal for the Study of Judaism		
JSNT	*Journal for the Study of the New Testament*		
		NRSV	New Revised Standard Version
JSNTSup	Journal for the Study of the New Testament Supplement Series	OTL	Old Testament Library
		PG	Patrologia Graeca, ed. J.-P. Migne, 162 vols. (Paris: Garnier and Migne, 1857–86)
JSOT	*Journal for the Study of the Old Testament*		
JSOTSup	Journal for the Study of the Old Testament Supplement Series	pl.	plural
		rev.	revised
		RSV	Revised Standard Version
JSQ	*Jewish Studies Quarterly*	SC	Sources chrétiennes
LCL	Loeb Classical Library	SFSHJ	South Florida Studies in the History of Judaism
loc. cit.	*loco citato*, in the place cited		
LXX	Septuagint, Greek translation of the Hebrew Bible	sg.	singular
		STDJ	Studies on the Texts of the Desert of Judah
MT	Masoretic Text		
n.	note	s.v.	*sub verbo*, under the word
NAB	New American Bible	trans.	translated by
NABRE	New American Bible (Revised Edition)	VTSup	Supplements to Vetus Testamentum
n.d.	no date	ZAW	*Zeitschrift für die alttestamentliche Wissenschaft*

Old Testament

Gen.	Genesis	Ruth	Ruth
Exod.	Exodus	1–2 Sam.	1–2 Samuel
Lev.	Leviticus	1–2 Kings	1–2 Kings
Num.	Numbers	1–2 Chron.	1–2 Chronicles
Deut.	Deuteronomy	Ezra	Ezra
Josh.	Joshua	Neh.	Nehemiah
Judg.	Judges	Tob.	Tobit

Jdt.	Judith	Ezek.	Ezekiel
Esther	Esther	Dan.	Daniel
1–2 Macc.	1–2 Maccabees	Hosea	Hosea
Job	Job	Joel	Joel
Ps(s).	Psalm(s)	Amos	Amos
Prov.	Proverbs	Obad.	Obadiah
Eccles.	Ecclesiastes	Jon.	Jonah
Song	Song of Songs	Mic.	Micah
Wis.	Wisdom (of Solomon)	Nah.	Nahum
Sir.	Sirach	Hab.	Habakkuk
Isa.	Isaiah	Zeph.	Zephaniah
Jer.	Jeremiah	Hag.	Haggai
Lam.	Lamentations	Zech.	Zechariah
Bar.	Baruch	Mal.	Malachi

New Testament

Matt.	Matthew	1–2 Thess.	1–2 Thessalonians
Mark	Mark	1–2 Tim.	1–2 Timothy
Luke	Luke	Titus	Titus
John	John	Philem.	Philemon
Acts	Acts	Heb.	Hebrews
Rom.	Romans	James	James
1–2 Cor.	1–2 Corinthians	1–2 Pet.	1–2 Peter
Gal.	Galatians	1–3 John	1–3 John
Eph.	Ephesians	Jude	Jude
Phil.	Philippians	Rev.	Revelation
Col.	Colossians		

Other Ancient Sources

2 Bar.	2 Baruch	LAB	Liber antiquitatum
4 Bar.	4 Baruch (Paraleipomena		biblicarum
	Jeremiou)		

INTRODUCTION

The field of modern biblical studies has not always been kind to the study of Christian doctrine. Deep in the mindset of every well-trained biblical scholar is the fear that his or her exegetical work will be labeled "apologetic." By that is meant a less-than-honest grappling with Scripture's literal sense and a willingness to let an objective enterprise be twisted into an act of special pleading for one's own religious predilections. For those working in the field of Old Testament there is an additional danger lurking: the tendency to allow Christian presuppositions to run roughshod over the literal sense of the scriptural text and in so doing impugn the dignity of the Hebrew Scriptures themselves.

In the following chapters I make the rather audacious claim that theological doctrines need not be a hindrance to exegesis but, when properly deployed, play a key role in uncovering a text's meaning. This is not to deny the challenges that modern sensitivities toward the historical character and development of biblical religion have posed for theologians. The epilogue will return to this problem and develop in more detail how the relationship of Scripture to doctrine should be understood. As will be clear from a reading of the entire volume, each doctrine is related to Scripture in its own unique way. There is no single method of reading that I wish to propound.

Each chapter will take up a doctrine and demonstrate how it illumines what the biblical writers wish to accomplish. I should note in advance, however, that this book understands the concept of a biblical author in terms of the presentation of the Bible in its final canonical form. In certain cases—one thinks of the doctrine of impassibility—it is not the case that the doctrine can be sustained on the basis of this or that singular textual example. Limiting the focus of one's investigation in that way would be a disaster for understanding the doctrine. Rather, borrowing the methodology of Brevard Childs, we will explore divine impassibility and other doctrines in light of several intertextually related examples.[1] In addition, the canonical readings offered here will not limit themselves to a single Testament but will often entail the challenging task of relating the Old Testament to the New. As has been a constant in all the exegetical work that I have done, I will propose christological readings of the Old Testament that take the Jewish character and integrity of the text with utmost seriousness. Obviously I would not expect Jewish readers to concur with what I propose, but I very much hope they will see the Jewish contours of these texts honored and respected. A good christological reading, in my opinion, ought to enhance a Christian's understanding of and reverence for the Jewish character of sacred Scripture, rather than the reverse.

I begin with a consideration of the doctrine of God. The first chapter grapples with one of the more troubling texts in Scripture. For reasons that go unexplained, the first two sons of Aaron, Nadab and Abihu, are incinerated when they approach the tabernacle to offer incense (Lev. 10:1–4). How are we to understand what appears to be an irrational outburst of Israel's God? Many modern readers have found this presentation of God's character a considerable impediment to a reverent reading of the story. The worries about Marcion's "God of the Old Testament" return with a vengeance here.

Over the course of my teaching career I have regularly taught a course on the tabernacle narrative (Exod. 25 through Lev. 10). Like several generations of scholars, I puzzled over just what Nadab and Abihu did to merit the punishment they received. The secondary literature on this question offers all kinds of solutions. Each explanation makes a certain degree of sense but only if you concede some important presupposition that is not in the text.

When I read Edward Greenstein's brilliant essay on the problem, it was like an epiphany. He picked up precisely where critical scholarship had left the problem: the text does not provide sufficient information to solve the problem, and additional information is, consequently, presumed. But rather than attempting to square this circle one more time by offering yet another ingenious scenario that the biblical author tacitly implied but did not explicitly state, Greenstein suggested that the very fact that the problem cannot be solved on the basis of the evidence at hand is the intention of the biblical writer. But

---

1. Childs's most important works are *Introduction to the Old Testament as Scripture* (Philadelphia: Fortress, 1979); and *Biblical Theology of the Old and New Testaments* (Minneapolis: Fortress, 1992).

if that is true, what motivated the writer to create such a puzzle? Greenstein turned to the literary theory of deconstruction in order to provide the proper answer. On the face of it this theoretical approach seems perfectly situated to make sense of our story. For in the mind of a deconstructionist reader, an aporia like this is precisely what we expect to find in texts. No matter how intent an author might be on conveying a logical, structurally sound story, it is in the design of narrative (and human life!) itself that some pieces will not quite fit together as intended.

But there are problems with this thesis. Though Greenstein opened his essay with a heavy dose of difficult deconstructionist theory—something, I am afraid, that probably drove away many biblical scholars—it was not altogether clear by the end of the essay, when he began to put this theoretical framework to work on the story of Nadab and Abihu, that it really worked as he intended. A proper deconstructionist wants to claim that every literary text is characterized by aporias, whereas Greenstein argued that the aporia of Lev. 10 was especially appointed by the authors for this story. In other words, the aporia of Lev. 10:1, if we can really call it that, was designed to make a point about human knowledge regarding the cultic order and the power of the liturgical actions themselves to compel the deity to act. In Greenstein's mind, the inability of the reader to figure out what Nadab and Abihu did wrong was meant to show that God is greater than the cultic order and cannot be fully governed by its sacred rites. The more I looked at the issue, the more I agreed with Greenstein's instincts, but at the same time I felt that the theory he used to explain it simply could not be sustained. But the answer was not to jettison the theory—after all, without the ancillary tool of deconstruction, I do not think that Greenstein could have made the discovery. All readings presuppose some sort of hermeneutical structure, even if the author of a reading is unaware of what it might be. But the theory had to be modified so that it could better account for the textual situation Greenstein had so ably described.

For this reason I suggested that we read the story through the lens of apophatic theology. Those who have followed the literature on apophasis will not be surprised by this move since there is considerable overlap between it and deconstruction. But apophatic theology claims that an aporia is not an indication of nihilism and thus of the inability of a text to convey its intended message. Rather, apophaticism claims that because God as an object of human knowledge is so fundamentally different from the human knower, no literary account, however detailed or brilliant it might be, can capture God's full nature. Something will always be left out. This circle cannot be squared. And so Nadab and Abihu's actions remain unexplained because the story wants to inscribe within the reader the sense that, no matter how powerful the tabernacle complex and the consequent control by priestly agents may appear, there will always be elements of the shrine that remain outside the ken of humans. There will always be danger for whoever dares to draw near. There is an irreducible danger to housing God.

This particular essay has always been a favorite of mine because it illustrates what I believe a properly theological reading of Scripture can accomplish. A survey of the standard historical approaches demonstrates that a different sort of literary imagination is required for the brilliance of this story to shine through. In the end, Pseudo-Dionysius represents not an end run around the historical-critical project but the needed tool for that project to achieve its intended goal. Doctrine can illumine what the exegete wishes to explain.

My discussion of impassibility in chap. 2 will surprise many. If there is one theological idea that would appear wholly nonbiblical, it would be this one. How could the deity of the Old Testament, a figure so emotionally engaged with the people who call on his name, be described as beyond emotional affectivity? This task is made all the harder for someone like me who believes that Yochanan Muffs's classic essay on prophetic intercession—an article that puts front and center the affectively engaged quality of Israel's God—is one of the best essays on the subject. Yet it was through a careful reading of his essay (perhaps after the fourth or fifth time through!) in conjunction with Uriel Simon's commentary on the book of Jonah that I came upon the solution to the challenge that it offers.

Central to solving this puzzle was a deeper inquiry into what the theological tradition has meant by the term *impassible*. One thing I have learned over the years is that the biblical guild rarely has much more than a surface understanding of how the various doctrines function in the work of a serious theologian. Nowhere is this problem more apparent than with the issue of impassibility. It is indeed fair to ask whether the doctrine of impassibility really does justice to the character of God depicted in the Bible. But to pursue this question with any integrity, one must begin by grappling with what the theological tradition intends by the doctrine. One might begin with Thomas Weinandy's excellent treatment of the origins of the doctrine and the work that it does in Christian thought.[2] For Cyril of Alexandria, the man associated with the origin of the term, it means not that God does not suffer but that he suffers in an impassible fashion. In this chapter, I explore how the biblical text, read canonically, confirms this theological insight.

2. *Does God Suffer?* (Notre Dame, IN: University of Notre Dame Press, 2000).

It may be worthwhile to say a bit more about reading canonically. One of the strongest influences in my own work has been Brevard Childs, the man who proposed the method of reading canonically. For Childs there were three important dimensions to a theological engagement with the Bible. First was attention to the diachronic developments and how they contributed to the final shape of each biblical book. Contrary to what many have asserted, Childs's "canonical method" was not interested solely in the final form of the text. For those who are dubious, I would recommend carefully reading his treatment of the passages about Immanuel in Isa. 6–12[3] or his very sensitive reading of the prose material into which the revelation of the Ten Commandments has been situated in the book of Exodus.[4] For Childs each level in the development of the biblical text is useful to the theological reader as long as it has relevance for and contributes to an understanding of the text's final form. The second dimension moves beyond the frame of a single biblical book and asks how the books included in the Old Testament are to be read, each in light of the others. For an excellent example of this, consider his groundbreaking treatment of the Psalm titles and their relationship to the books of Samuel.[5] And the final such relationship is that between the two Testaments of the Christian Bible. How is the Old to be read in light of the New, and how is the New to be read in light of the Old?

I will turn to the third dimension after saying a bit more about the second. In my chapter on impassibility, it is important to note how the book of Jonah (as read by Uriel Simon) comments on and deepens the presentation of prophetic intercession that Muffs so brilliantly depicts through the figure of Moses. Thus we can illumine a Christian doctrine by a careful reading from two outstanding Jewish biblical scholars.

The relationship between the two Testaments is an issue that has greatly challenged modern biblical scholarship. Aware of the tragic legacy of a supersessionism that presumed that the "primitive" features of the Old Testament were overcome in the New, many theologically sensitive exegetes have chosen to steer clear of the relationship between the Testaments for fear of offending Jewish sensibilities. I am in complete sympathy with such worries. The Christian treatment of the Old Testament in the nineteenth and twentieth centuries was not always respectful. Yet, the fear of correlating the Testaments—however noble that might appear—has had a very detrimental effect on the laity. Given the general suspicion in the public eye about "the

---

3. *Isaiah*, OTL (Louisville: Westminster John Knox, 2001), 60–81.
4. *The Book of Exodus*, OTL (Philadelphia: Westminster, 1974), 340–75.
5. "Psalm Titles and Midrashic Exegesis," *Journal of Semitic Studies* 16 (1971): 137–50.

God of the Old Testament," the reserve shown by scholars in dealing with both Testaments has unintentionally contributed to the isolation of the Old from the New.

It is particularly on this challenge that the approach of Childs is so productive. For in his mind the two Testaments, each in its own way, contributes to a deeper understanding of the figure of Jesus Christ. The chapters on the Fall of humanity and election (chaps. 4 and 5) provide concrete examples of how the Old might be read in light of the New. The doctrine of the Fall has not been well received by many modern exegetes. And perhaps for very good reason, since the doctrine gives the narrative of the sin in the garden a centrality it never possessed within the Old Testament itself. For many scholars this fact requires a bracketing of the doctrine of the Fall when one reads the Old Testament. This is, of course, easier said than done. For though it might make sense at one level to move all consideration of the doctrine to the New Testament, this would conflict with the explicit testimony of Paul that the idea has its grounding in his (Jewish) Bible. In this chapter I address the question from an angle already taken by Karl Barth and try to make a case for the doctrine on the basis of the Old Testament itself.

A particularly difficult problem for the theological reader of the Bible has been how to relate the doctrine of creation from nothing to Scripture (chap. 3). Contrary to what one might imagine, the earliest proponents of the doctrine do not center their interests on the question of the absolute beginnings of the universe. As a result, the grammatical challenge posed by Gen. 1:1 does not hold as central a place in the doctrine as many biblical scholars have imagined. One should note Thomas Aquinas's claim that the doctrine still stands even if the created order is eternal and does not have an absolute beginning point (though he believed that revelation requires that we posit such a point of origin). What is central is the relationship of God to the world. Unlike the Greeks, early Christian thinkers claimed that God is not just another being—albeit a superpowerful one—among the other beings of the universe. He is, instead, the ultimate cause of all being and in many important respects beyond being itself. All creation derives its being from him and depends on his gracious will to retain that being. As Kathryn Tanner has shown, a key piece of the doctrine involves describing the way in which God governs the created order. If God were just another being among beings, then the limits of the material order—which the Greeks held to be eternal, just as the gods are eternal—would limit what God could accomplish. The sovereignty of God would come at the cost of human free agency and vice versa. But given that Christian theology does not view God's relationship to the world in the way the Greeks imagined it, one is able to conceive of God's absolute sovereignty as not in conflict with the capacity of humans to act freely. When this concept is given the attention it is due, the question of the Bible's support (or nonsupport) of the doctrine looks very different from the way nearly every biblical scholar has approached the subject.

This book contains two chapters on the tabernacle, one of which goes in a christological direction, the other in a Mariological direction (chaps. 6 and 7). In the brief compass of this introduction, I cannot lay out in any detail what these chapters do. But I want to call special attention to the fact that, though both read the Old Testament with the New Testament in view, they do not efface what Christopher Seitz has called "the per se witness of the Old Testament." Indeed, a proper christological reading can only be mounted to the degree that the per se witness is the subject of the exegesis. I continue to probe the Old Testament in a christological fashion in chap. 8, an essay on Tobit (which will, in turn, set up my chapter on purgatory at the end of the book). In the figure of Tobit one sees an individual whose life recalls the Isaianic "suffering servant" and points forward to the distinctive narrative features of Jesus of Nazareth as presented in the Gospels. An important subtheme of this chapter is the claim that this sort of Christology requires the reader to take the Jewish identity of Jesus with utmost seriousness.

My final two chapters take up two (related) problems that are central to Catholic theology: the treasury of merits and the doctrine of purgatory. But I did not write either of these from the more limited perspective of the Catholic tradition per se. Like every other chapter in this book, these probe the biblical texts with a specific doctrine in hand, asking whether those very texts can be illuminated by it. Protestant worries about these particular doctrines are taken very seriously, and I hope that Protestant readers will be able to appreciate and respect the exegetical logic that informs these doctrines, even if they feel compelled to reject some of the conclusions I draw.

As is well known, the Reformers fought strenuously against what they thought was a deep Pelagian tendency in contemporary Catholicism. Reliance on the utter grace of God, they claimed, had been exchanged for a hubristic confidence in meritorious good deeds. I will not venture into whether the Protestant critique accurately captured the state of the Catholic Church in the sixteenth century. My interest is rather different. In the wake of Protestant concerns for safeguarding the character of divine grace considerable anxiety arose about the value of all human works. As a result, texts that had put meritorious deeds front and center such as Dan. 4:24 (4:27 Eng.; one of the most important texts for early Christian reflection on the forgiveness of sins) became subjects of great exegetical contention. A lengthy dissertation (or two!) could be written on the way this verse was understood in the sixteenth and seventeenth centuries.

When I began my research on this problem, I realized early on that I was out of my depth as far as the theological issues were concerned. To make up for this lack of knowledge, I began some extensive reading on the relationship of grace to merit in the thought of Augustine and Aquinas in particular. The work of Michael Root and Joseph Wawrykow helped me to see that there was a legitimate place for meritorious acts in both the Lutheran and Reformed wings of the Reformation. But the accents and emphases were not quite the same as one would find in subsequent Jewish and Roman Catholic thought.

The need for biblical scholars to attend to the theological literature became most apparent to me when I was rereading E. P. Sanders's landmark volume, *Paul and Palestinian Judaism*. He did an outstanding job of showing how commandment keeping was a way not of earning God's grace but of growing into the elected status that was conferred on every Jew at birth. Yet certain issues that dogged the Reformers continued to dog Sanders, even though he was not an overly theological reader himself. The Reformation has had a long reach. John Barclay has made considerable advances on this front.[6] This is certainly to the credit of Sanders, who provided the motivation and initial compass points for Barclay's efforts. But it is striking, nevertheless, that Barclay's insights, as important as they are, do not really take us much beyond the picture drawn by Aquinas, who was in turn shaped by the later works of Saint Augustine. Reading the Bible theologically is often a demanding enterprise that requires familiarity with the field of historical theology. Even nontheological readers can benefit from having some theological sophistication.

The chapter on purgatory probably needs a bit more explanation. In his book on charity David Downs takes me to task as a Catholic apologist—a label, as I mentioned at the beginning of this chapter, that no self-respecting biblical scholar would wish to bear.[7] A serious accusation indeed! Here we see firsthand the perils of engaging in theological exegesis, at least as a Catholic in a domain long ruled by Protestants. In this chapter, however, I do not make the strong claim that Downs would have a right to worry about. That

---

6. John Barclay, "Grace and Transformation of Agency in Christ," in *Redefining First-Century Jewish and Christian Identities: Essays in Honor of E. P. Sanders*, ed. Fabian E. Udoh (Notre Dame, IN: University of Notre Dame Press, 2008), 372–89.

7. *Alms: Charity, Reward, and Atonement in Early Christianity* (Waco: Baylor University Press, 2016).

is, my point is not to show the necessity of affirming the doctrine of purgatory for anyone who wishes to read Scripture correctly, as I do in my chapters on apophaticism and impassibility. My concerns are much more modest in scope. Granted that the notion of purgatory is nowhere explicitly stated in Scripture, is it possible nonetheless to see biblical warrants for affirming it? As I say near the end of the chapter, a contemporary retrieval of the doctrine will surely be subject to the theological predilections and ecclesial affiliation of the interpreter. But for those who do affirm it, I wish to lay out why the scriptural teaching on the forgiveness of sins makes such a notion plausible even if it cannot compel all and sundry to believe in it.

Let me conclude by saying a few words about the origins of this book. Over the course of my career I have taken a serious interest in the history of exegesis and the use of Scripture in theological argument. The chapters of this book are the fruits of these various explorations. Each of the chapters save one (that on *creatio ex nihilo*) originally appeared as a journal article or in a volume of collected essays. Some of them have been extensively revised for this book (e.g., the two chapters on the tabernacle), while others have been reprinted here in nearly the same form as their original publication (e.g., the chapter on apophatic theology). As a result of their disparate origins, some chapters reflect on the relationship of doctrine to exegesis in very explicit terms, and others address the subject in a more subtle and understated fashion.

The table of contents reflects the way the various essays sorted themselves out, not the logic that informed their composition. As a result, the chronological template (proceeding from creation to final consummation) should not be pushed too far regarding its hermeneutical intentions. One reader of the manuscript, for example, wondered whether the placement of the two chapters on Catholic doctrine at the very end of the book represented the true telos of the project, as if the author were orienting his readers toward Rome. That is certainly not the case. Though this book does not shy away from Catholic theology, it was written with the hope that Protestant and Jewish readers would also find it of value.

PART 1

"Who Is a God Like You?"

1

Apophatic Theology

The Transcendence of God and the Story of Nadab and Abihu

The story of the tragic deaths of Nadab and Abihu has bothered readers for centuries. As Edward Greenstein observes, the tale is a "model of undecidability. . . . It looks to most readers like a punishment in search of a crime."[1] In this chapter I suggest that this manner of formulating the problem points toward its solution. When read through an apophatic lens, the narrative shows us what we can and cannot know about God's presence in the liturgical life of ancient Israel. Apophatic theology does not simply solve a textual puzzle; rather, it allows the reader to plumb the depths of biblical religion.

One of the strangest stories in the Bible is that of Nadab and Abihu in Lev. 10. Immediately after the consecration of the priesthood (Lev. 8) and the miraculous consumption of the sacrifices on the eighth day (Lev. 9:24), these two priests offer *'ēš zārâ* ("strange fire") and are incinerated on the spot (Lev. 10:1–2). In the Jewish postbiblical liturgical reading cycle of the synagogue, this tale is paired with the death of Uzzah when he tries to steady the ark in 2 Sam. 6,[2] but Greenstein has argued that there are innerbiblical grounds for this association: "Uzzah was the son of Abinadab, and this name has been

---

1. Edward Greenstein, "Deconstruction and Biblical Narrative," *Prooftexts* 9 (1989): 43–71, here 56.
2. See Michael Fishbane, *Haftarot: The Traditional Hebrew Text with the New JPS Translation* (Philadelphia: Jewish Publication Society, 2002), 120–21.

constructed from Abi[hu] and Nadab."[3] Though my emphasis will be on Nadab and Abihu, I wish to claim that both stories explore the theme of divine holiness within the framework of God's choice to dwell among the Israelites.

The Danger of the Ark in Israel's History

The first thing the reader must bear in mind is the Bible's assumption that God has really taken up residence in the tabernacle. Michael Wyschogrod, in an essay on the notion of incarnation in the Jewish tradition, has argued: "God has undertaken to enter the world and to dwell in a place."[4] But this deeply "incarnational" character of the tabernacle carries a particular danger along with it: individuals will be tempted to co-opt either the building itself (cf. Jer. 7) or its most important artifact—the ark—to their own political and/or religious advantage and so compromise the freedom of God. We can see this danger enacted in the so-called ark narrative in the books of Samuel.[5] This narrative opens with Israel suffering a terrible defeat at the hands of the Philistines. The troops subsequently return to camp and the elders pose the obvious question: "Why has the LORD put us to rout today before the Philistines?" (1 Sam. 4:3a). The reader knows the answer: the sins of Hophni and Phineas, the sons of Eli. But the elders do not share this knowledge. Though they ask the right question, they do not wait for an answer. Their inquiry turns out to be less a lament over Israel's sin than a (subtle) challenge that God take immediate action: "Let us bring the ark of the covenant of the LORD here from Shiloh,

3. Edward Greenstein, "An Inner-Biblical Midrash of the Nadav and Avihu Episode" [in Hebrew], in *Proceedings of the Eleventh World Congress of Jewish Studies, Jerusalem, June 22–29, 1993* (Jerusalem: World Union of Jewish Studies, 1994), 71–78, here 71.

4. Michael Wyschogrod, "Incarnation," *Pro Ecclesia* 2 (1993): 208–15, here 210. For a more detailed discussion of the same, see Michael Wyschogrod, "A Jewish Perspective on Incarnation," *Modern Theology* 12 (1996): 195–209. I am, of course, eliding the dissenting voice of the Deuteronomist; see Benjamin D. Sommer, *The Bodies of God and the World of Ancient Israel* (Cambridge: Cambridge University Press, 2009), 99–108. But my point in this opening paragraph concerns the larger canonical picture, which was decisively shaped by the Priestly school.

5. The classic treatment is that of Leonhard Rost, *The Succession to the Throne of David*, trans. Michael D. Rutter and David M. Gunn (Sheffield: Almond, 1982). Still one of the best treatments is Patrick D. Miller and J. J. M. Roberts, *The Hand of the Lord: A Reassessment of the "Ark Narrative" in 1 Samuel* (Baltimore: Johns Hopkins University Press, 1977). For a survey of the literature, see Keith Bodner, "Ark-Eology: Shifting Emphases in 'Ark Narrative' Scholarship," *Currents in Biblical Research* 4 (2006): 169–97. The analysis found below was first expressed in Gary A. Anderson, "Towards a Theology of the Tabernacle and Its Furniture," in *Text, Thought, and Practice in Qumran and Early Christianity*, ed. Ruth A. Clements and Daniel R. Schwartz (Leiden: Brill, 2009), 161–94, here 164–66. It has subsequently been expanded in the dissertation of Mark Enemali, "The Danger of Transgression against Divine Presence" (PhD diss., University of Notre Dame, 2014).

so that he may come among us and save us from the power of our enemies" (4:3b). As André Caquot and Philippe de Robert conclude: "All this seems to suggest a certain arrogance in the attitude of the elders of Israel."[6]

This stratagem appears promising at first. For when the Philistines learn of the arrival of the ark, they quake in fear: "Woe to us! Who can deliver us from the power of these mighty gods? These are the gods who struck the Egyptians with every sort of plague in the wilderness" (4:8). But calmer heads prevail and they venture forth to battle. The results for the Israelites, however, are devastating: "So the Philistines fought; Israel was defeated, and they fled, everyone to his home. There was a very great slaughter, for there fell of Israel thirty thousand foot soldiers. The ark of God was captured; and the two sons of Eli, Hophni and Phinehas, died" (4:10–11).

The precise character and gravity of Israel's sin becomes clearer when we compare the Israelite reaction to their initial defeat with what happens to the Israelite armies at Ai (Josh. 7).[7] Just as in 1 Sam. 4, the Israelites suffer a terrible defeat due to an unknown sin: Achan (7:2–5), the narrator informs us, has taken booty for himself in violation of Mosaic law (7:1). After the return of the defeated soldiers, Joshua and the tribal elders tear their clothes, put ashes on their heads, and fall on their faces before the ark, imploring God to explain the reason for the defeat.

> Then Joshua tore his clothes, and fell to the ground on his face before the ark of the LORD until the evening, he and the elders of Israel; and they put dust on their heads. Joshua said, "Ah, Lord GOD! Why have you brought this people across the Jordan at all, to hand us over to the Amorites so as to destroy us? Would that we had been content to settle beyond the Jordan! O LORD, what can I say, now that Israel has turned their backs to their enemies! The Canaanites and all the inhabitants of the land will hear of it, and surround us, and cut off our name from the earth. Then what will you do for your great name?" (Josh. 7:6–9)

God is quick to answer: Achan's sin has led to Israel's defeat. They must attend to this misdeed before any other military action can be attempted (7:12–26).

---

6. This quotation and the proposal that bringing the ark constitutes a challenge to the deity to act can be found in André Caquot and Philippe de Robert, *Les livres de Samuel*, CAT (Geneva: Labor et Fides, 1994), 77. They also make the astute observation that the elders' proposal to bring the ark into battle constitutes a sin at least as grave as, if not more grave than, that of Hophni and Phineas: "But the taking of the ark, which appears as an exceptional act, a sort of last resort before a failure, will cause a much more serious failure, and the author wants to accent the respective responsibilities" (78).

7. The importance of this intertext has been neglected in much of the secondary literature. The only reference I could find was that of Robert Chisholm, *1 and 2 Samuel*, Teach the Text Commentary Series (Grand Rapids: Baker Books, 2013), 27.

It is striking how differently the Israelites behave in 1 Sam. 4. Instead of taking the opportunity to appeal to God in the deliberate and solemn fashion that we find in Joshua (tearing of clothes, placing ashes on their heads, and falling on their faces before the ark), they simply pose what appears to be a perfunctory question: "Why has the LORD put us to rout?" Eschewing a posture of penance and allowing God no time to respond, the elders concoct their own solution: they race to the shrine and remove the ark of the covenant, believing that its sacramental agency can assure them a victory. By failing to address the sin that occasioned the terrible defeat, the elders have unwittingly turned the ark into something of a lucky charm.

We can contrast this aberrant understanding of the power of the ark with David's understanding in 2 Sam. 15:25. Here is a man who possesses a divine promise regarding the eternal character of his kingdom (2 Sam. 7), but even with this promissory note in hand, when he is driven from the city of Jerusalem by his upstart son, Absalom, he refuses to use the ark as a guarantee of safe return.

> Abiathar came up, and Zadok also, with all the Levites, carrying the ark of the covenant of God. They set down the ark of God, until the people had all passed out of the city. Then the king said to Zadok, "*Carry the ark of God back into the city. If I find favor in the eyes of the LORD, he will bring me back and let me see both it and the place where it stays. But if he says, 'I take no pleasure in you,'* here I am, let him do to me what seems good to him." . . . So Zadok and Abiathar carried the ark of God back to Jerusalem, and they remained there. (2 Sam. 15:24–26, 29, emphasis added)

David realizes that everything that is taking place is the result of his dalliance with Bathsheba, just as the prophet Nathan predicted. Though David has no doubts about the power of the ark, he is spiritually mature enough to realize that it will provide no advantage in his penitential state.[8] The freedom of God is honored precisely in respect to the object to which God has tied his presence.

For this reason the ark narrative comes to a preliminary conclusion in 1 Sam. 6 with the story of the ark's return to Israel and the slaying of those in Beth-Shemesh who greeted its arrival improperly.[9] In response to their grave

8. This is not to say that David has altogether set aside any concern for his future. His advice that Hushai return to Jerusalem to counter the counsel of Ahithophel indicates that David knows that God's providence requires his own active agency. But this action only sets in broader relief David's refusal to use the ark as an aide in securing his restoration to the throne.

9. I call this a "preliminary conclusion" intentionally. Miller and Roberts claim that the relocation of the ark to Kiriath-jearim brings the narrative to full closure (*Hand of the Lord*, 35–36). To be sure, a lesson has been learned about the danger of using the ark as a "lucky charm,"

misdeed, the people cry out: "Who is able to stand before the LORD, this holy God?" (1 Sam. 6:20). The implied answer is obvious: no mortal should presume to be safe when standing before the God of Israel.[10] This is the lesson to be learned from the improper treatment of the ark back at the beginning of the ark narrative. God's presence in the ark is not to be taken lightly. The ark is no lucky charm. The men of Beth-Shemesh do the rational thing: they forward this dangerous cargo to the inhabitants of Kiriath-jearim.

What Did Nadab and Abihu Do Wrong?

This brings me to the subject of this chapter, the incense offering of Nadab and Abihu. The story follows upon the theophany that was the climax of the ceremony of consecration on the eighth day: "Fire came out from the LORD and consumed the burnt offering and the fat on the altar; and when all the people saw it, they shouted and fell on their faces" (Lev. 9:24). Immediately thereafter we read:

> Now Aaron's sons, Nadab and Abihu, each took his censer, put fire in it, and laid incense on it; and they offered strange fire [ʾēš zārâ] before the LORD, such as he had not commanded them. And fire came out from the presence of the LORD and consumed them, and they died before the LORD. Then Moses said to Aaron, "This is what the LORD meant when he said,
>
>> 'Through those who are near me
>>   I will show myself holy,
>> and before all the people
>>   I will be glorified.'"
>
> And Aaron was silent. (Lev. 10:1–3 NRSV alt.)

The story about Nadab and Abihu's cultic error has puzzled interpreters for centuries—going all the way back to Philo of Alexandria.[11] Christian Frevel sums things up well: "The short episode raises more questions than it

---

but the Israelites remain uneasy as to the nature and character of the ark. The close of 1 Sam. 6 points logically toward 2 Sam. 6, when the ark will find its final resting spot in Jerusalem. The text in question (1 Sam. 6:13) is quite difficult. See the standard commentaries for a discussion of the text-critical problems. In this instance, lower and higher criticism cannot be separated.

10. The connection of this question to that posed to pilgrims in Pss. 15:1 and 24:3 is obvious and important. All three texts inscribe within the reader the concern not to presume on the Lord's presence within the ark.

11. The literature on the reception history of this pericope is rather large. For a survey, see Robert Kirschner, "The Rabbinic and Philonic Exegeses of the Nadab and Abihu Incident (Lev. 10:1–6)," *JQR* 73 (1983): 375–93; Avigdor Shinan, "The Sin of Nadab and Abihu in Rabbinic

answers."[12] Before entertaining some of the proposed solutions to the challenges this text poses, let us look at the story within its present canonical environment.

A few basic structural factors must be borne in mind before we can ask what Nadab and Abihu have done wrong. First of all, it is important to note that chaps. 8–10 open with a reference to the "taking" of various materials that are necessary for the ritual:[13]

> The LORD spoke to Moses saying: "*Take* Aaron and his sons with him, the vestments, the anointing oil, the bull of sin offering." (Lev. 8:1–2)

> On the eighth day Moses . . . said to Aaron: "*Take* a bull calf for a sin offering." (Lev. 9:1–2)

> Now Aaron's sons, Nadab and Abihu, each *took* his censer. (Lev. 10:1)

The first two narrative examples take special care to underscore that the "taking" in question was done according to a legitimate command:

> And Moses did as the LORD commanded him. (Lev. 8:4)

> They brought what Moses commanded. (Lev. 9:5)

But our third example, Lev. 10, diverges abruptly from this pattern:

> Nadab and Abihu, each took his censer . . . such as [the LORD] had not commanded them. (10:1)

James Watts has noted that the last clause of 10:1 ("as [the LORD] had not commanded them") is not simply different from what was said in 8:4 and 9:5. Rather, it stands athwart seven citations of this compliance formula ("Moses/Aaron did as the LORD commanded him") in chap. 8 and three more in chap. 9. Watt captures the literary effect quite well: "The intrusion of the negative

---

Literature" [Hebrew], *Tarbiz* 48 (1978–79): 201–14; and Jacob Milgrom, *Leviticus 1–16*, AB 3 (New York: Doubleday, 1991), 633–35.

12. "Die kurze Episode löst mehr Fragen aus, als daß sie Antworten gibt." Christian Frevel, "'Und Mose hörte (es), und es war gut in seinen Augen' (Lev 10,20): Zum Verhältnis von Literargeschichte, Theologiegeschichte und innerbiblischer Auslegung am Beispiel von Lev 10," in *Gottes Name(n): Zum Gedenken an Erich Zenger*, ed. Ilse Müllner et al., HBS 71 (Freiburg: Herder, 2012), 104–36, here 114.

13. Thomas Hieke, *Levitikus 1–15*, HThKAT (Freiburg: Herder, 2014), 377–78; cf. Milgrom, *Leviticus 1–16*, 596.

particle ["such as he had *not* commanded them"] comes like a thunderclap, an aural shock to a listening audience just as YHWH's consuming fire presented a visual shock to the watching Israelites in the story."[14] This raises an important question: Why did Nadab and Abihu bring incense in the first place?

For some interpreters, that Nadab and Abihu did something that was not commanded is all we need to know to explain the punishment. Because the cult stands squarely under the authority of God, any freelancing is strictly forbidden. Nadab and Abihu are punished for going beyond what was prescribed. This sounds eminently reasonable, but the literary character of Lev. 9 suggests another way of understanding the problem.

Ritually, we must distinguish Lev. 8 from chaps. 9–10. Chapter 8 describes the ordination of Aaron and his sons to the priesthood, which takes place over seven days. Chapter 9, on the other hand, describes the rituals of the eighth day, which lead to the dramatic theophany that climaxes the entire tabernacle narrative. Leviticus 8 is distinctive in that every ritual action that takes place has been carefully scripted in Exod. 29:1–37. Compare, for example, the commandment regarding the burnt offering in Exod. 29:15–18 with the execution of that command in Lev. 8:18–21:

> Then you shall take one of the rams, and Aaron and his sons shall lay their hands on the head of the ram, and you shall slaughter the ram, and shall take its blood and dash it against all sides of the altar. Then you shall cut the ram into its parts, and wash its entrails and its legs, and put them with its parts and its head, and turn the whole ram into smoke on the altar; it is a burnt offering to the LORD; it is a pleasing odor, an offering by fire to the LORD. (Exod. 29:15–18)

> Then he brought forward the ram of burnt offering. Aaron and his sons laid their hands on the head of the ram, and it was slaughtered. Moses dashed the blood against all sides of the altar. The ram was cut into its parts, and Moses turned into smoke the head and the parts and the suet. And after the entrails and the legs were washed with water, Moses turned into smoke the whole ram

---

14. James Watts, *Leviticus 1–10*, HCOT (Leuven: Peeters, 2013), 512–13. Gordon Wenham says much the same thing:

> Throughout chs. 8 and 9 the obedience of Moses and Aaron is constantly stressed (8:4, 9, 13, 17, 21, 29, 36; 9:5, 7, 10, 21). Every step they take is in obedience to a divine command directly given or mediated by Moses. Both chapters open with such a word (v. 2). But the action in ch. 10 commences without any divine directives. In language very reminiscent of ch. 8 we learn of Nadab and Abihu taking the initiative themselves. The alert listener or reader at once senses that there is something wrong. This scene does not begin like the previous two. It is structured differently. Almost immediately the narrative explains what is wrong: the fire they offered was "not commanded." (*The Book of Leviticus*, NICOT [Grand Rapids: Eerdmans, 1979], 134)

on the altar; it was a burnt offering for a pleasing odor, an offering by fire to the LORD, as the LORD commanded Moses. (Lev. 8:18–21)

The same is true, *mutatis mutandis*, for the relationship of all the sacrificial instructions in Exod. 29 to their execution in Lev. 8. Nothing has been left to chance. God has laid out all the rules in precise detail.

In comparison to this, the rites of the eighth day, described in Lev. 9, unfold very differently.[15] In this chapter Aaron and his sons must consult the general rules for sacrifice laid out in Lev. 1–7 and discern which ones apply to the current circumstances.[16] Contrast, for example, the pattern found in Lev. 8, wherein Moses executes the commands already given and is commended for acting "just as the LORD commanded [him]," with what we find in Lev. 9:16: "He presented the burnt offering, and sacrificed it *according to regulation* [כמשפט]." The phrase "according to regulation" refers the reader back to the generic laws (what I will call "the priestly manual") for the burnt offering in Lev. 1.[17]

This is no small difference. In a word, the period of Mosaic supervision has drawn to a close, and from now on the responsibility will rest on the priests to "check the manual," so to speak, as to what comes next. As we have seen, this is exemplified in the case of the people's burnt offering (Lev. 9:16). But we could argue similarly with respect to Nadab and Abihu's incense offering. As scholars have long noted, the telos of the tabernacle narrative is described in Exod. 29:42b–46, a text that is sandwiched between the laws for the daily animal and incense offerings (29:38–42a and 30:1–10).[18] Indeed, the laws for the animal *tāmîd* blend almost imperceptibly into a description

---

15. On the enormous difference between these two chapters, see Andreas Ruwe, "The Structure of the Book of Leviticus in the Narrative Outline of the Priestly Sinai Story (Exod. 19:1–Num. 10:10*)," in *The Book of Leviticus: Composition and Reception*, ed. Rolf Rendtorff and Robert A. Kugler, VTSup 93 (Leiden: Brill, 2002), 55–78, here 67. But it should be noted that I do not agree with Ruwe's claim that the book of Leviticus as a whole should be divided into two parts, chaps. 1–8 and 9–26. Chapters 8–10 remain something of a unity in my mind, notwithstanding the significant caesura between 8 and 9.

16. See Rolf Rendtorff, *Leviticus*, BKAT 3 (Neukirchen-Vluyn: Neukirchener Verlag 1985), 298; and Ruwe, "Structure," 68: "The sacrificial regulations in 1:1–7:37, however, refer only to the first offering of Israel through Aaron and the Aaronites, celebrated *following the consecration*, and all further offerings of the people." Of course, we should not overstate the matter: the sin offering that the priests offer for themselves will vary from what was prescribed in Lev. 4.

17. For a similar use of the phrase "according to regulation" (כמשפט), see Lev. 5:10, which also functions as an abbreviation of a rite and refers the reader back to the sacrificial law of Lev. 1.

18. Among others, see Erhard Blum, *Studien zur Komposition des Pentateuch* (Berlin: de Gruyter, 1990), 297; Christophe Nihan, *From Priestly Torah to Pentateuch*, FAT 25 (Tübingen: Mohr Siebeck, 2007), 34; and Sommer, *Bodies of God*, 100.

of God's indwelling the tabernacle complex—the presumption being that once the tabernacle has been constructed (Exod. 40) and the priests ordained (Lev. 8, fulfilling the commands of Exod. 29:1–37), the morning and evening *tāmîd* ("regular") offerings are to begin. This would include the offering of a sheep at the outer bronze altar (Exod. 29:38–41) and the incense offering at the inner golden altar (30:7–10).[19] Given the structure of Exod. 29:1–30:10 (seven days of ordination followed immediately by the two *tāmîd* offerings), one might have expected that once the commands regarding priestly ordination had been completed in Lev. 8 that Aaron and his sons would commence their regular daily routine with respect to the *tāmîd* offerings. The synagogue mosaic at Sepphoris depicts the rites of Lev. 9 in just this fashion.[20] To our surprise, however, Lev. 9 opens with a set of unexpected commands regarding the ritual of the eighth day that are ordered to secure the public theophany at the close of the chapter (v. 24).

The animal *tāmîd* offerings, however, have not been forgotten, just displaced. In an offhand remark in the middle of the eighth-day ceremony we learn that Aaron has attended to the requirements of the animal *tāmîd*:[21] "He presented the grain offering, and, taking a handful of it, he turned it into smoke on the altar, *in addition to the burnt offering of the morning*" (Lev. 9:17, emphasis added). Since the animal *tāmîd*, "the burnt offering," had already been offered and was clearly in accord with a divine command, one could infer that the incense *tāmîd* should follow. This position was suggested by Rashbam and followed by the late medieval Jewish interpreter Seforno (d. 1550).[22] Though I think this is the best explanation, it is by no means

19. Many modern readers have been misled by the chapter divisions to think of Exod. 30:1–10 as a new literary unit. But the Masoretes were sensitive to the Priestly writer's own division when they identified 30:11 as the next literary unit. P divides the discourse of Exod. 25:1–31:18 into seven discrete units, the first of which is the longest and extends from 25:1 to 30:10. On this, see Peter Kearney, "Creation and Liturgy: The P Redaction of Ex 25–40," ZAW 89 (1977): 375–87. Critical scholarship has been so focused on the "misplacement" of the instructions to build the incense altar (30:1–6)—positing that they should have been found in Exod. 25—that it has overlooked the fittingness of the instructions to offer incense (30:7–10). Strikingly, the Samaritan version, which does relocate the incense legislation, attaches it to 26:35 rather than chap. 25.

20. Ze'ev Weiss, *The Sepphoris Synagogue: Deciphering an Ancient Message through Its Archaeological and Socio-Historical Contexts* (Jerusalem: Israel Exploration Society, 2005), 77–94, esp. 91–94.

21. Milgrom notes that it is unusual that our text has mentioned the daily *tāmîd* in association with the grain offering (v. 17) rather than with the burnt offering in the previous verse (v. 16). But he offers the reasonable explanation that "the writer presumes that the burnt offering and cereal offering are an inseparable pair and are sacrificed together" (*Leviticus 1–16*, 584).

22. Rashbam can be found in *Miqra'ot Gedolot: Wayyiqra* (Ramat Gan: Bar-Ilan, 2013), at Lev. 10:1; for Seforno, see *Bi'ur al Ha-Torah le-Rabbi Obadiah Seforno* (Jerusalem: Mosad Ha-Rav Kook, 1980), at Lev. 10:1.

conclusive (as is little in the first few verses of Lev. 10!). David Hoffman rejects this view on the supposition that the daily incense offering was offered by one priest rather than two. He concludes that "it is more accurate to explain the offering along the lines found in the Mekhilta de-Millu'im that the sons of Aaron wanted to bring a special freewill offering of incense in order to express their joy."[23] But whatever position one takes, it is clear that Nadab and Abihu did not intend to stray from divine teaching. In any event, the question becomes, what did they do wrong?

Various Attempts at an Answer

This is a challenging matter. After some two millennia of inquiry no consensus has emerged. One common solution locates the problem with the fire. Menahem Haran, for example, explains:

> Nadab and Abihu intended to make an offering of incense in their censers (Lev. 10:1–3). They were punished because they offered it to Yahweh in "strange fire," that is, fire other than that which was kept burning on the altar for the daily sacrifice. Nadab and Abihu *apparently* [emphasis added] took their fire from somewhere outside the altar-area and placed it in their censers, as it is stated: "each took his censer and put fire in it."[24]

At first blush, this explanation seems obvious. But Greenstein has called our attention to Haran's use of the word "apparently." Assumptions are being made here; a closer inspection reveals that the text says nothing about the *source* of the fire.

But the difficulty goes deeper. "Indeed, a persistent problem with this reading," Greenstein explains, "is the fact that the 'fire' is presented first as mere, unqualified 'fire' (so 10:1a: "put fire in it"). It is modified as 'strange' only after it had been offered with incense before YHWH (10:1b)."[25] This suggests

23. David Hoffman, *Das Buch Leviticus*, 2 vols. (Berlin: Poppelauer, 1905–6), 1:292.

24. Menahem Haran, *Temples and Temple-Service* (Oxford: Clarendon, 1978), 232. This interpretation is found already in Bruno Baentsch, *Exodus, Leviticus, Numeri* (Göttingen: Vandenhoeck & Ruprecht, 1903), 349, and in many others since: Roland Gradwohl, "Das 'fremde Feuer' von Nadab und Abihu," *ZAW* 75 (1963): 288–96, here 290–91; John C. H. Laughlin, "The 'Strange Fire' of Nadab and Avihu," *JBL* 95 (1976): 559–65, here 560–61; and Milgrom, *Leviticus 1–16*, 598.

25. Edward Greenstein, "Deconstruction," 58. Nihan has noted the same thing:
> Yet as already observed by Dillman, if the same notion was intended in Lev. 10, the profane provenance of the fire used by Nadab and Abihu should have been specified at the *beginning*, not at the end of the description of the ritual act undertaken by Aaron's sons, when the fire they used was mentioned for the first time, exactly as is the case

that the fire, in and of itself, was not the problem. Accordingly, the medieval Jewish commentary known as the Hizquni (thirteenth century) remarks: "All incense offerings involve fire; it was in fact the incense, not the fire, that was 'alien.'"[26] Baruch Levine echoes this sentiment when he writes: "Hebrew *ʾēš zārāh* 'alien fire' refers to the incense itself. [This phrase] could be translated 'an alien [incense offering by] fire.'"[27] Additional, but certainly not conclusive, support for this explanation can be found in the law for the incense offering itself. In Exod. 30:9 Moses explicitly warns the priests not to offer "strange incense" (*qəṭōret zārâ*) at the altar. Some have suggested that the offering of Nadab and Abihu falls under the umbrella of this specific warning.[28]

Another reason for not adopting Haran's suggestion too quickly is found in Lev. 16. Prior to laying out the rules for the rites of Yom Kippur, we read: "The LORD spoke to Moses after the death of the two sons of Aaron, when they *drew* [*too*] *near* [בקרבתם] before the LORD and died" (16:1).[29] This verse suggests that it was neither the incense nor the fire that was problematic but rather the decision by these two minor priests to encroach upon an area they did not have privileges to enter. In this respect, the sin of Nadab and Abihu looks a lot like that of Korah in Num. 16–17, a favored point of comparison for many modern interpreters. Arie Noordtzij, for example, has argued: "*Apparently* they intended to offer daily incense that only the high priest was authorized to do."[30] But as Greenstein quickly adds: "The telltale 'apparently' admits to a high degree of doubt, leaving room for the contrary claim [of Gordon Wenham]: 'Along with Aaron and their brothers, Eleazar and Ithamar, [Nadab and Abihu] had just been ordained as priests. It *may be assumed*, therefore, that they had the right to offer incense.' The

---

in the instructions of Lev. 16:12–13 and Num. 17:11. Instead, the formulation of 10:1 suggests that the "profane fire" results from the addition of incense (קטרת) on the fire burning in Nadab's and Abihu's censers. (*From Priestly Torah to Pentateuch*, 581–82)

26. *Hizquni on the Torah* (Jerusalem: Mosad Ha-Rav Kook, n.d.), at Lev. 10:1.

27. Baruch Levine, *Leviticus*, JPS Torah Commentary (Philadelphia: Jewish Publication Society, 1989), 58.

28. So, Levine, *Leviticus*, 59.

29. I am following the lead of the MT, the *lectio difficilior*. Numbers 3:4 and 26:61 offer a different understanding. The matter would be different if we followed the LXX or the targums, which have adjusted the text of Lev. 16:1 to harmonize it with Num. 3:4 and 26:61. On this problem, see Milgrom, *Leviticus 1–16*, 598, though Milgrom adopts the reading of the LXX.

30. Arie Noordtzij, *Leviticus*, Bible Student's Commentary (Grand Rapids: Zondervan, 1982), loc. cit. (emphasis added). The comparison of Lev. 10:1–3 with the narrative of Num. 16–17 is frequent. See more recently, Benedikt Jürgens, *Heiligkeit und Versöhnung: Levitikus 16 in seinem literarischen Kontext*, Herders Biblische Studien (Freiburg: Herder, 2001), 280–83; Reinhard Achenbach, *Die Vollendung der Tora: Studien zur Redaktionsgeschichte des Numeribuches im Kontext von Hexateuch und Pentateuch*, Beihefte zur Zeitschrift für altorientalische und biblische Rechtsgeschichte 3 (Wiesbaden: Harrassowitz, 2003), 93–97; and Hieke, *Levitikus 1–15*, 385.

need to 'assume,'" Greenstein concludes, "bespeaks the undecidability of the sense."[31]

Several commentators have suggested that Nadab and Abihu's incineration arose from a dispute between two rival priestly parties.[32] Such a view, ironically, often follows from the observation about how difficult it is to discern the nature of the sin.[33] Accordingly, Erhard Gerstenberger writes: "In the case of Nadab and Abihu, there was a divine death sentence involving death by fire for the guilty parties. Put plainly: A formerly influential, rival priestly group was eliminated. *The alleged occasion for their elimination is of no interest as such.* One need only allude to it, and not really designate it."[34]

The point I wish to make is that no single explanation has garnered a consensus and it is highly unlikely that after centuries of reflection any will ever do so. The fact that most modern commentators reflexively append words such as "apparently" or "it may be assumed" to their explanations says about all one needs to know about the nature of the problem. The claim that the text is really about tensions between different priestly parties is also a form of testimony to the difficulty of resolving the nature of the crime (so Gerstenberger). A few recent commentators, however, have been more forthright about the intractable nature of the problem. Benjamin Sommer, for example, concludes that the various solutions are unpersuasive due to "the severely enigmatic nature of Leviticus 10."[35] James Watts is sharper still: "The endless attempt by interpreters to explain what Nadab and Abihu did wrong is

31. Greenstein, "Deconstruction," 58, citing Wenham, *Book of Leviticus*, 154 (emphasis added).

32. Frank Moore Cross, *Canaanite Myth and Hebrew Epic* (Cambridge, MA: Harvard University Press, 1973), 204–5; Martin Noth, *Leviticus: A Commentary*, OTL (Philadelphia: Westminster, 1977), 84; and Erhard Gerstenberger, *Leviticus: A Commentary*, OTL (Louisville: Westminster John Knox, 1996), 117. I find this explanation hard to accept because the chapter as a whole finds fault with all four of Aaron's sons. Can we really imagine that the Priestly source polemicized against Aaron's entire line? But just such a case has been made by Reinhard Achenbach, "Das Versagen der Aaroniden: Erwägungen zum literarhistorischen Ort von Leviticus 10," in *"Basel und Bibel": Collected Communications to the XVIIth Congress of the International Organization for the Study of the Old Testament, Basel, 2001*, ed. M. Augustin and H. M. Niemann, BEATAJ 51 (Frankfurt am Main: Peter Lang, 2004), 55–70. On this claim, see the weighty critique of Nihan, *From Priestly Torah to Pentateuch*, 606–7.

33. So Cross (*Canaanite Myth*, 204) writes: "Nadab and Abihu . . . offered 'strange fire,' whatever that may be, before Yahweh."

34. Gerstenberger, *Leviticus*, 117 (emphasis added). Finally I might mention the attractive suggestion of David Damrosch (*The Narrative Covenant: Transformations of Genre in the Growth of Biblical Literature* [Ithaca, NY: Cornell University Press, 1991], 267–78) regarding various points of overlap between the account of Lev. 10 and the sin of Jeroboam in 1 Kings 13–15. But as this approach is mainly interested in literary parallels and has little to say about the nature of the sin in Lev. 10, I will not give it consideration.

35. Sommer, *Bodies of God*, 112. Note that he cites Greenstein's work with approval.

pointless."[36] Such comments remind me of what Robert Jenson once said about the doctrine of the atonement: "It is one of the most remarkable and remarked-upon aspects of theological history that no theory of atonement has ever been universally accepted. By now, this phenomenon is itself among the things that a proposed theory of atonement must explain."[37]

Has the Answer Been Deliberately Withheld?

This is, in fact, the approach Greenstein takes. He starts from the premise that the biblical text intentionally withholds the reason and then asks why this might be. It would be difficult to establish such a thesis solely on the grounds that scholars have not agreed. In this sense our text would be no different from hundreds of others in the Hebrew Bible. A lack of consensus is not a rare thing in biblical scholarship. To be persuasive, we must establish a good reason that the text is silent about such an important question. We will turn to the matter of a material cause shortly. But let us look for a moment at some formal features of our text that may confirm Greenstein's thesis.

Commentators often divide Lev. 10 into two parts: the first half pertains to the sin of Nadab and Abihu and its aftermath (vv. 1–11), while the second deals with the consumption of the various sacrificial pieces and concludes with the apparent error of Eleazar and Ithamar (vv. 12–20).[38] What is most striking about the second half of the chapter is the way Moses inspects the activity of the priesthood in regard to their sacrificial responsibilities. In each of the subunits (meal offering [vv. 12–13], offering of well-being [vv. 14–15], sin offering [vv. 16–20]) Moses documents how the priests' actions tally with the laws given in Lev. 1–7 (another reference back to "the manual") and explicitly notes whether the actions accord with the divine commandments or not.

This last point is worth bearing in mind as we consider another point of structural congruity. As has often been noted, the chapter provides two very different pictures of how Aaron reacts to the errors of his children.[39] In the first he acquiesces to the divine punishment, but in the second he argues strongly on behalf of his sons against the claims of Moses, and his words carry the day.

36. Watts, *Leviticus 1–10*, 187.
37. Robert Jenson, *Systematic Theology*, vol. 1, *The Triune God* (Oxford: Oxford University Press, 1997), 186.
38. See Achenbach, "Das Versagen," 63.
39. On Aaron's response to Moses at the end of the chapter, see Frevel, "Und Mose hörte (es)," 104–35 and the literature cited therein.

Error of Nadab and Abihu (Lev. 10:1–3)	Error of Eleazar and Ithamar (Lev. 10:17–20)
Then Moses said to Aaron, "This is what the LORD meant when he said, 'Through those who are near me I will show myself holy, and before all the people I will be glorified.'"	"Why did you not eat the sin offering in the sacred area? For it is most holy, and God has given it to you that you may remove the guilt of the congregation, to make atonement on their behalf before the LORD. Its blood was not brought into the inner part of the sanctuary. You should certainly have eaten it in the sanctuary, as I commanded."
And Aaron was silent.	And Aaron spoke to Moses,
	"See, today they offered their sin offering and their burnt offering before the LORD; and yet such things as these have befallen me! If I had eaten the sin offering today, would it have been agreeable to the LORD?"
	And when Moses heard that, he agreed.

What is striking is that in the case of Eleazar and Ithamar, Moses spells out very specifically what law has been violated ("Its blood was not brought into the inner part of the sanctuary"; cf. Lev. 6:23). But this careful correlation of sacrificial law with its subsequent execution is precisely what is missing in the first few verses of the chapter. Moses's explanation of the affair is just as mysterious as the sin itself: "This is what the LORD meant when he said, 'Through those who are near me I will show myself holy, and before all the people I will be glorified'" (10:3).[40] When did God say this and how does it clarify the character of Nadab and Abihu's sin? These questions cannot be answered. The contrast between the errors committed by these two sets of sons is vividly drawn. The literary structure of Lev. 10 confirms Greenstein's contention that Nadab and Abihu's error is cloaked in mystery.[41]

One should also observe that the biblical author had antecedent material before him that could have explained the error. Exodus 30:7–10 documents

40. Milgrom (*Leviticus 1–16*, 600) poses the obvious question: "But where did he say [this]?" Recognizing that there is no clear antecedent, Milgrom interprets the clause prospectively: "This is what the Lord has decreed, saying: 'through those near to me . . .'" Yet this interpretation—which says nothing about the nature of the deed but only something about what it reflects concerning the deity—only further underscores that our narrator is withholding from the reader the cause of the punishment.

41. It is worth noting that the end of the chapter has its own enigma. It is by no means clear what the force of Aaron's explanation is that eventually assuages the anger of Moses. Commentators have, for the most part, thrown up their hands. It would appear that the narrator has drawn a curtain between the (implied) lay reader and the sacerdotal office. I agree with Watts (*Leviticus 1–10*, 515) when he writes: "The text's ambiguity indicates that the authors' interests lie elsewhere. The writers of Leviticus 10 did not intend to decide a particular issue of ritual practice by telling this story, but instead wanted to demonstrate Aaron's newly granted authority in action."

how the incense offering is to be made and explicitly warns against desecration (v. 9). It is striking and hardly accidental that our author makes no reference to this text.

A Deconstructionist and Apophatic Reading

So we are left with the question of why Nadab and Abihu's sin is not identified. Greenstein has suggested that a deconstructive reading strategy may be of assistance. Deconstruction is a valuable tool for a text like this because it openly acknowledges structural limitations in regard to all human knowing. No single reading, no matter how well conceived philologically or trenchantly argued historically, can provide a "stable or impregnable meaning."[42] The integrity of the story will always stand athwart any attempt to domesticate it. Hebrew narrative "is as stubborn as Job in the face of his friends' contentions," Greenstein writes. "In the end God supported Job. Interpretation runs into difficulty—Derrida's aporia—at precisely those points at which it seeks to impose order."[43]

But Greenstein does not follow Derrida to the letter (nor will I).[44] For Derrida believes that *every* text we encounter—no matter what the author may intend—resists domestication because *all* meaning is subject to endless deferment. Greenstein, however, contends that there is a particular reason (or "logos") that conditions the difficulty of discerning the nature of Nadab and Abihu's cultic error. In order to appreciate this nondeconstructive detail we need to step back for a moment and look at Lev. 10 in light of the lengthy tabernacle account that precedes it.

The first thing to be observed is the parallelism between the creation of the world in Gen. 1 and the building of the tabernacle in Exod. 25–Lev. 9. As Peter Schäfer has put the matter: "The creation of the world is not, if one accepts this view, solely the work of God but also the work of man: only when Moses erects the tabernacle is God's created order brought to completion."[45] The role ascribed to human agency in this narrative is not to be overlooked. Human actions have become a nonnegotiable part of the way God has chosen

---

42. Greenstein, "Deconstruction," 62.

43. Ibid., 60.

44. Watts (*Leviticus 1–10*, 513) makes a similar criticism, but he then proceeds to dismiss the rest of Greenstein's arguments. The text's purpose is not to make a claim about the character of God, Watts argues, but to buttress priestly claims to power. As I will claim below, almost all of what Greenstein has argued can be retained if we just recast his Derridean terminology into its Dionysian counterpart.

45. Peter Schäfer, "Tempel und Schöpfung," *Kairos* 16 (1974): 132.

to direct human history. A second and closely related point is the manner in which this building project succeeds in capturing the presence of God. Moses opens the rites of the eighth day with the warning to do exactly as God has commanded (Lev. 9:6–7). Aaron complies with complete obedience and succeeds in attracting the divine presence to the sacrificial altar ("Fire came out from the LORD and consumed the burnt offering and the fat on the altar; and when all the people saw it, they shouted and fell on their faces," 9:24). In allowing the tabernacle to be built and the cult to begin, God has invited Israel to participate in the divine life. But along with this gracious condescension comes considerable risk. Because Israel's liturgical actions are allowed to attain such theurgic capabilities, God's freedom is put at risk. Has the priesthood gained the upper hand over the being of God? Can the mastery of cultic law allow the priesthood to conjure the divine presence at will? *Mē genoito* [May it never be]! As Thomas Hieke puts the matter: "This dramatic narrative dispels the misunderstanding that one can compel God to behave in a certain way through human—or more exactly—ritual action."[46]

Greenstein would certainly agree with this sentiment, but he would want to say more. Because of the limitations inherent to human knowing, *every* approach to God will be dangerous. (One thinks of the Israelites' cry at the close of the Korah episode: "Everyone who approaches the tabernacle of the LORD will die. Are we all to perish?" Num. 17:27 [17:13 Eng.].) God lessens this danger by revealing a protocol for drawing near to his presence (Lev. 1–7). But the danger involved in approaching God will always exceed any finite list of precautionary measures. *However much law a priest may master, every approach to the altar constitutes a potential danger.* The spirituality of Ps. 24 and the ark narrative returns with a vengeance: "Who can ascend the mountain of the LORD, who may stand in his holy place?" (Ps. 24:3 AT). Hieke captures this well when he writes: "[Lev. 1–9] gives the impression that the priests have a marvelous world at their disposal with their own office at the center in which they can flourish. Leviticus 10, however, makes it clear that the priests have been given the dangerous task of drawing near to God again and again as the representatives of the people."[47]

46. Hieke, *Levitikus 1–15*, 379. Also see his remarks on 332: "The narrative of the dramatic death of Nadab and Abihu in Leviticus 10 forms a contrast to the ideal-cult and serves as an example of warning that the careful observance of liturgical rites should not lead the priest to think he can manipulate God through ritual actions." Sommer (*Bodies of God*, 120–21) registers similar concerns about the theurgic dimensions of Priestly theology. In his opinion the non-Priestly sources have better resources for dealing with this challenge. But if my argument about Lev. 10 holds, the Priestly source holds its own on this matter.
47. Hieke, *Levitikus 1–15*, 379. See also Watts, *Leviticus 1–10*, 513–17.

Though Greenstein has chosen to express these theological ideas in Derridean vocabulary, I think that his approach finds a better vehicle in the realm of negative, or apophatic, theology. On this view I would interpret the numerous commands that God has given Moses about the foundation and operation of the cult as a witness to the *kataphatic* side of revelation. God provides enough information about himself and the world he has created that the priesthood can attract his physical presence to a structure built by human hands and tend to his daily needs. But *kataphasis* always requires an *apophatic* corrective.[48] There remains an infinite gap between creature and creator, and no matter how much cultic law one might master, God will not be reduced to an object subject to human control. Lest the priesthood become inebriated by the power God has conferred upon it, the radical otherness of God's majestic glory breaks out and reestablishes his utter transcendence.

Let us look at how Greenstein concludes his argument, but allow me to gloss his Derridean vocabulary with words that could have been drawn from the father of apophatic theology, Pseudo-Dionysius, also known as Saint Denis. Derrida's thoughts are "under erasure" while the words of Saint Denis are in italics.

> The story of Nadab and Abihu, as narrative, intrudes into the exposition of cultic law that precedes and follows it. It may strike the reader as disrupting the text as violently as the flash of fire annihilated the young priests. As the narrative genre of the episode disturbs the legal landscape by its otherness, so does its representation of a possibly opaque and nonverbal—*suprarational* irrational—God upset the orderliness of the cultic system. Notwithstanding the cultic regulations . . . God has not in fact explained everything. The system contains terrible dark secrets; YHWH may strike without warning. . . . In our reading [the disruption on the eighth day shows us that] God is *greater than* above/beyond the cultic order. A God worthy of name cannot be *wholly contained* trammeled by rules any more than an infinite God can be contained by names, by language. The priest can only control what the priest does; he cannot control God. Behind the orderly veneer of priestly ritual, behind the *parokhet* that screens off YHWH's quasi-condensed presence from the human observer, is the inscrutable Other. YHWH can hardly be better comprehended

48. For a gentle introduction to the themes of apophatic theology, see Bernard McGinn, *The Foundations of Mysticism: Origins to the Fifth Century* (New York: Crossroad, 1994), 157–82; Denys Turner, *The Darkness of God: Negativity in Christian Mysticism* (Cambridge: Cambridge University Press, 1995), 19–49. For the briefest primer possible: Jaroslav Pelikan, *The Melody of Theology: A Philosophical Dictionary* (Cambridge, MA: Harvard University Press, 1988), s.v. "apophatic."

than the motives of Nadab and Abihu and the question of whether they had done anything amiss.[49]

It is striking how minor these corrections are. We get nearly the same results with Saint Denis but avoid the theological (and literary!) errors that accompany Derrida.[50]

I would like to emphasize, before concluding, that on this view we will never know what Nadab and Abihu did wrong. Because if we could, our propensity to theurgic hubris would not be lessened (which is the intention of our text), but rather abetted. The biblical author does not want us so much to "learn" from their example (that is, they did X wrong and I will never do that again) as to develop a sense of wariness about the altar of God (I will never master all that is required for this job).[51] In this sense, the story of Nadab and Abihu has much in common with the story of Cain and Abel. For God's acceptance of Abel's sacrifice and rejection of Cain's raises problems very similar to those of Nadab and Abihu. What did Cain do wrong? Not surprisingly, commentators have come to no agreement on this, most likely because the text itself does not wish to disclose the motive. The preference for Abel over Cain, like that of Jacob over Esau, is grounded in the mystery of election, a domain of divine activity that is closed off to full human comprehension.[52]

49. Greenstein, "Deconstruction," 63–64.

50. For a similar point, see Bryan Bibb, "Nadab and Abihu Attempt to Fill a Gap: Law and Narrative in Leviticus 10:1–7," *JSOT* 96 (2001): 83–99. He says that God "reminds the people that the problem is not that there is no order in his divinity. The problem is that the limited understanding and ability of humans can only take a few steps toward comprehending the true reality, with its blessings and dangers. The narrative not only exposes the depth of the problem, it also motivates them to think more about the limitations of their cultic system" (95–96).

51. Which is not to say that there is no lesson to be learned here. Obviously Nadab and Abihu did violate some law—God does not act irrationally when he takes their lives. But for reasons that I have spelled out, the text is not interested in providing the reader with an explanation. The point of the author is to instill within the reader the sense of danger that should attend every approach to the altar. As Milgrom (*Leviticus 1–16*, 577) notes, the *Sifra* had a feeling for the wariness that overtook Aaron as he prepared to assume his priestly office. One could also compare Aaron's worries to the young Martin Luther who shook in fear the first time he approached the altar to offer the Eucharistic sacrifice. He later said that had he not been restrained he would have fled and never raised the host. See Martin Brecht, *Martin Luther: His Road to the Reformation, 1483–1521* (Philadelphia: Fortress, 1985), 70–76. My suspicion is that many modern commentators lack the necessary theological imagination that attends the real presence of the deity to appreciate the religious world of the Bible. On precisely this point, see the perceptive comments of Mary Douglas in her essay "The Bog Irish," in *Natural Symbols: Explorations in Cosmology* (New York: Pantheon Books, 1970), 37–53. Her comparison of Pope Paul VI's comments on the Eucharist in *Mysterium Fidei* with West African practices (see 47–48) is right to the point.

52. On the impossibility of determining Cain's error and its significance for the book of Genesis, see Jon D. Levenson, *Death and Resurrection of the Beloved Son* (New Haven: Yale

There is good reason then, why interpreters have found it difficult to locate the precise character of the error of Nadab and Abihu. Our text, which hitherto has been so deeply invested in the kataphatic process of revelation, recoils in worry that the reader who has mastered the many details of Levitical law may believe that he or she has acquired the formula for conjuring the divine presence. In some senses, the story of Nadab and Abihu and that of the ark in the books of Samuel are of a piece, as the lectionary cycle of the synagogue has long suggested.[53] Both narratives address the question of divine freedom from a context in which God has apparently given human beings considerable control over his person. In Samuel the issue is: What is the role of God's saving presence in the ark? Scripture is clear about God's condescension to dwell on the ark and his intention to venture forth with Israel's armies to victory in battle. This raises an obvious question: Will the ark "work its magic" regardless of the moral status of those who attend it? The ark narrative answers that question with a resounding "no."

In Lev. 10 the theological challenge is slightly different. Here God's condescension through ritual law has granted the priesthood the power to conjure God's presence. Rashi captures this aptly when he comments on the promise Moses makes at Lev. 9:6: "Through the works of [Aaron's] hands, God will make his presence manifest." This grants a considerable degree of power to the cultic procedures that Moses is about to hand over to Aaron and his sons. But Lev. 10 shows us that the power granted to the priesthood is far more complex than it may have appeared at first. Not only do the commands require human discernment in order to be obeyed, but the cost of even the slightest error is frightfully high. No wonder the Israelites recoil in fear at the prospect of attending the altar.

Let me conclude by saying that my thesis can be articulated in both a softer and a stronger sense. At the softer end, I hope I have cogently argued that the final canonical form of our text is patient of an apophatic reading. If Rashi is to be trusted, one of the prominent issues at stake in Lev. 8–10 is the liturgical power placed in the hands of the clergy. The reader who is sensitive to these theurgic possibilities cannot help but wonder what checks are in place to remind the priest of his status as a vulnerable and radically dependent creature. "Who would ascend the mountain of the LORD" is a question not only for the lay pilgrim but for the servant of the altar as well. As Greenstein argues, "A God worthy of the name cannot be *wholly contained* ~~trammeled~~ by rules

---

University Press, 1993), 71–75. I will return to the theological challenges represented by such a text in chap. 5.

53. Fishbane, *Haftarot*, 120–21.

any more than an infinite God can be contained by names, by language. . . .
The priest can only control what the priest does; he cannot control God."[54]

But my claim, truth be told, has been slightly stronger than this. I have
suggested that not only is the text patient of such a reading but it invites or
even solicits it (but note that I do not claim that it demands this reading). To
that end I suggested that the irresolvability of the episode is reflected in the
literary character of Lev. 10 as a whole. The author *underscores* obedience or
disobedience to very specific sacrificial requirements: incense, grain, well-being,
and sin offerings (vv. 1, 13, 15, 18). In each of the final three instances—grain,
well-being, and sin offerings—the requirements are easily traceable to laws
found in the priestly manual of Lev. 1–7. Only the incense offering departs
from this pattern. In this instance alone we do not learn about the specifics
but are simply told that the violation is testimony to the holiness of God:
"This is what the LORD meant," Moses explains, "when he said,

> 'Through those who are near me
>   I will show myself holy,
> and before all the people
>   I will be glorified.'" (Lev. 10:3)

This is, of course, an answer that explains nothing (check the commentaries!). And that is precisely my point. Perhaps recourse to apophatic theology
gives us at least one way of making sense of this striking literary feature of
our chapter.

---

54. Greenstein, "Deconstruction," 64.

2

The Impassibility of God

Moses, Jonah, and the Theo-Drama of Intercessory Prayer

The story of Moses's intercession on behalf of Israel is full of drama. After the sin of the golden calf, God seems intent on destroying the people he redeemed from slavery. Thankfully, Moses is brave enough to step into the breach and intercede for the people. This tale, as has long been noted, makes a powerful case for the importance of intercessory prayer. Save for the words of Moses, all would have been lost. But doesn't this elevation of prayer come at the risk of God's providential plans? What if Moses had not interceded? Would God have been overcome by his anger? On its own, the book of Exodus does not give us sufficient data to answer these questions. But when read alongside the book of Jonah, a solution emerges. The doctrine of impassibility reflects the portrait of God that results from a close reading of these two prophetic narratives.

Basic to the identity of Jesus in the thinking of the early church were his representative nature and his impassibility. God did not just resurrect a man on Easter Sunday; rather, in that act he committed himself to raising all those who are joined in faith to him. Robert Jenson puts the matter in a characteristically laconic fashion: While Jesus rests in the grave, the Father faces a dilemma. He can either "have his Son and us with him into the bargain, or he can abolish us and have no Son, for there is no Son but the one who said, 'Father, forgive them.'"[1] Certainly, one of the reasons

---

1. Robert Jenson, *Systematic Theology*, vol. 1, *The Triune God* (Oxford: Oxford University Press, 1977), 191.

the early church labored so hard to make sure that Jesus was fully man was so that this representative aspect would be efficacious. What has not been assumed cannot be healed.

The other feature basic to Christ's identity was his impassibility. Christ became one with us through his suffering on the cross. But suffering is of course a dangerous element to introduce into the Godhead, because suffering is something that happens *to* a person, and as a result, it can *change* a person. When Jesus prays in Gethsemane that his cup of suffering be removed, an element of reservation is introduced. Is Jesus a free agent in this story?[2] Most readers are going to answer, vigorously, Yes! But if Jesus really doubted, that is, if he experienced the sort of vacillation that is common to the human condition, is it possible that the larger project of human salvation was truly at risk? Had the man Jesus not come down on the right side of the matter, was all lost? Christian theology has never wanted to assert this. And so the Christian tradition has coined an impossible phrase to account for this conundrum: Christ suffered *impassibly*. The doctrine of divine impassibility in Christian dress has meant that God's intimate involvement with the human condition did not set at risk his providential purpose of redeeming the created order. David Hart has put the matter well: "For God to pour himself out . . . as the man Jesus is not a venture outside of the trinitarian life of indestructible love, but in fact quite the reverse: it is the act by which creation is seized up into the sheer invincible pertinacity of that love, which reaches down to gather us into its triune motion."[3]

The question I would like to pose in this chapter is whether these two notions that appear so quintessentially christological—representation and impassibility—have an analogy in the Old Testament.

Moses and the Nature of Representation

Certainly, one of the most dramatic moments of intercession in the Old Testament is the moment when Moses speaks to God just after Israel has venerated the golden calf (Exod. 32:1–6). No sooner has Israel been given a

2. On this problem, see Robert Jenson, "Identity, Jesus, and Exegesis," in *Seeking the Identity of Jesus: A Pilgrimage*, ed. Richard B. Hays and Beverly Roberts Gaventa (Grand Rapids: Eerdmans, 2008), 43–59.

3. David Bentley Hart, "No Shadow of Turning: On Divine Impassibility," *Pro Ecclesia* 11 (2002): 184–206, here 202. One should also compare the judicious and informative treatment of the problem by Ellen Davis in her essay "Vulnerability, the Condition of Covenant," in *The Art of Reading Scripture*, ed. Ellen F. Davis and Richard B. Hays (Grand Rapids: Eerdmans, 2003), 290–93.

set of commands that solemnize its election as God's very own people than it violates one of the most important of them. God, in understandable indignation, turns to address his prophet Moses:

> Go down at once! Your people, whom you brought up out of the land of Egypt, have acted perversely; they have been quick to turn aside from the way that I commanded them; they have cast for themselves an image of a calf, and have worshiped it and sacrificed to it, and said, "These are your gods, O Israel, who brought you up out of the land of Egypt!" (Exod. 32:7–8)

It is worth noting that already in this first address to Moses, God sets up a peculiar triangular relationship: he takes Moses into his confidence to discuss the matter of Israel's sin, but in so doing he indicates from the very inception the state of alienation between himself and Israel. Israel, God declares, is not my people but *your* people; it is *you, Moses*(!), who brought them up out of Egypt. This peculiar turn in diction creates the necessary space between God and Israel that will allow God to deal with this people in a less than salutary fashion.

Having shown his hand, God gets right to the point: "I have seen this people, how stiff-necked they are. Now let me alone, so that my wrath may burn hot against them and I may consume them; and of you I will make a great nation" (32:9–10). Israel's disobedient nature is inarguable; it is established on the grounds of the quickness with which the nation has overturned the mandates of the recently minted Sinaitic covenant.[4]

What is most striking here is the textual echo of the story of Noah.[5] Early in Genesis, not long after the creation of the world itself, God became indignant at the lawlessness and violence that was rampant on the face of the earth and decided to destroy the world. Only Noah was found worthy to survive this cataclysm, and he was told to build an ark so that he, his immediate family, and a representative sample of the animal kingdom might survive the chaotic waters.

Yet there is a significant difference between these two stories. Noah, though a survivor of the flood, achieved this status in a more or less passive manner. True, he built the ark and loaded it with animals, but he took no stance for or against what God had decreed. Not to put too fine a point on it, he

---

4. I have called this the Bible's doctrine of "immediate sin," which is not really different from what the Christian West would call "original sin." See chap. 4 on the Fall of humanity in the present volume.

5. On this point, see the excellent discussion by R. W. L. Moberly, *At the Mountain of God: Story and Theology in Exodus 32–34*, JSOTSup 22 (Sheffield: JSOT Press, 1983), 92.

simply went along for the ride. Whereas Noah was simply "remembered" by God (Gen. 8:1), Moses stridently demands that God remember his prior commitments:

> "Remember Abraham, Isaac, and Israel, your servants, how you swore to them by your own self, saying to them, 'I will multiply your descendants like the stars of heaven, and all this land that I have promised I will give to your descendants, and they shall inherit it forever.'" And the LORD changed his mind about the disaster that he planned to bring on his people. (Exod. 32:13–14)

Unlike Noah, Moses is taken into God's confidence and consulted about what is going to transpire. For if God simply wished to announce a judgment, he could say: "I have seen this people, how stiff-necked they are. And so I will let my wrath burn hot against them and consume them; and of you I will make a great nation." Such a statement would draw an almost exact analogy to the story of the flood. And so we could justly wonder whether Marcion was not correct about the irascible nature of Israel's jealous God.[6] But note what God in fact says: "I have seen this people, how stiff-necked they are. *Now let me alone*, so that my wrath may burn hot against them and I may consume them; and of you I will make a great nation" (32:9–10, emphasis added).

In acting this way, God sets a condition on his rage and practically requests Moses's permission before he proceeds. A rabbinic midrash captures the tenor of this request well:

> God said to Moses after the incident of the Golden Calf, "Let me at them, and my anger will rest on them and I will get rid of them." Is Moses holding back God's hand, so that God must say "Let go of me"? What is this like? A king became angry at his son, placed him in a small room, and was about to hit him. At the same time the king cried out from the room for someone to stop him. The prince's teacher was standing outside, and said to himself, "The king and his son are in the room. Why does the king say 'stop me'? It must be that the king wants me to go into the room and effect a reconciliation between him and his son. That's why the king is crying, 'Stop me.'" In a similar way, God said to Moses, "Let Me at them." Moses said, "Because God wants me to defend Israel, He says, 'Let Me at them.'" And Moses immediately interceded for them.[7]

6. Marcion, an influential second-century heretic, taught that there was a radical dichotomy between the Old and New Testaments. Indeed, for him, the jealous God of the Old Testament was inferior to the God of Jesus.

7. *Exodus Rabbah* 42.9 as cited in Yochanan Muffs, "Who Will Stand in the Breach? A Study of Prophetic Intercession," in *Love and Joy: Law, Language, and Religion in Ancient Israel* (New York: Jewish Theological Seminary, 1992), 34.

It is not solely that God requests Moses's help in this matter; he also signals the manner by which Moses can be most effective. God tells Moses that if he leaves God alone God will make of him a "*great nation.*" But this way of putting the matter clearly calls to mind the earlier promise God made to the very father of the nation he wishes to destroy (Gen. 12:2). By framing his request this way, God sets up the most formidable argument that can be used against him. God cannot destroy Israel, because of the *promise* to which he is eternally bound.

Moses begins his argument, however, from a slightly different direction. First, he categorically denies any degree of ownership over this people. Though God has "flattered" Moses by naming him as the one who brought Israel out of Egypt (Exod. 32:7), Moses will have none of this. "O LORD, why does your wrath burn hot against your people, whom you brought out of the land of Egypt with great power and with a mighty hand?" (32:11). Having laid the responsibility for the exodus on God's shoulders, Moses considers the tremendous investment God himself has made in this very venture. He reminds God that one of the central concerns in leading Israel out of Egypt with all sorts of supernatural deeds ("with great power and with a mighty hand") was to make it publicly clear to one and all just who was the true sovereign Lord. Pharaoh had his own doubts about the matter right from the start and so refused to release Israel. "Who is the LORD that I should heed Him?" he jeeringly asked Moses in reply to his request (5:2). As a result of such insolence, God let Pharaoh persist in his stubborn refusals so that "I will gain glory for myself over Pharaoh and all his army; and the Egyptians shall know that I am the LORD" (14:4). And now, Moses reminds God, if you destroy Israel in the wilderness, your *glorious reputation* that you worked so hard to win will come to naught. "Why should the Egyptians say," Moses remarks, "'it was with evil intent that he brought them out to kill them in the mountains, and to consume them from the face of the earth'" (32:12).

But Moses does not let the case rest here. He rejoins the opening that God has provided him. He recounts how God bound himself to a specific people when he first promised to make *them* "a great nation" (32:10; cf. Gen. 12:2): "Remember Abraham, Isaac, and Israel, your servants, how you swore to them by your own self, saying to them, 'I will multiply *your* [plural] descendants like the stars of heaven, and all this land that I have promised I will give to *your* [plural] descendants, and they shall inherit it forever'" (32:13, emphasis added). Having been reminded of his obligations, "the LORD changed his mind about the disaster that he planned to bring on his people" (v. 14).

A key feature of this entire narrative is the strongly *representational* role that Moses plays. As Yochanan Muffs has argued so brilliantly, Moses is not simply an exemplary human being standing before God. *He, in fact, represents part of God to God.*[8] He assumes a part of the divine personality such that one cannot properly pick out the full characterization or identity of God by attending only to what the subject identified as "God" in the story says. Indeed, to follow the literal sense in this fashion is to fall quickly into heresy. For good reason Marcion latched onto this text and questioned whether any sober-minded reader could abide such a capricious God; and more recently, Harold Bloom has vigorously nodded in agreement with this second-century figure.[9]

But Muffs sidesteps this difficulty by arguing that who God is in this story is represented by a combination of what both God and Moses say. "God allows the prophet to represent in his prayer His own attribute of mercy," Muffs declares, "the very element that enables a calming of God's [angry and vindictive] feelings."[10] Because the prophet is a necessary, nonnegotiable element in the rendering of the identity of God, the midrash can go so far as to say that God wept when Moses was ready to hand over his soul to death: "God said, Who will stand against Me on the day of wrath? [cf. Ps. 94:16]. This means, Who shall protect Israel in the hour of My anger? And who will stand up in the great eschatological war for My children? And who will speak up for them when they sin against Me?"[11] Moses is a *necessary* actor in the narrative that depicts God's character. The identity of God would be different without him.

Yet Moses's psychic connection with God is not the only representational aspect on the table. Moses is also strongly tied to the people Israel. Indeed, as the dialogue between Moses and God continues and the immediate threat of destruction is set aside, a new issue surfaces: whether God will renew his close ties to Israel and personally accompany the people to the promised land. Again, God tries to sever Moses from the people Israel. But when Moses sees the great favor he has won in God's eyes, he is not in any way content. For Moses, favor becomes a valuable commodity only when it is deployed to Israel's benefit. "Now if I have found favor in your sight," Moses answers, "show me your ways, so that I may know you and find favor in your sight. Consider too that this nation is your people." God replies, "My presence will go with

8. Muffs, "Who Will Stand in the Breach?," 33–34.

9. Harold Bloom, *The Book of J* (New York: Grove Weidenfeld, 1990).

10. Muffs, "Who Will Stand in the Breach?," 33.

11. See *Midrash Tanhuma* to the *parasha* (weekly Torah portion) *Va-ethanan* (Deut. 3:23–7:11), as cited in Muffs, "Who Will Stand in the Breach?," 33.

you, and I will give you rest" (Exod. 33:13–14). Clearly, God is interested only in Moses, as he ignores the second half of Moses's request ("Consider, too . . ."). So Moses must step back into the breach to confront his benefactor: "If your presence will not go, do not carry *us* up from here. For how shall it be known that I have found favor in your sight, *I and your people*, unless you go with *us*? In this way, *we* shall be distinct, *I and your people*, from every people on the face of the earth?" (33:15–16, emphasis added). At this point the Lord acquiesces. Israel is fully back in his good graces, and God agrees to accompany Israel personally to the promised land.

Only one portion of Moses's request has not been addressed. Moses prayed that God would make known to him his ways. In order to do this, God has Moses ascend Mount Sinai a second time to receive a second set of the stone tablets. And on top of that mountain, the Lord passes by Moses and proclaims:

> The Lord, the Lord,
> a God merciful and gracious,
> slow to anger,
> and abounding in steadfast love and faithfulness,
> keeping steadfast love for the thousandth generation,
> forgiving iniquity and transgression and sin,
> yet by no means clearing the guilty,
> but visiting the iniquity of the parents
> upon the children
> and the children's children,
> to the third and the fourth generation. (34:6–7)

These attributes of God—which become known as the "thirteen attributes" in Jewish tradition—are often reused in the Bible by various intercessors to remind God of his compassionate nature and to persuade him to show mercy to his people.[12]

This remarkable revelation of God's overwhelmingly compassionate nature will be an important tool for Moses's subsequent intercession on behalf of Israel. For in the book of Numbers, when Israel is given the opportunity to enter the land of Canaan to lay claim to what God has promised, the people will think twice and refuse to enter. As a result of Israel's disobedience, God will react in a manner very similar to his response to the golden calf. The accompanying table lays out the parallel texts:

---

12. On these attributes, see Muffs, "Who Will Stand in the Breach?," 20–24. For a sample of how they are used elsewhere in the OT, consult Neh. 9:17; Pss. 86:15; 103:8; 145:8; Joel 2:13. See also the discussion by Uriel Simon, *Jonah: The Traditional Hebrew Text with the New JPS Translation*, JPS Bible Commentary (Philadelphia: Jewish Publication Society, 1999), 35 and 37.

Exodus 32	Numbers 14
[9]The Lord said to Moses, "I have seen this people, how stiff-necked they are. [10]Now let me alone, so that my wrath may burn hot against them and I may consume them; and of you I will make a great nation."	[11]And the Lord said to Moses, "How long will this people despise me? And how long will they refuse to believe in me, in spite of all the signs that I have done among them? [12]I will strike them with pestilence and disinherit them, and I will make of you a nation greater and mightier than they."
[11]But Moses implored the Lord his God, and said, "O Lord, why does your wrath burn hot against your people, whom you brought out of the land of Egypt with great power and with a mighty hand? [12]Why should the Egyptians say, 'It was with evil intent. . . .'	[13]But Moses said to the Lord, "Then the Egyptians will hear of it, for in your might you brought up this people from among them, [14]and they will tell the inhabitants of this land. . . .
[13]Remember Abraham, Isaac, and Israel, your servants, how you swore to them by your own self, saying to them, 'I will multiply your descendants like the stars of heaven, and all this land that I have promised I will give to your descendants, and they shall inherit it forever.'"	[17]And now, therefore, let the power of the Lord be great in the way that you promised when you spoke, saying,
	[18]'The Lord is slow to anger, and abounding in steadfast love, forgiving iniquity and transgression, but by no means clearing the guilty, visiting the iniquity of the parents upon the children to the third and the fourth generation.' [19]Forgive the iniquity of this people according to the greatness of your steadfast love, just as you have pardoned this people, from Egypt even until now."
[14]And the Lord changed his mind about the disaster that he planned to bring on his people.	[20]Then the Lord said, "I do forgive, just as you have asked."

The key difference between these two prayers is the introduction of the thirteen attributes into the body of the second. What Moses desires to know in Exod. 33:13 ("Now, if I have found favor in your sight, show me your ways . . .") turns out to be much more than a moment's curiosity. The knowledge he receives establishes the very basis of subsequent appeals for clemency. God has provided Moses with the legal grounds on which to pursue his claims against God.

Clearly, one part of the christological analogy is in place. Moses, like Jesus of Nazareth, has been called to represent his people before God. Indeed, the representation is so strong that the delineation of our characters in the simple plotlines of Exod. 32:7–14 and Num. 14:11–20 turns out to be quite complex. Because Moses, as Muffs puts the matter, assumes the role of one side of the divine personality, it is not clear that the dialogue is between a human prophet and a God who is totally other. Rather, God has involved Moses in this prayer in such a profound manner that the character we can pick out as "God" is portrayed by the combination of what our human and divine subjects say.

If we were to paraphrase Jenson, we could say that the God of Israel faces a dilemma: he can either have his prophet and Israel with him into the bargain, or he can abolish Israel and have no Moses, for there is no Moses but the one who says, "How shall it be known that I have found favor in your sight, *I and your people*, unless you go with *us*? In this way, *we* shall be distinct, *I and your people*, from every people on the face of the earth?" (Exod. 33:16, emphasis added).[13]

This is a powerful story, but also a potentially disturbing one. If we concede that God's identity is revealed by the interaction of prophet and Lord, we still leave open the question of what would happen should the prophet prove unfit for the job. Does all of Israel's sacred history stand in the balance? Is Moses's own psychic strength, which allows him to stand in the breach before God, that trustworthy? The midrash, as we saw, gives voice to these very fears when it depicts God as crying when Moses hands his soul over to death: "Who will protect Israel from Me now that Moses is gone?" God laments. This is a gripping yet troubling account. Is God so much a part of the natural order that he becomes totally dependent on fallible human intermediaries? Even the most reverent reader of the Bible hesitates here. In order to shed further light on the problem, let us turn to the figure of Jonah.

Jonah and the Nature of Impassibility

The book of Jonah is structured around two themes: getting Jonah to Nineveh so that he can deliver his message, and teaching this reluctant prophet why his task is necessary. Let us begin with the first.

---

13. Tertullian (ca. 160–ca. 225 CE) saw the christological analogy at work here and found in this text a potent witness to the christological mystery:

> Pitiable are ye . . . since you know not Christ, prefigured in the person of Moses, as the one who prayed to the Father, and offered His own life for the salvation of the people. It is enough, however, that the nation was at that instant really given to Moses. That which he, as a servant, was able to ask of the Lord [an allusion to Moses's response to God: "Thou shalt not do this; or else destroy me along with them"], the Lord required of Himself. For this purpose did He say to His servant, "Let me alone, that I may consume them," in order that by his entreaty, and by offering himself, he might hinder (the threatened judgment), and that you might by such an instance learn how much privilege is vouchsafed with God to a faithful man and a prophet. (*Against Marcion* 2.26, trans. Peter Holmes, *ANF* 3:318, alt.)

Jonah's mission to the Ninevites opens with the Lord's command in 1:1 and resumes again in 3:1 with a reiteration of the same. It is useful to see just how similar the opening lines of these respective chapters are.

Jonah 1	Jonah 3
[1]Now the word of the LORD came to Jonah son of Amittai, saying, [2]"Go at once to Nineveh, that great city, and cry out against it; for their wickedness has come up before me." [3]But Jonah set out to flee to Tarshish from the presence of the LORD.	[1]The word of the LORD came to Jonah a second time, saying, [2]"Get up, go to Nineveh, that great city, and proclaim to it the message that I tell you." [3]So Jonah set out and went to Nineveh, according to the word of the LORD.

One might assume that the intervening narrative about Jonah's experience on board the ship has taught him that the Lord's call is impossible to flee, and so now, in chap. 3, he is voluntarily complying with it. This, however, does not seem to be the case. First, although Jonah has learned that he cannot flee from his prophetic task, instead of confessing the error of his ways and telling the sailors to drop him off at the next harbor (a distinct but unmentioned possibility), he informs them that they must cast him overboard in order to have respite from the storm. Jonah, by this action, anticipates his more brazen attitude of chap. 4: it is better to die than to comply with a command that one finds morally repugnant. But God will not let the matter rest at that. It seems he is bound and determined that Jonah will reach Nineveh. For this reason, a fish is appointed to swallow Jonah and disgorge him upon dry land.

But just as Jonah refused to pray while in the hold of the ship even after being discovered by the ship's captain (1:6), so he is silent upon entering the fish. Only after three days—a common idiom in the Bible for denoting the passage of a period of time that is long but not overly so[14]—does he finally pray. This scene reminds one of the famous remark ascribed to Mark Twain, recounting his travel by ship to Europe. "After one day I was so sick I was afraid I was going to die," he quipped; "a few days later I was afraid I wasn't going to die!" Jonah's prayer of contrition is forced from his mouth by an aggressive God hell-bent on getting him to Nineveh.

While in Nineveh, Jonah makes a perfunctory trip through the city proclaiming that in a mere forty days the city will be no more. Just as he feared, his cry of judgment falls on receptive ears, and all the inhabitants of the city, from the king to the lowly oxen, undergo acts of self-mortification amid the hope that God will relent from his decree and show mercy.

14. See Simon, *Jonah*, 19.

Indeed, God does just that. Jonah, for his part, is greatly distressed and has harsh words for God:

> O Lord! Is not this what I said while I was still in my own country? That is why I fled to Tarshish at the beginning; for I knew that you are a gracious God and merciful, slow to anger, and abounding in steadfast love, and ready to relent from punishing. (4:2)

Jonah's displeasure is shocking. As readers, we are ignorant at the beginning of the tale as to what motivates Jonah's flight from God (1:1–3). Is it the difficulty of the job (large city, many sinners?), the fact that the city is some distance from his home, fear about his prophetic reputation, or maybe the fact that the people are not Israelites?[15] To the reader, any of these is possible, but Jonah's answer briskly brushes them all aside. This prophet is in agony because he knows that God is "gracious . . . and merciful, slow to anger, and abounding in steadfast love, and ready to relent from punishing" (4:2). In short, the very formula bequeathed to Moses as a means of forestalling a harsh decree turns from being beneficent to just the opposite! What should be the primary means of averting the wrath of God becomes the source of Jonah's moral outrage.

Jonah, the reader learns, is a rigorous moralist. He believes that the world's affairs should be conducted according to the exacting standards of the law and that any divergence to the right or left is worthy of quick and sure punishment.[16] In spite of, or perhaps *because of*, being forced to deliver a quite different message, Jonah will not give up on his sense of dissatisfaction bordering on outrage. Rather than returning home—*west*, toward Israel—Jonah declares his desire to die and obstinately heads *east*. There he builds a shelter in which to sit and watch what will become of the city. Evidently, he hopes that God's initial leniency will be shown to have been hopelessly optimistic, if not downright foolish, and the destruction of the wicked city will shortly take place.

What is striking here is that we see what happens when our appointed Mosaic prophet does not rise to the accepted standard of his office. It is not the case that all bets are off and that God's rage will now burst forth unchecked.

---

15. This last reason is a favorite explanation among many modern Christian readers. It simply does not work in the context of the book.

16. See the discussion of Thomas Aquinas on justice and mercy (*Summa Theologiae* 1.21.3). It is not unjust for God to show mercy toward the guilty; it is like someone paying a creditor 600 denarii when only 200 are owed. It is not an unjust action; it is an excessive one. And just as the sinner will "owe" a punishment of some sort for his crimes, so God is free to take less payment (measured in terms of punishment) than is due.

In fact, God had the system rigged from the beginning. He was going to get Jonah to Nineveh no matter what.

And here is the answer to the theological problem raised by the story of Moses's prayer of intercession. There we worried about the manner in which God seemed to tie his identity to the role of a certain human agent. If that agent proved fallible, would God's wrath get the better of him? In the story of Jonah, we see the bottom line: if we have to choose between a narrative that will preserve human free choice but compromise God's mercy and a narrative that will compromise human choice in order to effect God's mercy, the direction God will take is clear. And this, I would argue, is precisely what the theological tradition has tried to affirm through the doctrine of impassibility. It is not that God is indifferent to his creation in the way in which the Greek philosophical world saw things. God is intimately bound to his creation, but that boundedness cannot and will not compromise his providential ends. John Webster has put the matter well:

> Precisely because God's will is sovereign, it can freely and without loss or impairment take the prayers of creatures into its service, and allow itself to hear in the creature an echo of itself. God is not constituted by these others; his will is not battered into submission; rather, through them God demonstrates the kind of liberty which is proper to Himself, a liberty which is not threatened by but exercised in Moses's prayer, Jonah's refusal, and the Son's anguish in the Garden.[17]

But the story does not end here. For the genius of the book of Jonah is the way it underscores the theme of prophetic participation in the life of God. God could leave Jonah in his funk and, like a mother or father faced with a toddler's tantrum, simply hope that with the passage of time things will change. Or he could give up on Jonah altogether. Why not? Is it not God's prerogative to do such? Yet just as God *provided* a fish to make Jonah do his bidding, God now *provides* a plant to grow up over Jonah's head and offer some shade: "The Lord God *provided* a ricinus plant, which grew up over Jonah, to provide shade for his head and save him from his distress [$r\bar{a}'\hat{a}$]. Jonah was very happy about the plant" (4:6 AT).

This plant, which arises to shade Jonah's head, seems also to be a token of God's care and concern for Jonah's emotional welfare. For the masculine suffix ("*his* distress") unequivocally informs us that the distress in question concerns Jonah's own person, not what the sun might produce. Moreover,

17. John Webster provided these comments as a response to a version of this paper at the Society of Biblical Literature conference in Philadelphia, November 2005.

a rich set of ironies is put in place. Just as we could say that penance and contrition saved the Ninevites from the consequences of their wickedness (*rāʿâ*, 1:2; 3:8, 10), so this plant has been sent to "save" (*ləhaṣîl*) Jonah from his distress (*rāʿâ*).[18] Jonah perceives that this token of "salvation" is God's act of trying to make amends after all is said and done. He apparently understands the plant as something sent to placate his anger, a token that he is not completely in the wrong.

But this is not God's design. The distress from which he wishes to deliver Jonah is Jonah's own strict moral calculus about how the world's affairs should be administered. Evidently, God has determined that no rational argument is going to win the day with Jonah. If anything has been learned up to now, it is the strength of Jonah's resolve. God will have to use other means to show Jonah that he is not as self-sufficient as he has thought. And it is for this pedagogical purpose that the plant has been sent in the first place. No sooner has it been given than it is taken away. This provides God the opportunity to allow Jonah to indict himself.

Compare Jonah's attitude toward Nineveh with his attitude toward the plant. When Jonah sees that Nineveh has been sustained by God's mercy, he assumes the attitude we saw earlier on the ship—he wishes to die: "Please take my life from me, for it is better for me to die than to live" (4:3). A world bereft of justice, he believes, is not worth inhabiting. God, in evident perplexity, asks: "Is it right for you to be angry?" (4:4), which we might gloss: "Are your moral scruples that rigorous that turning a benign eye on this city really does you in?" Jonah does not answer this query. As at the beginning of the book, he departs in silence, evidently hoping that the city will soon return to its wayward ways so that he can enjoy a moment of *Schadenfreude* at God's expense. Justice is no trifling matter to this earnest prophet.

God intervenes by providing Jonah with a plant that offers him some shade, an act that appears to be a gesture of reconciliation. But as soon as Jonah begins to take solace in it, God sends "a sultry east wind" to destroy the plant so that the sun can beat down on him. Jonah is forlorn and mutters to himself, "It is better for me to die than to live" (4:8). Now God has Jonah in a corner. He poses his question again: "Is it right for you to be angry," to which he adds a brief clarification, "*about the plant?*" (4:9 NRSV alt.). For the first time in the story, this model of self-control loses his cool. Jonah breaks his silence, lashing out at God in defiant anger: "Yes [I am very angry,

---

18. Even better, one could say that just as the acts of self-mortification taken on by the Ninevites demonstrated their dependence on God, so the sun sent to smite Jonah demonstrates his own dependence on God—as great as that of the Ninevites he despises.

indeed, about that plant!], angry enough to die." In this fashion, Uriel Simon writes, "Jonah unwittingly passes sentence on [himself by] the disproportion of his reaction: the fact is that he was not nearly as troubled by the salvation of Nineveh as he is by the death of the plant. He confesses that the broad assault on divine justice did not provoke him nearly as much as the personal attack on his own well-being."[19]

Given the ridiculous position that Jonah has now put himself in, God can close the book with a sharp question, which we never hear Jonah answer: "And should I not be concerned about Nineveh, that great city, in which there are more than a hundred and twenty thousand persons who do not know their right hand from their left, and also many animals?" (4:11). According to Jewish tradition, Jonah answers God by reciting the closing lines of the prophet Micah:

> Who is a God like you, pardoning iniquity
>   and passing over transgression
>   of the remnant of your possession?
> He does not retain his anger forever,
>   because he delights in showing clemency.
> He will again have compassion upon us;
>   he will tread our iniquities under foot. (Mic. 7:18–19)

Whatever Jonah's response, the reader sees the untenable position he has put himself in. God is not content simply to use this reluctant prophet to forgive Nineveh; he wishes also to educate the prophet. For ideally the prophet is supposed to represent both God to the people (in order to proclaim justice) and the people to God (in order to plead for mercy).

Conclusion

It is God's fundamental desire that any prophet who would speak to and for Israel would participate in God's manner of conducting the affairs of the world.[20] Sometimes, as in the case of Moses, this means being sufficiently

---

19. Simon, *Jonah*, 44.
20. So Hans Urs von Balthasar:
    The whole dialogue between God and man passes through Moses in such a way that he must not only continuously represent God's standpoint over against the people, but can equally continuously set out before God the standpoint of the people, where this is at all defensible. . . . [YHWH], who has bound himself to Israel, is quite simply no longer free. . . . The mediator must defend what is divine against God: God's commitment and obligation against God's freedom, God's will to bestow grace against his punitive

knowledgeable about God's *character* (the thirteen attributes) and *promises* that he can remind God of them in time of need.[21] The biblical narrative is constructed such that this is a *real* act of bargaining.[22] Absent Moses and his bravery, Israel will cease to exist.

But the story fails as soon as we reduce it to some theory of divine accommodation. For attributing to God the expression of wrath is not the same as attributing to God such bodily appendages as hands or feet. *The expression of divine wrath or grief is necessary in order to bring the importance of human participation into highest relief.* The point is worth repeating: when Moses and God go head to head in Exod. 32–34, the identity of God is not represented solely by what the character marked "God" says in the dialogue. The identity is fleshed out by the combination of the two voices. Through the prophets, God has invited Israel into his own person, and unlike Noah the people have a material effect on how the world's affairs are conducted. In the midrash, God rues the day Moses departs from this world. As Muffs has so clearly shown, God has not only left himself open to intimidation; he has *required* it. Yet God has not been so cavalier as to hand over his providential designs to a wayward and often fickle humanity lock, stock, and barrel. His providential plan will not be deterred.

In the book of Jonah, we see what happens if the prophetic counterpart refuses to play his part. Given a choice between human participation and God's intentions to forgive and heal, the latter must always win. But even in

righteousness, ultimately God's "weakness" against his strength. (*The Glory of the Lord*, vol. 6, *Theology: The Old Covenant*, trans. Brian McNeil and Erasmo Leiva-Merikakis [San Francisco: Ignatius, 1991], 191)

21. Karl Barth writes, in regard to Moses's prayer: "Is not this to flee from God to God, to appeal from God to God?" (*Church Dogmatics* 4/1, trans. G. W. Bromiley [Edinburgh: T&T Clark, 1956], 426). Or consider Barth on the person of Moses himself:

[Moses] was the man who heard and mediated the Word of God, advising and leading and, in fact, ruling the people, not in his own power, but in that of the Word of God which he heard and mediated. And we know, too, that he was the man who prayed for Israel in his solitariness with God, in a sense forcing himself upon God, keeping Him to His promises and earlier work as the covenant Lord of Israel, and being approved and heard by God. He was the man who anticipated in his relationship to Israel the mission ordained for it in its relationship with the nations as the meaning and scope of the covenant which God had concluded with it. He steadfastly represented the people before God even at the risk of his own person and his own relationship with [YHWH]. . . . The mystery of the grace of God is the mystery of this man, and of the connexion between him and that One. The elevation of Israel stands or falls with his election. . . . To look to God meant to Israel to look to this man, to hear God to hear the word of this man, to obey God to follow his direction, to trust God to trust his insight. (*Church Dogmatics* 4/1, 429–30)

22. Aquinas, who believes in the predestination of the saved and the damned alike, nevertheless declares with full confidence that the prayers of the elect contribute to another's predestined state. See his discussion in *Summa Theologiae* 1.23.8.

this case, it is not sufficient simply to "win." A forgiven Nineveh is not the same as an educated prophet. The book does not end with the success of the prophetic mission (Jon. 3:10). Rather, the whole book turns on the drama of chap. 4 and whether Jonah can learn what his role in this affair should have been, with the hope that he will play it more faithfully should the occasion arise again.

In brief, representation and impassibility in their Old Testament inflections take seriously God's intimate emotional involvement with humankind. Yet however passionate the divine-human encounters may appear, they never call into question the benevolent ends toward which God is driving the story. God is love, and as such he desires to involve humankind in the administration of the world to which he is so devoted. Moreover, as the close of the book of Jonah shows so clearly, it is not enough for God to impose obedience. God wants his prophets to offer their service willingly. God allows himself to be dependent upon the prayers of Israel's great intercessors, but in so doing he does not set his providential plans at risk. For it is precisely God's sovereignty that makes our freedom possible.

Perhaps this is the answer the Old Testament would provide to the conundrum of Gethsemane. The man Jesus makes a free decision, but there is no way to imagine that the Son would do anything but obey the Father and drink that cup. The advantage of the Old Testament is that we need not explore this thorny problem in the context of a single moral agent. The Old Testament can split the problem (precisely because the idea of "incarnation" is present in a less concentrated form[23]) across two narratives and so ask and answer a question that cannot be put to the person of Jesus. Placing Moses and Jonah in Gethsemane, we can see that God, through the agent appointed to represent God before humanity and humanity before God, does suffer—but he does so impassibly.

---

23. On the notion that God incarnates himself within the people Israel, see Michael Wyschogrod, "Incarnation," *Pro Ecclesia* 2 (1993), 208–15, esp. 212–13.

PART 2

"In the Beginning"

3

Creation

Creatio ex Nihilo *and the Bible*

The doctrine of creation out of nothing has been a challenge for modern biblical scholars. For most commentators, everything turns on how we understand the first few words of Genesis. As a result defenders of the doctrine have felt compelled to reject recent translations of this initial clause: "When God began to create . . ." (NJPS). But this has made the more philologically astute readers worry: Can doctrine trump grammar? A solution to this problem requires us to return to the origins of the doctrine itself. This doctrine's central concerns focus on the relationship of God to the world; worries about the absolute beginning of the universe are secondary. By attending to the way the doctrine arose in the early church, we will better understand its biblical grounding.

The relationship of the doctrine of *creatio ex nihilo* to the Bible has been a much-debated issue since the rise of historical criticism. All the standard prooftexts for the doctrine have been shown to lack the clarity and precision they were once thought to possess. This chapter will come at this challenge from three directions. First, I will begin with an examination of Gen. 1:1–3, the standard point of departure for every student of the doctrine. Second, I will turn to the central theological concerns that the doctrine addresses. Here I will take up Janet Soskice's important claim that the theological center of *creatio ex nihilo* should not be restricted to the question of the origins of the universe.[1] Gerhard May's influential work on the origin of the doctrine

1. Janet Soskice, "Creation and the Glory of Creature," *Modern Theology* 29 (2013): 172–85.

is not the only account that can be given.[2] To fill this out I intend to consider Kathryn Tanner's brilliant study, *God and Creation in Christian Theology*, a book which goes a long way toward reorienting the terms of discussion.[3] For Tanner the doctrine explains how the Bible can speak of God's utter transcendence from and immanence to the world in a noncontradictory fashion. A different set of biblical texts will need to be examined in order to test the viability of this approach. My final point concerns the affective character of the doctrine, something I have learned from the writings of John Webster and David Hart. "The Christian vision of the world," Hart has observed, "is not some rational deduction from empirical experience, but is . . . a moral and spiritual labor."[4]

Genesis 1 and *Creatio ex Nihilo*

Let me begin with the Bible. The two texts most commented on are Gen. 1:1 and 2 Macc. 7:28.[5] For many modern scholars, 2 Maccabees appears to be the better candidate of the two, for it seems to contain an explicit denial of the pre-existence of matter: "Look at the heaven and the earth and see everything that is in them, and recognize that God did not make them out of things that existed." But, as scholars have shown, the assertion that God did not make the world out of things that existed could have merely implied that he fashioned the world from unformed matter. For we have contemporary Greek evidence for the use of an almost identical idiom to describe the engendering of children by their parents.[6] But we should be careful to underscore that this does not mean that the author of 2 Maccabees understood the term this way. At the same time, that possibility cannot be ruled out. As a result this text fails as a decisive prooftext for the doctrine. The most we can say is that 2 Maccabees is patient of the doctrine of *creatio ex nihilo*.

The so-called Priestly creation story, Gen. 1:1–2:4a, is also a contested text. The consensus among scholars (with which I agree), is that the first three verses depict God forming the world out of pre-existent matter. On

2. Gerhard May, *Creatio ex Nihilo: The Doctrine of "Creation out of Nothing" in Early Christian Thought*, trans. A. S. Worrall (Edinburgh: University of Edinburgh Press, 1994).

3. Kathryn Tanner, *God and Creation in Christian Theology: Tyranny or Empowerment?* (Minneapolis: Fortress, 1988).

4. David Bentley Hart, *The Doors of the Sea: Where Was God in the Tsunami?* (Grand Rapids: Eerdmans, 2005), 58.

5. For an example of this, see Paul Copan and William L. Craig, *Creation out of Nothing: A Biblical, Philosophical, and Scientific Exploration* (Grand Rapids: Baker Academic, 2004) and the literature cited therein.

6. May, *Creatio ex Nihilo*, 8.

this view, the first two verses constitute a set of subordinate clauses that set up the main clause in v. 3:

> [1]When God set out to create the heavens and the earth, [2]the earth was a formless void and darkness covered the face of the deep, while a wind from God swept over the face of the waters. [3]Then God said, "Let there be light"; and there was light. (NRSV alt.)

On this understanding, v. 2 describes the chaotic substrate that preceded God's first creative act. To this we can add the problem of the "darkness" that is mentioned in v. 4 ("And God saw that the light was good; and God separated the light from the darkness."). It precedes God's creative work of making light.

One way out of this impasse is to appeal to the Greek translation of the Hebrew original. The Septuagint renders Gen. 1:1 as an independent sentence and thus portrays the making of the heavens and the earth as the first act of creation and the subsequent description of the chaotic nature of the earth, heavens, and waters as a description of how they appeared after this first creative act. Indeed, as Menahem Kister has shown, it is a short step from the Septuagint to an early Jewish exegetical tradition that understood all the items listed in Gen. 1:2 as items created by God.[7] The adoption of the Septuagint translation in the prologue to the Gospel of John lends considerable authority to this particular translation for the Christian reader of the Bible.[8] Although I am very sympathetic to using both the Septuagint and John to supplement what we learn from Gen. 1, I do not think we should abandon the Hebrew text as a lost cause. Let me explain why the first chapter of the Bible may still be of some value for *creatio ex nihilo*.

A crucial point to bear in mind is a distinction that Brevard Childs has made between a discrete textual witness and its underlying subject matter.[9] We have the discrete, literary witnesses of each biblical author whose distinct, perspectival voice must be heard. But there is also an underlying subject matter that these various witnesses are grappling with, something that Childs

---

7. "*Tohu wa-Bohu*, Primordial Elements and *Creatio ex Nihilo*," *JSQ* 14 (2007): 229–56.

8. This is the tack that Ian A. McFarland takes in *From Nothing: A Theology of Creation* (Louisville: Westminster John Knox, 2014). For him, the significance of the Gospel of John is twofold. First, it does not mention the formless waste of Gen. 1:2. Second, in John "the sole precondition . . . for creation is God." And not a solitary God, McFarland is quick to add, but a God who is defined by his relationship to his Word: "In this way, at the same time that John 1 stands as the most explicit biblical statement of the unconditional character of God's creating work, it also signals that creation from nothing is not merely a claim about God's relation to the world, but also a statement about God's own identity" (McFarland, *From Nothing*, 23).

9. Brevard S. Childs, *Biblical Theology of the Old and New Testaments: Theological Reflection on the Christian Bible* (Minneapolis: Fortress, 1992), 80–90.

identifies with the Latin word *res* or the German *Sache*. As an example let us consider the person of Jesus Christ. The biblical scholar is responsible for two things: first, hearing the distinctive voices of each of the various New Testament authors and allowing them to speak about Jesus in their own singular fashion and without harmonization. The Lukan Jesus, for example, must not be confused with the Johannine. But the scholar must also take an additional step and address the underlying reality of the Jesus who is confessed in the creeds. To limit the task of exegesis to that of uncovering different voices is to abandon the theological task proper to exegesis in the first place.

When biblical scholars address the literary shape of Gen. 1:1–3, one of the first things to be noted are the parallels with the Mesopotamian story of creation, the *Enuma Elish*. But just as significant are the differences between the two accounts. As biblical scholars have pointed out, the material that pre-exists creation is presented in vastly different ways in the two cosmogonies. The *Enuma Elish* presumes an epic battle between the God who will emerge as sovereign and the powers of chaos, while the Bible describes the creation of the world as taking place without any opposition.[10] As Jon Levenson succinctly puts the matter: "Genesis 1:1–2:3 *begins* near the point when the Babylonian poem *ends* its action!"[11]

To put a point of emphasis on the dramatic turn that Gen. 1 takes, let us consider what happens to the figure of Leviathan or to the sea dragons in the course of creation's six days. As is well known, a wide variety of biblical texts trace a path not unlike what is found in Assyrian and Canaanite materials. In these texts the sea dragon (sg. *tannîn*, pl. *tannînîm*) appears as a primordial chaos monster acting with purposes athwart those of God. Consider, for example, Ps. 74:13: "You divided the sea by your might; you broke the heads of the dragons [*tannînîm*] in the waters," or Isa. 51:9: "Was it not you . . . who pierced the dragon [*tannîn*]?" But also important to note is the way in which the term for the sea dragon can stand as a poetic variant of other terms for primeval monsters: "On that day the LORD . . . will punish Leviathan the fleeing serpent . . . he will kill the dragon [*tannîn*] that is in the sea" (Isa. 27:1).

10. In the world of Gen. 1, the only ground for explaining the emergence of evil is human sin. So Ronald Hendel (from a typescript of his forthcoming AB commentary):

> God's perception of the goodness of things in Genesis 1 is reversed at the beginning of the P flood story, when God sees that the earth and all flesh have become corrupt (6:12). In the intertextual relations between Gen 1 and 6:12, the initial goodness of things turns out to be a somewhat fragile quality, capable of being disrupted and corrupted by violent deeds. The goodness of things seems to be God's intention, but it is an ideal condition which living things can spoil, and which then requires a (cleansing) destruction and re-creation.

11. Jon Levenson, *Creation and the Persistence of Evil: The Jewish Drama of Divine Omnipotence*, 2nd ed. (Princeton: Princeton University Press, 1994), 122 (italics in original).

In stark contrast to all of these examples stands the witness of Gen. 1:20–23:

> And God said, "Let the waters bring forth swarms of living creatures, and let birds fly above the earth across the dome of the sky." So God created the great sea monsters [*tannînîm*] and every living creature that moves, of every kind, with which the waters swarm, and every winged bird of every kind. And God saw that it was good. God blessed them, saying, "Be fruitful and multiply and fill the waters in the seas, and let birds multiply on the earth." And there was evening and there was morning, the fifth day.

Here the sea monster is created by God and wholly under his control. No longer an adversary of any kind, he can be included in the formula of approbation: "And God saw that [what he had made] was good." Jon Levenson summarizes the novelty of Gen. 1 in this fashion: "In Genesis there is no active opposition to God's creative labor. He works on inert matter. In fact, rather than *creatio ex nihilo*, 'creation without opposition' is the more accurate nutshell statement of the theology underlying our passage."[12]

At one level there is nothing to dispute here. But at the same time, this evaluation is not completely satisfying. We must recall that *creatio ex nihilo* is a doctrine that arises in a Greco-Roman environment—that is, in a world in which the eternity of matter implied that the gods were constrained by its limitations when they created the world. But this particular problem is not something the biblical writer ever faced or could even imagine.

This is an important clarification because many commentators make the strong claim that Gen. 1 refutes *creatio ex nihilo*. But if we are pursuing this question strictly from the perspective of what our textual witnesses allow, it would be fairer to say that God does not face any opposition to his creative endeavors, as is the rule in the ancient Near East. True, matter is pre-existent, but one must concede that this datum means something quite different when we import it into a Greco-Roman environment. For there the issue of pre-existent matter connotes a significant qualification of divine power.

Here is where the notion of the text's *res* or *Sache* comes into play. There can be no doubt that the author of Gen. 1 inherits an account of creation that presupposes the need to destroy the forces of chaos first. These so-called *Chaoskampf* texts have been well studied by biblical scholars. But the author of Gen. 1 has consciously and utterly rejected this idea. If we were to sit down with our priestly scribes and give them a brief introduction to Greek cosmology, emphasizing for them the fact that pre-existent matter necessarily restricts what God can accomplish in the material world, can we imagine

12. Ibid., 122.

that they would accept such a notion? Though certainty obviously eludes us, I find it hard to imagine.

But let me return to the issue of the chaos substrate. As Levenson has noted, the materials listed in Gen. 1:2 form a primordial chaos. But, as he goes on to say, the same holds true for darkness.

> Light, which is God's first creation, does not banish darkness. Rather it alternates with it: "there was evening and there was morning" in each of the six days of creation. . . . The priority of "evening" over "day" reminds us of which is primordial and recalls again that chaos in the form of darkness has not been eliminated, but only confined to its place through alternation with light.[13]

On this understanding, darkness is part of the primordial chaos substrate that confronts God as he sets out to create the world. Like the "matter" of Greek cosmogonies, it would appear to limit God.

Yet such a notion is overturned by a close reading of the entire narrative. For, as countless commentators have noted going all the way back to the rabbinic period, the seventh day does not append the formula that was standard for the previous six days: "There was evening and there was morning, the Xth day." On the seventh day, all trace of this primordial darkness disappears. Gerhard von Rad writes:

> The Sabbath at creation, as the last of the creative days, is not limited; the concluding formula ("and it was evening and it was morning . . .") is lacking, and that too, like everything else in this chapter, is intentional. Thus Gen 2.1ff. speaks about the preparation of an exalted saving good for the world and man, of a rest "before which millennia pass away as a thunderstorm" (Novalis). It is tangibly "existent" protologically as it is expected eschatologically in Hebrews [chap. 4].[14]

And Jon Levenson adds:

> No wonder the Mishnah can call the eschatological future, "a day that is entirely Sabbath and rest for eternal life" and designate Psalm 92, the song "for the Sabbath day," as the special hymn for that aeon. The reality that the Sabbath represents—God's unchallenged and uncompromised mastery, blessing, and hallowing—is consistently and irreversibly available only in the world-to-come. Until then, it is known only in the tantalizing experience of the Sabbath.[15]

13. Ibid., 123.

14. Gerhard von Rad, *Genesis: A Commentary*, rev. ed. (Philadelphia: Westminster, 1972), 62–63.

15. Levenson, *Creation*, 123.

But it is not just the Mishnah that makes this move. As Yair Zakovitch points out, Isa. 60 utilizes a tradition about the special light that was available for the first days of creation to describe the conditions that will define the city of Jerusalem at the eschaton.[16] Verses 19–20 read:

> The sun shall no longer be
> > your light by day,
> nor for brightness shall the moon
> > give light to you by night;
> but the LORD will be your everlasting light,
> > and your God will be your glory.
> Your sun shall no more go down,
> > or your moon withdraw itself;
> for the LORD will be your everlasting light,
> > and your days of mourning shall be ended.

What is striking about this text—indeed something it shares with the seventh day in Genesis—is that darkness is not some sort of primordial chaos that God must work around. Rather, it is an element of the cosmos that not only is under God's providential power but can and will be eradicated at the close of the world's history.

Robert Wilken noted that the Roman thinker Galen had intimated the doctrine of *creatio ex nihilo* prior to its appearance in the works of Theophilus and Irenaeus. Galen observed that the Bible describes the created order as arising from the power of the divine word alone and not limited by the physical characteristics of matter. Though Galen's remarks were based on some knowledge of Gen. 1, it is not hard to imagine that Isa. 60 would have been just as bothersome to him. Light, in his mind, required the mediating agency of the sun and stars. Summarizing Galen's train of thought, Wilken writes:

> Certain things are impossible by nature and God does not—indeed cannot—do such things. He chooses the best possible way, the way according to reason. . . . The world of nature cannot be understood unless it is recognized that all things, including the creator, are governed by unalterable laws according to reason. The laws determine the way things are and always will be, not because God decided they should be this way, but because that is the best way for them to be. God is part of nature. He is, in the hymn of the Stoic Cleanthes, "leader of nature, governing all things by law."[17]

16. Yair Zakovitch, *Mašmîʿa šalom məbaśśer ṭôv* (Haifa: Haifa University Press, 2004), 38–43.
17. Robert Wilken, *The Christians as the Romans Saw Them* (New Haven: Yale University Press, 2003), 87.

The only conclusion I think we can draw from the Bible's final canonical form is that the existence of darkness at creation must be something God permits rather than something he is obligated to confront. Or, putting the matter differently, Gen. 2:1–3 (read in conjunction with Isa. 60) provides the standard historical-critical interpretation with an aporia. As we have seen, reading Gen. 1:1 in light of the *Enuma Elish* suggests that God is both confronted with and limited by the state of the universe prior to creation, hence the modern propensity to treat Gen. 1:1 as a subordinate, temporal clause. But by the time we get to the seventh day (or the eschaton), this assumption must be qualified. In other words, the close of the first creation story forces the reader to go back and rethink what is described at the beginning. But let me be clear. I am not suggesting that this changes how we view the grammar of 1:1. Grammar remains grammar. But the close of this story stands in some tension with the beginning. Though Gen. 1 does not teach *creatio ex nihilo* in the way early Christian theologians might have thought of it, it does not rule it out as decisively as many modern readers have assumed.

The Relationship of Divine Grace to Human Freedom

Let me turn from the first creation story to what systematic theologians have identified as the central theological concerns of the doctrine. The reason for doing so is that many biblical scholars have presumed that the doctrine stands or falls on the interpretation of Gen. 1. But, if the doctrine is more than just an account of the world's origin, then Soskice is certainly correct in exhorting us to widen our frame of reference as to what counts as biblical evidence. I will take as my point of departure McFarland's book *From Nothing: A Theology of Creation*.

He begins his account with the figure of Theophilus of Antioch, a bishop who around the year 180 CE wrote a treatise titled *To Autolycus*. Therein we find the claim that "God brought everything into being out of what does not exist, so that his greatness might be known and understood through his works."[18] Irenaeus of Lyons, of course, makes the very same claim. But the larger issue at stake here, it is important to note, is not so much how the world came to be as how the world is governed. Theophilus and Irenaeus want to establish that God's transcendence over the world does not come at the cost of his intimate oversight of its affairs.

18. *To Autolycus* 1.4, as cited by McFarland, *From Nothing*, 1.

The concern of governance can be seen in the striking contrast between the way Justin Martyr on the one hand and Theophilus and Irenaeus on the other treat the relationship between divine transcendence and immanence. Because Justin is beholden to the Platonic notion of pre-existent matter, "God is unable to act directly on or be immediately present to creation: God is and remains outside the phenomenal world."[19] For Irenaeus, on the other hand, God's transcendence does not connote remoteness from the material order. Quite the contrary. McFarland writes:

> This divine fullness establishes the most profound intimacy between Creator and creature: the same God "who fills the heavens and views the depths . . . is also present with everyone of us. . . . For his hand lays hold of all things, . . . is present in our hidden and secret parts, and publicly nourishes and preserves us." God's transcendence does not imply distance from creatures, but is rather the ground for God's engagement with them.[20]

As R. A. Norris summarizes the matter: "What makes God different from every creature—his eternal and ingenerate simplicity—is thus, for Irenaeus, precisely what assures his direct and intimate involvement with every creature."[21] In a world in which matter stands over against God, God is necessarily limited by the constraints matter imposes. Though divine transcendence is not at risk, the degree of intimacy that God can have with the world is severely qualified.

This distinctive feature of *creatio ex nihilo* is the subject of Kathryn Tanner's remarkable book *God and Creation in Christian Theology*. In this work, she shows how this doctrine enables one to affirm both divine immanence and transcendence without qualifying one in terms of the other. The blurb that Eugene Rogers provides on the back cover of the book is most illuminating. He writes: "Before I read *God and Creation*, I thought Christians had to choose between grace and free will. If they chose grace, so much the better. As I read, I found myself moved. Grace and free will were not rivals but companions."

Rogers's candid remark reveals the deep philosophical assumptions that most readers bring to the Bible. Even two thousand years into the Christian project, readers still think of divine grace as an external power that stands over against human free will. If an action, for example, requires 80 percent grace, then we contribute the other 20 percent. But Tanner would call such

19. McFarland, *From Nothing*, 11. In support of this position, McFarland cites this passage from Justin Martyr's *Dialogue with Trypho*: "He who has but the smallest intelligence will not venture to assert that the Creator and Father of all things would leave behind everything above heaven and appear on a little portion of the earth."
20. Ibid., 12.
21. R. A. Norris, *God and World in Early Christian Theology* (New York: Seabury, 1965), 86.

a worldview more Greek than biblical. In other words, because God's being is not distinct from the being of everything else that exists, he must establish his identity over against everything else. This is what the eternity of matter entails. *Creatio ex nihilo*, on the other hand, allows one to conceive this relationship quite differently: both God and the human agent can contribute 100 percent to any particular action. Tanner puts the matter thus: "Since divine agency is necessary for any action of the creature at all, it cannot be proper to say that God's activity is added on to the creature's." To which she adds this quotation from Karl Barth:

> In the rule of God we do not have to do first with a creaturely action and then—somewhere above or behind, but quite distinct from it . . .—with an operation of God Himself. To describe *concursus divinis* we cannot use the mathematical picture of two parallel lines. But creaturely events take place as God Himself acts.[22]

One way to appreciate the importance of this teaching is to consider an exegetical example. A doctrine, after all, is useful only to the degree that it makes us better readers of the biblical text. In his work on divine and human agency in Saint Paul's writings, John Barclay articulates a position that closely resembles Kathryn Tanner's.[23] And importantly he arrives at this view as a result of a close reading of several key passages in the Pauline correspondence.

For my part, I would like to turn to two of the most important moments in Abraham's life and the challenge they have posed for biblical commentators. In Gen. 12:1–3 Abraham is called by God "out of the blue":

> Now the LORD said to Abram, "Go from your country and your kindred and your father's house to the land that I will show you. I will make of you a great nation, and I will bless you, and make your name great, so that you will be a blessing. I will bless those who bless you, and the one who curses you I will curse; and in you all the families of the earth shall be blessed."

At this point in the story, Abraham has done nothing to merit the stupendous promise that he receives. This point was not lost on ancient exegetes, who proceeded to invent a myriad of stories to fill this lacuna. In so doing, they simply accented the fact that there is no explanation for the choice. Gerhard

---

22. Tanner, *God and Creation*, 94. The Barth quotation is from *Church Dogmatics*, 3/3.

23. John Barclay, "Grace and Transformation of Agency in Christ," in *Redefining First-Century Jewish and Christian Identities: Essays in Honor of E. P. Sanders*, ed. Fabian E. Udoh (Notre Dame, IN: University of Notre Dame Press, 2008), 372–89.

von Rad, along with innumerable other commentators, sees God's choice of Abraham as an excellent example of divine grace.[24] Everything depends on the will of the electing deity.

When we come to Gen. 22, however, after Abraham's extraordinary act of obedience to God's command to sacrifice his beloved son, the terms of the covenant are now reformulated but this time as a fitting reward for his obedience.

> The angel of the LORD called to Abraham a second time from heaven, and said, "By myself I have sworn, says the LORD: Because you have done this, and have not withheld your son, your only son, I will indeed bless you, and I will make your offspring as numerous as the stars of heaven and as the sand that is on the seashore. And your offspring shall possess the gate of their enemies, and by your offspring shall all the nations of the earth gain blessing for themselves, because you have obeyed my voice." (Gen. 22:15–18)

The important thing to note here is that the terms of the promise in both texts are similar, but the grounds for the promise could not be more different. Whereas Gen. 12 places the matter wholly in God's hands, Gen. 22 ascribes the promise to the merits of Abraham's deed: "Because you have done this . . . I will indeed bless you." It is striking to observe that von Rad makes no mention of this repetition of the promise. Although one cannot be certain, it is likely that this silence has to do with the author's discomfort with meritorious human actions. If so, von Rad enacts in his commentary the same position Rogers confessed before he grappled with the doctrine of *creatio ex nihilo*: divine grace and human merit are irreconcilable.

Tanner's work shows us that, had von Rad digested Barth or Aquinas on this issue, he could have done justice to the text in question.[25] One need not see the Bible's emphasis on human merit in Gen. 22 as canceling out the grace that was given in Gen. 12. To adopt the vocabulary of Thomas Aquinas, we could understand the act of election in Gen. 12 as the moment of "justification," when grace is given by God apart from any human merit. Having received this grace, Abraham is then enabled by this divine power to effect meritorious deeds that mark his progress toward sanctification. Barclay's description of Paul's "participationist" soteriology could easily be transferred to the book of Genesis: "Grace does not just invite 'response' but itself effects the human participation in grace, such that 'every good

---

24. Von Rad, *Genesis*, 159.

25. But the point I want to make is more Websterian—the doctrine depends on the spiritual affection of human wonder. We should not reduce it to a piece of objective knowledge. As Tanner's work shows, the modern world has demonstrated a massive forgetfulness about what the doctrine teaches even by those who affirm it!

work' can be viewed as the fruit of divine power as much as the product of believers themselves."[26]

It is striking that Barclay's amplification of what he learned from E. P. Sanders is already evident in the thinking of Athanasius. In a key passage, Athanasius writes: "When we render a recompense to the Lord to the utmost of our power, . . . we give nothing of our own, but those things which we have before received from Him, this being especially of His grace, that He should require, as from us, His own gifts."[27] And Khaled Anatolios explains as follows:

> Our response to God's grace both is and is not our own. It is not our own insofar as even this response derives from God's grace and is "received." And yet it is our own precisely because we do actually receive it: "those things which you give Me are yours, as having received them from Me." Moreover, it is precisely their becoming "our own" through our having received them which makes it possible for us to "give" them back to God. If they do not become our own, we would not be able to give them back to God; neither would God be able to require them back of us. But the fact that they do become our own means that the reciprocity of human and divine continues in an ascending cycle: God gives us grace and requires it back of us; we receive it and offer it back to God. "Virtue" and "holiness" are thus conceived in terms of this ascending dialectic, as the "offering back" as gift, of what is already received as gift. Here we see how a perceived dichotomy between striving for virtue and the participation in grace is really quite far from the more complex conception of Athanasius.[28]

The last sentence speaks volumes for the theological problem we have been tracing. It is almost impossible not to think of striving for virtue and participation in grace as irreconcilable opposites. One of the principal functions of the doctrine of *creatio ex nihilo* is to allow the reader of the Bible to make sense of passages in which divine grace and human free will seem to be set against one another. And that, I would suggest, is the sine qua non of any Christian doctrine. *Creatio ex nihilo* provides a metaphysical account of the world that allows for a deeper engagement with the way the Bible characterizes divine activity and human agency. As John Webster puts the matter, "The notion of creation out of nothing served to spell out the ontological entailments of the distinction between the eternal creator and the temporal, contingent creatures

26. Barclay, "Grace and Transformation," 385.

27. Athanasius, *Letter* 5.4 (*NPNF*[2] 4:518).

28. Both the citation from Athanasius and the commentary by Anatolios come from *Athanasius: The Coherence of His Thought* (New York: Routledge, 1998), 174–75.

who are the objects of his saving regard, resisting ideas of the creator as one who merely gave form to coeval matter, and so accentuating the limitless capacity and freedom of God."[29]

Creatio ex Nihilo and Charitable Acts

Let me dwell on the subject of these "ontological entailments" just a little longer. Robert Wilken, let us recall, showed us that Galen intuited the doctrine of *creatio ex nihilo* before the Christians themselves had come to broad agreement about it. In particular, Wilken argues that the Christian view of God's providential power offended Greek and Roman sensibilities:

> God, in the Greek view, dwelt in a realm above the earth, but he did not stand outside of the world, the *kosmos*. Earth and heaven are part of the same cosmos, which has existed eternally. The world is not the creation of a transcendent God. The cosmos has its own laws, and all that exists—the physical world, animals, man, and the gods—are subject to nature's laws. "Certain things are impossible to nature," said Galen, and "God does not even attempt such things at all." Rather, "he chooses the best out of the possibilities of becoming."[30]

We have already noted the challenges posed by Gen. 1:3 and Isa. 60. Both texts claim that God can illumine the world without recourse to the means that nature has provided—the sun, moon, and stars. Another offense against reason can be found in the revolutionary way that wisdom texts (and eventually the New Testament and early Christian thinkers) came to understand the charitable act. In these materials, showing kindness to the suffering was not just a good deed but an alignment of one's actions with the structure of the universe. One could argue that a discussion of the virtue of charity fits better within a theology of creation than in a discussion of religious ethics.

Peter Brown's magnificent book *Through the Eye of a Needle* has highlighted the significance of the theological shaping of this distinctive practice. Greco-Roman citizens, he observes, were not miserly. Wealthy donors funded lavish public buildings all over the empire. But their generosity always included the expectation that honor and other public accolades would come their way. In a world ruled by what Brown calls the iron laws of reciprocity, "it was considered bad luck to dream that one gave money to a beggar. Such

---

29. "Creation out of Nothing," in *Christian Dogmatics: Reformed Theology for the Church Catholic*, ed. Michael Allen and Scott R. Swain (Grand Rapids: Baker Academic, 2016), 129–30.
30. Wilken, *Christians as the Romans Saw Them*, 91.

dreams portended death: 'For Death is like a beggar,' the saying went, 'who takes and gives nothing in return.'"[31]

In the synagogue and church, however, a different construal of the charitable act was taking shape. The fact that the poor could not repay was a crucial ingredient for the value of giving alms, not out of a concern for unadulterated altruism—that is more a modern than an ancient value—but because of what such deeds of charity say about the way God governs the world.

This point is made well in a story that the rabbis told about an encounter between Rabbi Gamliel and an unnamed pagan philosopher.[32] The latter was bothered by the Torah's command that one should assist the poor and have no second thoughts while doing so. Acting so carelessly would bankrupt the man of means and the result would be two indigent persons, not just one. As we consider Rabbi Gamliel's response, it is important to make one point clear: in the Bible, a gift to the poor was often understood to be a no-interest loan.

> R[abbi] Gamliel said: "If a poor man sought a loan from you, would you consent?" He replied, "No!" "And if he brought a deposit?" He replied, "Yes!" "And what if he brought you the governor as surety?" He replied, "Yes."
>
> "Isn't it a matter of *a fortiori* logic: If you will issue a loan when a person of means goes surety, how much the more so when 'He who spoke and made the world' goes surety. For Scripture says, '*He who is generous to the poor makes a loan to God, and God will surely repay*'" (Prov. 19:17).[33]

The retort of Rabbi Gamliel is astounding. Our Greco-Roman philosopher imagines the charitable act solely within the framework of interhuman reciprocity. "Certain things are impossible to nature," Galen had claimed, "God does not even attempt such things at all." That neatly sums up why this pagan thinker rejected Rabbi Gamliel's understanding of charitable action. But in the biblical understanding, charity is an action that God directly oversees. The ways of providence conform with the intentions of the creator when he made the world.

Creatio ex nihilo—recalling the words of John Webster—rejects the idea that the creator simply gave form to coeval matter. If that was the case, then the rules of reciprocity ought to govern charitable behavior. Matter, we must

31. Peter Brown, *Through the Eye of a Needle: Wealth, the Fall of Rome, and the Making of Christianity in the West, 350–550 AD* (Princeton: Princeton University Press, 2012), 76.

32. For a strikingly similar Christian version of this story, see the passage from Saint Basil that I discuss in *Charity: The Place of the Poor in the Biblical Tradition* (New Haven: Yale University Press, 2013), 30–32.

33. My translation (AT) from *Midrasch-Tannaïm zum Deuteronomium*, ed. David Hoffmann (Berlin: Itzkowski, 1908), 84.

assume, restricts what God can do. The fact that the world does not operate within the ambit of these expectations gives eloquent testimony to "the
limitless capacity and freedom of God" in creating and governing the world.

It may be worth recalling that Christian charitable practices were envied by
many in the Roman world. Julian the Apostate famously attempted to import
them into a non-Christian setting. Yet his ambitions failed. Rodney Stark's
explanation of that failure is worth noting: "For all that [Julian] urged pagan
priests to match these Christian practices, there was little or no response because *there were no doctrinal bases or traditional practices* for them to build
upon."[34] The doctrine that was conspicuously lacking was *creatio ex nihilo*,
a doctrine that allowed Christian thinkers to see that the gracious intentions
of the creator were not limited by the materials at his disposal. Rather, it was
through those very materials that those intentions were granted expression.
Inserting Christian charitable practices into a pagan context was something
like transplanting an organ into a new body. Without powerful drugs in place,
the recipient's body will not recognize the new organ and will reject it. For
Christian charity to flourish, a radical new way of thinking about God's
relationship to the world had to take root.

Grace and Affirmation of the Doctrine

This leads to my final point, which I will make more in the way of a suggestion than a detailed argument. Affirming *creatio ex nihilo* is, as David Hart
asserts, "not some rational deduction from empirical experience, but . . . a
moral and spiritual labor."[35] Nowhere is the truth of this better reflected than in
the way the virtue of charity is enacted in the life of Tobit. Tobit is something
of a Joban figure: his heroism in assisting the poor is not rewarded; instead,
it leads to blindness and what threatens to be a premature and tragic death.
And yet, in spite of these challenges, he holds fast to the commandment. With
characteristic insight, Augustine captures nicely the irony of the moment:

> Tobit was blind, yet he taught his son the way of God. You know this is true,
> because Tobit advised his son, *Give alms, my son, for almsdeeds save you from
> departing into darkness* (Tob. 4:7, 11); yet the speaker was in darkness himself.
> . . . He had no fear that his son might say in his heart, "Did you not give alms
> yourself? Why, then, are you talking to me out of your blindness? Darkness is

34. Rodney Stark, *The Rise of Christianity* (Princeton: Princeton University Press, 1996),
88 (italics in original).
35. David Bentley Hart, *Doors of the Sea*, 58.

where almsgiving has evidently led you, so how can you advise me that *alms-deeds save you from departing into darkness?*" (*Enarratio in Psalmum* 96.18)[36]

The confidence of Tobit is altogether puzzling. "How could Tobit give that advice to his son with such confidence?" Augustine goes on to ask. And this is the answer he provides:

> Only because he habitually saw another light. The son held his father's hand to help him walk, but the father taught his son the way, that he might live.—And the "other light" that Tobit saw, of course, is the light of *faith*! (*Enarratio in Psalmum* 96.18)[37]

The notion that Tobit saw another light recalls an important passage from *The Confessions*. At the end of this work, when Augustine is commenting on the story of creation, he makes an astute observation about the literary structure of that narrative. During the first six days of creation—which describe the world that we live in—God concludes his successive efforts with an affirmation of the goodness of what he has made. This judgment is given special emphasis at the close of the sixth day in which God declares that all that he has made is "*very* good."[38]

But this raises an important question. Can we, as readers of the biblical text, affirm what God declares to be the case? The only way to do so, Augustine argues, is through divine grace (*Confessions* 13.31, 46):

> But as to those who do by Your Spirit see these things, it is You who see in them. Thus when they see that these works are good, it is You who see that they are good; when anything pleases us because of You, You are what pleases us in that thing, and when by Your Spirit something pleases us, it pleases You in us. "*For what man knows the things of a man, but the spirit of a man, which is in him?*

---

36. *Expositions of the Psalms*, vol. 2, *Psalms 73–98*, trans. Maria Boulding, The Works of Saint Augustine: A Translation for the 21st Century (Hyde Park, NY: New City, 2002), 456.

37. Ibid.

38. But Augustine also knows that the world that God fashioned in the first six days is not "the best of all possible worlds," to quote Leibniz's expression. That awaits the seventh day, that is, the eschaton. The *Catechism of the Catholic Church* (§310) puts it this way:

> But why did God not create a world so perfect that no evil could exist in it? With infinite power God could always create something better (*STh* [Aquinas, *Summa Theologiae*] I,25,6). But with infinite wisdom and goodness God freely willed to create a world 'in a state of journeying' towards its ultimate perfection. In God's plan this process of becoming involves the appearance of certain beings and the disappearance of others, the existence of the more perfect alongside the less perfect, both constructive and destructive forces of nature. With physical good there exists also physical evil as long as creation has not reached perfection (*SCG* [Aquinas, *Summa contra Gentiles*] III,71).

So the things also that are of God, no man knows, but the spirit of God. Now we have received not the spirit of this world, but the spirit that is of God, that we may know the things that are given us from God" (1 Cor. 2:11).[39]

In this text we see the two themes we have been following tightly stitched together. On the one hand there is the ability to discern the goodness with which God not only made the world but continues to uphold and guide it. As that pagan philosopher with whom Rabbi Gamliel spoke knew so well, the world does not present itself as a place directed by divine mercy. The Greeks were not unwise to presume that one would be better off relying on the principle of reciprocity. Even the gods are constrained by the ways of nature. For Rabbi Gamliel (and Saint Basil) only divine revelation (in this case, Prov. 19:17) could enable one to see the astonishing manner in which God is related to the world. But revelation on its own is not sufficient. One also needs the assistance of the Holy Spirit to act in accordance with the commandments God has given. In his stupendous obedience to the command to offer his only son, Abraham was not earning his salvation—full stop. Rather, he was enabled to complete this meritorious deed in a way that honored both divine and human agency. "In crowning our merits," Augustine had said, "you are crowning your own gifts." And so for the affirmation of the goodness of the created order. The world, as it is presently constituted, does not present itself as good to the sensitive observer. We can only speak of it as such when we are graced to see it as God sees it. Affirming the doctrine of *creatio ex nihilo* is not simply an exegetical task; it requires the supernatural gift of faith.

The relationship between doctrine and biblical exegesis is both complex and fraught with controversy. A hallmark of modern approaches to the Bible is the independence of the exegete from the disputes that have arisen in interconfessional contexts. Given the fact that many presentations of *creatio ex nihilo* ground the concept on a faulty reading of Gen. 1:1–3, a consensus has arisen that the doctrine has little to do with the Bible itself. But in the early Christian sources themselves, Gen. 1:1 is not the most important piece of the puzzle. As Anatolios, for example, has shown, the doctrine is more interested in the dependence of the created order on God than in the conditions of its initial origin. As we saw in the second part of this essay, a major concern of the doctrine is to clarify how human and divine agency interrelate. I suggested that one way of testing its biblical character would be to ask whether

---

39. *The Confessions of St. Augustine*, trans. F. J. Sheed, 2nd ed. (Indianapolis: Hackett, 2006), 317.

the doctrine can help us exegete biblical texts where the question of divine and human agency is at issue.

In addition to this, because the doctrine puts such a premium on dependence, the practice of charity also provides confirmation of the doctrine. As I have argued at great length elsewhere, early Christian charity has more to do with metaphysics than morals. That is, the teaching about charitable actions and the rewards they generate is meant to reveal the (wondrous) type of world God has created and—on the basis of this information—how one might flourish in it. Roman thinkers greatly esteemed Christian charity, and some like Julian tried to import these patterns of living into the pagan realm. Yet those efforts were unsuccessful because they lacked the requisite theological underpinning. Behind the practice of charity as taught in the Bible is the presumption that God superintends such acts and that those who give in this sacrificial fashion will ultimately be rewarded. The reward, it is important to emphasize, is not so much a motivator of the behavior in question as an indicator of the type of world God has fashioned. To pagan thinkers, this was an irrational assertion. Matter restricts what the gods can do. Better to conduct one's affairs in accord with the "ironclad laws of reciprocity" than to cherish notions about divine sovereignty that do not hold water.

In both these instances (charity and grace/merit) certain metaphysical assumptions are presumed. God governs the natural order in a way that respects human autonomy and rewards sacrificial generosity. God does not operate within the rules of interhuman (and so, this-worldly) reciprocity. Though I do not claim that Gen. 1:1–3 establishes this, I have shown that Gen. 2:1–3 profoundly qualifies the independence of matter that might be inferred from the first three verses of the Bible. This, plus the evidence of Second and Third Isaiah, strongly pushes the reader of the Bible toward the doctrine itself. It is a trajectory internal to the larger canonical witness. The fact that as early as the book of *Jubilees* we have texts claiming that God created the primordial matter of Gen. 1:2 provides confirmation of this. It is on these grounds that the doctrine has deep biblical roots.

4

Original Sin

The Fall of Humanity and the Golden Calf

Biblical scholars regularly maintain, with good reason, that the story of Adam and Eve is not a "fall" story in the conventional sense of the word. Some have gone a step further and adopted a reading more in keeping with ancient Gnosticism, that the story is more about the maturation and elevation of the human race than its fall. But if the concern is to establish a theological anthropology that is properly biblical, it is hard to ignore the dim view of the human condition that is found in most of the Old Testament. Attention must be paid to the other stories of origin in the Bible that address this subject more directly. What we see in these materials is the propensity of human actors to rebel against God almost immediately after receipt of an extraordinary blessing. From this vantage point, one can cast a glance backward at Gen. 2–3 and appreciate the theological and exegetical logic that informed the apostle Paul's famous reading of this text.

Rabbi Abbahu said: Just as I led Adam into the garden of Eden and commanded him and he transgressed my commandment, whereupon I punished him by dismissal and exile . . . so also did I bring his descendants into the land of Israel and command them, and they transgressed my commands and I punished them by dismissal and exile.

Genesis Rabbah 19.9 (AT)

The modern age has not been kind to the traditional interpretation of the story of Adam and Eve. Since the rise of modern biblical studies in the early part of the eighteenth century, more than a modicum of doubt has been cast upon the standard Christian understanding of that story as "the Fall."[1] If

1. This story has been rehearsed so many times that it is not necessary to review it here. For one statement of the matter, see James Barr, *The Garden of Eden and the Hope of Immortality*

the transgression of Adam really does usher in the reign of sin and death from which the rest of the biblical odyssey will seek redress, why is Adam's sin and its consequences *never* mentioned until the writings of Paul? Could the story really have such intrinsic significance and yet be completely ignored by the rest of the Old Testament and the teachings of Jesus?

The problem is a real and profound one and must be engaged. On the one hand, I am in definite agreement with most of my biblical colleagues that the story of Adam and Eve, on its own terms, does not lead inevitably to the Christian notion of "the Fall." Yet, I do not believe that focusing on the *bare narrative* of Gen. 2–3 is the proper way to approach this doctrine. If we wish to place the Fall on solid biblical grounds, we will need to expand our notion of what creation entails in the minds of our biblical authors. And, armed with this datum, we will be better prepared to understand, with some sympathy, why the fathers of the church read Gen. 1–3 as they did.

Two Creation Stories

Reading the Bible's story of creation has never been a simple matter. Modern readers have puzzled over the relation between these ancient descriptions of the world's beginnings and the alternative accounts provided by scientific investigation. But there are other, even more basic problems. Consider, for example, the long-known fact that the Bible contains not one, but two accounts of creation. And these two accounts are presented back to back at the very beginning of Genesis.

The earliest interpreters of the Bible, both Jewish and Christian, thought that both accounts came from the hand of Moses. In the first (Gen. 1:1–2:4a), Moses provided only the barest essentials about creation. His diction was grand and majestic; God creates the world through the power of his word. "Let there be light" God commands, "and there was light" (1:3). "Let us make humankind in our image" (1:26), God suggests (to whom?!), and humans were made. If this first chapter were set to music, one would expect its setting to include a large chorus and orchestra.

In the second story of creation, Moses dispenses with these broad brush-strokes and gives a far more detailed presentation (Gen. 2:4b–3:24). The impersonal and majestic portrait of God is displaced momentarily in favor of a more

---

(Minneapolis: Fortress, 1992), 1–20. See also the important articles of R. W. L. Moberly, "Did the Serpent Get It Right?," *Journal of Theological Studies* 39 (1988): 1–27; and R. Di Vito, "The Demarcation of Divine and Human Realms," in *Creation in Biblical Traditions*, ed. R. Clifford and J. Collins, CBQMS 24 (Washington: Catholic Biblical Association of America, 1992), 39–56.

informal approach. "The LORD God formed every animal of the field," Moses writes, "and brought them to the man to see what he would call them" (2:19). Later, when Adam and Eve have sinned, God appears in the cool of the day to pass judgment (Gen. 3:8), but before he sternly evicts the couple from his garden of delights, he pauses to clothe them with "garments of skin" (Gen. 3:21).

If the first story provides the reader a majestic conception of creation in its entirety, the second is a far more intimate examination of a detail or two within that created order. The tenor is tragic, yet homespun. It eschews the elaborate architectonic structure of the first story in favor of a more impressionistic and consequently incomplete presentation of the events.

The author of the first creation story uses similar language to that found in the priestly legislation of Leviticus. He takes great interest in the division of all life into its various species; he asserts that the task of the sun and moon is to order humans' calendrical cycles, and he grounds Sabbath rest in the created order. All these characteristics are developed in elaborate detail in Leviticus. Genesis 1 is but a brief foretaste or précis of what is to follow.[2] Because of the numerous parallels between this account of creation and the book of Leviticus, modern scholars have ascribed Gen. 1 to the Priestly school.

The author of the second story uses a unique name to identify the deity, YHWH-Elohim. This writer, unlike the Priestly source, does not show the same fastidiousness about the personal name of Israel's God. He feels free to use the name YHWH prior to its formal revelation to Moses.[3] As a result, he is identified as the circle of J, a convention that comes from the German form of YHWH (i.e., JHWH). There is profound disagreement as to whether J was supplemented by another source (often abbreviated E) or whether J was written before or after P.[4] We need not worry about these details; for our purposes the first four books of the Bible are divisible into Priestly (P) and epic (J, or perhaps better, JE) sources. What is agreed upon, however, is that in the final editing of the Torah, there was a conscious decision made to place the P story first. It was intended to introduce the story that followed.[5]

2. See the comments of Brevard S. Childs in his *Biblical Theology of the Old and New Testaments* (Minneapolis: Fortress, 1992), 112: "Although the Priestly creation account ends with the completion of God's work and its blessing, it is only in the Sinai events that the writer unfolds the mystery of Israel's role in the plan of creation as the dwelling place of God on earth."

3. I am simplifying here. The issue of the revelation of the names is more complicated than I can do justice to in this chapter. See the important work of R. W. L. Moberly, *The Old Testament of the Old Testament: Patriarchal Narratives and Mosaic Yahwism*, Overtures to Biblical Theology (Minneapolis: Fortress, 1992), 5–104. He argues for a coherent reading of the revelation of the name irrespective of source divisions.

4. Handbooks on the source-criticism are numerous. The most competent scholarly account of the issues at hand is that of Joseph Blenkinsopp, *The Pentateuch* (New York: Doubleday, 1992).

5. Childs has observed that P now introduces the J account and "the J material thereafter functions, not as a duplicate creation account, but as a description of the unfolding of the

The Priestly Story of Creation and the Tabernacle

The modern discovery of the sources of the Pentateuch has revolutionized the way in which the Bible is read. Outside of those conservatives who have an a priori commitment to the notion of a single Mosaic author for the Pentateuch, the thesis that Gen. 1–3 comes from two different literary sources is accepted by nearly all. Still the division of these chapters into two different literary sources should not obscure the responsibility of the interpreter to account for their assemblage into a single text. The final editor of the Bible clearly intended these two stories to be read together. The question is, how?

The first thing to be noted is that the biblical writer does link his account of creation's beginnings with the end toward which creation points, although the links are only apparent after the whole story has unfolded. Our own conceptions of creation are far more scientific in outlook, and we expect creation stories merely to disclose the rudiments of nature's origins. Not so the ancients. They told creation stories with the primary purpose of providing a cosmic foundation for the meaning and purpose of human life. Creation of human life could not be understood fully without relating creation to its appropriate telos. Because the Babylonians imagined the building of great cities and temples as the supreme task of the human being, it should be no surprise that their stories of creation culminated in the building of Babylon and the descent of the office of king from heaven.[6]

The Priestly writer makes a similar move, but achieves it in a *very* different fashion. In between the opening narratives about the creation of human beings and the end toward which this points—the election of Israel at Mount Sinai—we find a lengthy set of stories about Israel's pre-Sinaitic ancestors. Unlike other myths of origin, the biblical story takes a long time before it discloses its ultimate intention. No doubt this delay is intentional; it allows Israel's appearance in the story—like Israel's election itself—to emerge as a surprise, a completely unexpected event from the perspective of Gen. 1–11.

At Sinai the purpose of creation comes into focus. Moses ascends the mountain in the presence of his fellow Israelites. "The glory of the LORD settled on Mount Sinai," the P writer reveals, "and the cloud covered it for six days; on the seventh day he called to Moses out of the cloud" (Exod. 24:16). While he is protected within this cloud-covered peak, God reveals directions for the

---

history of mankind as intended by the creation of the heavens and the earth" (*Biblical Theology of the Old and New Testaments*, 113). We will return to the relation of Gen. 1 to Gen. 2–3 at the end of this chapter.

6. John van Seters, "The Creation of Man and the Creation of the King," *ZAW* 101 (1989): 333–42.

sanctuary he will inhabit (Exod. 25–31). Having heard this revelation, Moses descends the mountain. His face is aglow as a result of his close audience with the Creator (Exod. 34:29–35). When he reaches the Israelites, Moses discloses the plans for the sanctuary, and the people proceed to construct it (Exod. 35–40).

As scholars have long noted, the building of this sanctuary parallels the creation of the world.[7] Like Gen. 1, the story of the tabernacle's construction is patterned after a sevenfold activity beginning immediately after Moses ascends Mount Sinai. He waits there for six days, and then on the seventh God draws him near to his very presence (Exod. 24:15b–18). The initial plans for the tabernacle are given to Moses in a set of seven addresses that conclude with the command to observe the Sabbath rest of the seventh day (Exod. 25:1; 30:11, 17, 22, 34; 31:1, 12). The fashioning of priestly vestments is marked by the sevenfold refrain he did "as the LORD had commanded Moses" (Exod. 39:1, 5, 7, 21, 26, 29, 31), as is the erection of the tabernacle itself (Exod. 40:19, 21, 23, 25, 27, 29, 32).

The narrative describing the construction of the tabernacle ends with the remark, "Moses finished the work" (Exod. 40:33). This recalls the conclusion of creation in Gen. 2:1–2, where almost the same terminology is used to describe God's completion of creation.[8] Just as Gen. 1 ends with divine rest on the Sabbath, so at the end of Exod. 40 God's glory descends and fills the tabernacle (v. 34). The indwelling of this shrine after seven works of construction parallels the sacralizing of the Sabbath day on the seventh day of creation. The "rest" to be provided by the sanctuary is an apt and fitting parallel to the Sabbath rest. Just as the Sabbath stands both within and outside time, so the hallowed ground of the sanctuary is situated on earth yet points beyond earth's finite contours.

But there is a significant advance in this Sinaitic moment. Whereas in creation God's sacralizing of the Sabbath takes place apart from human knowledge and participation, *at Sinai God involves humans in the process of creation itself.* God finishes the creation of the world in seven days, but it is Moses who constructs the tabernacle, through seven deeds. At Sinai, unlike creation, God approaches Israel and draws the people near to himself. The rabbis caught the high valuation of this human act of world-building when they describe the purpose of Moses's action as causing the divine presence (the *Šəkînâ*) to dwell within *a work of human hands.* Peter Schäfer summarizes the rabbinic position: "The

---

7. Jon Levenson, *Sinai and Zion* (San Francisco: Harper & Row, 1987), 142–45.

8. See the studies by J. Blenkinsopp, *Prophecy and Canon* (Notre Dame, IN: University of Notre Dame Press, 1977), 56–69; and M. Weinfeld, "Sabbath, Temple, and the Enthronement of the Lord—The Problem of the Sitz im Leben in Gen 1:1–2:3," in *Mélanges bibliques et orientaux en l'honneur de M. Henri Cazelles*, ed. A. Caquot and M. Delcor (Neukirchen-Vluyn: Neukirchener Verlag, 1981), 501–12.

creation of the world is not, if one accepts this view, solely the work of God but also the work of humankind: only when the man Moses erects the tabernacle is God's created order brought to completion."[9] Subsequently, when explaining why the completion of the tabernacle was necessary to complete creation itself, Schäfer concludes: "The world, from its beginning onward, requires that God be in relationship with humanity; without such a relationship between God and humans, the creation of the world would be senseless and superfluous."

Creation has been mimed in the building and consecration of the tabernacle and its sacerdotal attendants. But the point is more profound than that of mere literary parallel. *The construction of the tabernacle is the climax of creation.* At Sinai, God descended to earth and drew Israel to himself. Creation remained unfinished until the day the tabernacle was completed.[10]

The Heart of the Jewish Bible: Lighting the Sacrificial Pyre

According to the theology of P, once the tabernacle and its altar had been consecrated by Moses, the preparatory work of the liturgy was finished. This point must be underscored: when the daily sacrifices began (Exod. 29:38–42 = Lev. 9) *the goal of all creation would be consummated.* The promise of God is now on the verge of realization: "I will dwell among the Israelites, and I will be their God" (Exod. 29:45). The people, in turn, offer a public response to God's decision to reside in the tabernacle. Rather than pledging words of obedience to the Torah, as they do in J, the people fall on their knees in praise and trembling at his awesome appearance:

> Moses and Aaron entered the tent of meeting, and then came out and blessed the people; and the glory of the LORD appeared to all the people. Fire came out from the LORD and consumed the burnt offering and the fat on the altar; and when all the people saw it, they shouted and fell on their faces. (Lev. 9:23–24)

The moment of lighting the sacrificial pyre is the very apogee of the Torah. And, as Avigdor Hurowitz has so carefully shown, this moment of wonder and glory has ample parallels in the ancient Near East.[11] The moment of temple

---

9. Peter Schäfer, "Tempel und Schöpfung," *Kairos* 16 (1974): 132–33.

10. It should be no surprise that Christian interpreters from the patristic era forward saw the tabernacle as a type of the womb of the Virgin Mary. Both tabernacle and womb became the "bearers of God," and both were seen as the focal point of God's creative design. See chap. 8 for a fuller discussion.

11. Avigdor Hurowitz, "The Priestly Account of Building the Tabernacle," *JAOS* 105 (1985): 21–30; and the same author's *I Have Built You an Exalted House: Temple Building in the Bible*

building *always* ushers in an age of peace and tranquillity. Because the temple was in microcosm what the world was in macrocosm, ancient Near Eastern texts are quite happy to compare the erection of a temple to the act of creating the world. Some scholars have reconstructed an earlier form of P that would make the biblical tale look very much like these ancient Near Eastern models. Moses received a divine blueprint of the tabernacle and its founding rites (Exod. 25–31), which he then put in place (Exod. 35–40; Lev. 8); when the installation of the building was completed, the altar was lit amid great festivity and joy (Lev. 9).

But our biblical writer does not honor this script in the final form of the story, a detail that is nearly always lost on those scholars who content themselves with reconstructing more primitive versions of the canonical story. *For as soon as the sacrificial pyre has been sanctified by fire, it is profaned.* Or, to put it in a slightly different way: this foundational moment did not culminate in beatitude but in cultic error. Just as fire issued from the holy of holies to consume the first sacrifices, so fire miraculously and immediately issues forth and devours the first offenders of the liturgy.

> "Fire came out from the LORD and consumed the burnt offering and the fat on the altar." (Lev. 9:24)

> "Fire came out from the presence of the LORD and consumed them." (Lev. 10:2)

It is easy to see from the parallelism of these two texts why the Jewish medieval commentator Rashbam argued that one and the same fire both consumed the sacrifices and incinerated Nadab and Abihu.[12]

Nor is this the end of the matter. A sacrificial rite is not concluded until all the flesh of the animal has been properly disposed of.[13] This can be done by incineration on the altar, disposal outside the camp, or consumption by a qualified person, the specific means depending on the type and grade of sacrifice. It turns out that Aaron's other two sons, Eleazar and Ithamar, had failed to eat the purification sacrifices they had prepared in Lev. 9:15. And so the story of the founding of the cult ends with guilt distributed among the entire priestly family: Aaron and his four sons have been found negligent of their duties and Moses must conclude the episode with a harsh rebuke (Lev. 10:16–20). It is not until Lev. 16, the first rite of atonement, that these priestly

---

in the Light of Mesopotamian and North-West Semitic Writings, JSOTSup 115 (Sheffield: JSOT Press, 1992).

12. *Commentary on Leviticus*, at 10:1.
13. See, e.g., the treatment of the purification offering in Lev. 4:13–21.

sins are rectified.[14] Israel's first public penitential moment is motivated by the errors of its cultic beginnings.

The Chasm between Leviticus 8 and 9

Let us pursue the issue of priestly error from a slightly different angle. We have set this story against its ancient Near Eastern environment, but its placement within the literary framework of Leviticus is also revealing. Most readers of Leviticus do not notice the major disjuncture that exists between Lev. 8 and 9. In Lev. 8 Aaron and his sons have been, more or less, passive participants in a seven-day rite of consecration. It is Moses who brings them forward to the altar, washes and clothes them, and supervises and performs nearly all the rites at the altar. We should also add that Moses performs all these actions according to the precise decrees given in Exod. 29:1–37; nothing in Lev. 8 is left to human improvisation or chance. Seven times, the narrator underscores, Moses completes a portion of the ritual "as the LORD commanded." This sevenfold refrain is repeated over seven days and ties the entire ceremony back to creation itself, which was also completed over a seven-day sequence.[15]

Enter Lev. 9 and the mold is broken. The foundation rites end as do the sequences of sevenfold cultic actions. Moreover, unlike Lev. 8, the ritual narrated in Lev. 9 has no corresponding command section and so *it is the first act since the arrival at Sinai that P has not pre-scripted*. The period of careful design, oversight, and execution through the agency of God and Moses has drawn to a close. And as soon as the closely superintending hand of God is removed and a space is created for human autonomy, things begin to unravel.[16]

The picture drawn by P is striking. Although creation began with an account of what took place during the first six days, it did not reach its true climax until Moses and the Israelites had arrived at Mount Sinai. When the priesthood was consecrated and the altar lit, God's purpose for the world was

14. The introduction to the rites prescribed for the Day of Atonement read as follows: "The LORD spoke to Moses *after the death of the two sons of Aaron* [= Lev. 10:1–2], when they drew near before the LORD and died. The LORD said to Moses: Tell your brother Aaron not to come just at any time into the sanctuary inside the curtain before the mercy seat . . ." (Lev. 16:1–2).

15. On the importance of the septenary structure, see J. Milgrom, *Leviticus 1–16*, AB 3 (New York: Doubleday, 1991), 542–44.

16. In this vein, it is no doubt significant that Lev. 9 provides us with the first example of a ritual that is described in shorthand form. Rather than detail each and every aspect of the purificatory and burnt offerings of the people, our writer simply notes that the purification offering was sacrificed like that of the earlier sacrifice of the priest and that the burnt offering was done according to the command (9:15–16). We have left the rigor and exactitude of those foundation rites, where punctilious attention to each detail is necessitated to assure that the cult not be established on shifting sands. In the more quotidian world of Lev. 9 the priesthood is on its own, practicing its craft according to its received legal custom.

completed. He had elected the nation Israel and commanded them to draw near to his presence and tend to his daily needs. But no sooner had creation come to a close than its very centerpiece, the tabernacle, was violated.[17] In consequence of this, the Day of Atonement served to set creation aright.[18]

The Story of the Golden Calf in J

The structural significance of Lev. 10 has been lost on many readers of the Bible, both ancient and modern.[19] The reason for this is easy to uncover. The final editors of the Torah were not content to leave the story of the founding of the tabernacle in the form that P had bequeathed to them. Instead of moving in a seamless fashion from the blueprint (Exod. 25–31) to its completion (Exod. 35–40), a catastrophe intervenes: the construction of the golden calf and the beginning of idolatry. The foundation narrative of the cult was marred by human sin even before the first tent peg had been secured. This textual insertion had grave consequences for the understanding of Nadab and Abihu's sin as set forth by P. In the eyes of most, the sin of the golden calf

17. Let me summarize this interpretation of Lev. 10 by underscoring what the text does not say. Although P will not allow the story of the founding of the cult to end in utter beatitude, he is also loath to assert in any dogmatic way that the error of Nadab and Abihu was an act of obstreperous rebellion against, or even wanton disregard for, the God of Israel. We are left, as Edward Greenstein has shown so ably, completely in the dark about the motivation of these two wayward priests and the specific nature of their sin ("Deconstruction and Biblical Narrative," in *Interpreting Judaism in a Postmodern Age*, ed. S. Kepnes [New York: New York University Press, 1996], 45–46). God's presence in the tabernacle, P seems to imply, is elusive. Ritual prescriptions seek to safeguard the practice of the cult, but they do not eliminate all danger. To house even a portion of God's being on earth (his *Shekinah*, in rabbinic vocabulary) is a daunting task, and no code of cultic law, however detailed, can head off all dangers. But this ambiguity about the motives of Nadab and Abihu should not blind us to the structural significance of their error. In P's view, the prescriptions for behavior around sancta are not graded as to weight of sin or level of human intentionality. A. Toeg has caught this sensibility well (*Matan Torah be-Sinai* [Jerusalem: Magnes, 1977], 150): "Inasmuch as a complex and detailed set of laws oversees the promise that God will dwell in the tabernacle, any sin, insofar as it is a sin, is serious. For all that, if there is room to distinguish between a grave and a light sin, the grave sins can be found precisely in the area closest to the focal point of holiness and not in a far distant arena such as that of idolatry." All errors, in other words, in close proximity to the holy are grave. The "strange fire" of Nadab and Abihu has marred the otherworldly beatitude that should have attended the inauguration of the cult.

18. Note how Israel's rite of atonement begins: "The LORD spoke to Moses *after the death of the two sons of Aaron* [= Lev. 10:1], when they drew near before the LORD and died" (emphasis added).

19. For exceptions to this rule, see the excellent essay of Benjamin Sommer, "Expulsion as Initiation: Displacement, Divine Presence, and Divine Exile in the Torah," in *Beginning/Again: Towards a Hermeneutics of Jewish Texts*, ed. S. Magid and A. Cohen (New York: Seven Bridges, 2002). Also see David Damrosch, *The Narrative Covenant: Transformations of Genre in the Growth of Biblical Literature* (San Francisco: Harper & Row, 1987), 266–78.

was far more serious than the improper offering of the two sons of Aaron. To commit a wanton act of idolatry at the foot of Mount Sinai was to show such disregard for the covenant that the very election of Israel itself might be called into question. Indeed, for a moment God thought to destroy the entire nation and start over again with the figure of Moses (Exod. 32:9–10).

Peter Kearney has argued that the introduction of the golden calf into the middle of the tabernacle narrative has resulted in a sequence of creation (Exod. 25–31), fall (Exod. 32–34), and then restoration (Exod. 35–40).[20] If we exclude Lev. 8–10 from our picture, this reading would be attractive but still troublesome. In spite of a brilliant job of editing, there is no evidence that the Priestly narrative about the construction of the tabernacle (Exod. 35–40) "knows" a tradition about the calf. Kearney has not done justice to what Geoffrey Hartman has aptly called the "frictionality" of biblical narrative.[21] It is easier and simpler to understand the placement of the calf as an editorial act of upping the ante of original sin. *If the P narrator had placed the act at the conclusion of the tabernacle cycle, the shapers of the canon were determined to do him one better: the act of original sin would precede the ceremony of installation.* Israel constructed this bovine idol at the very moment Moses received the final instructions for the heavenly tabernacle, in direct violation of the commandments received just a few weeks previous. By attending to how the biblical story expanded over time we can see that the text is more interested in establishing the *immediacy* of human disobedience than it is in creating a seamless whole that can be read with a minimum of friction.

Indeed, "immediacy" may be the best way to define "original sin" in its Old Testament context. As soon as Israel receives the benefaction of election, the people offer not praise and gratitude but rebellion. This pattern defines the narrative not only of Israel's election but of other founding moments in the Hebrew Scriptures as well. Consider the establishment of the northern kingdom under King Jeroboam.[22] At the close of Solomon's reign, the prophet Ahijah announced that all the tribes of Israel save one would be ripped from the house of David and given to Jeroboam and his successors

20. P. J. Kearney, "Creation and Liturgy: The P Redaction of Ex 25–40," *ZAW* 89 (1977): 375–87.

21. "Struggle for the Text," in *Midrash and Literature*, ed. G. Hartman and S. Budick (New Haven: Yale University Press, 1986), 13.

22. This parallel was suggested to me by Moshe Greenberg (oral communication) and has been made by others as well. See Damrosch, *Narrative Covenant*, 266–78; Edward L. Greenstein, "The Formation of the Biblical Narrative Corpus," *AJSR* 15 (1990): 151–78, esp. 171; and James Nohrenberg, *Like unto Moses: The Constituting of an Interruption* (Bloomington: Indiana University Press, 1995), 280–96.

(1 Kings 11:26–40). Indeed, only because of an earlier promise that God had made (11:32) would David's house be able to keep even Judah and Jerusalem.

The granting of this new kingdom to Jeroboam is truly a wondrous affair. The character of his royal office—*in potential*—looks every bit as grand as that of David (11:38). And like David, as soon as Jeroboam is elected as king, he is driven from the land. He takes refuge in Egypt (11:40). When Solomon dies, his son Rehoboam assumes the throne and puts the entire nation under harsh slave-like labor. Jeroboam is subsequently called out of Egypt to redeem the Israelites from these oppressive conditions. The parallels to an earlier story of departure from Egypt are patent.

But no sooner has Jeroboam come forth from Egypt and liberated his people than he erects golden calves and demands that his citizens worship before them rather than at the altar in Jerusalem (1 Kings 12:25–33). Jeroboam's words of instruction exactly match those spoken about the first golden calf: "Here are your gods, O Israel, who brought you up out of the land of Egypt" (1 Kings 12:28, cf. Exod. 32:4). The punishment is swift and sudden; a prophet denounces the act and declares that the northern kingdom is henceforth doomed to destruction as a result of this apostasy (1 Kings 13:1–2). And certainly not by accident, Jeroboam's two sons, Abiyah and Nadab—recalling the sons of Aaron—die tragic deaths. The entire cycle of Exodus has been relived. Jeroboam's opportunity to realize another Davidic dynasty ends as quickly as it begins.[23]

Rabbinic interpreters were very attentive to the theme of Israel sinning immediately upon reception of a benefaction. According to one rabbinic elaboration (*Exodus Rabbah* 42.7–8), the thought of building the first calf was entertained just moments after the Israelites heard the command that forbade it. The biblical prophet Ezekiel was even more extreme: he put the moment of original apostasy all the way back in Egypt (20:6–10).[24] Another well-known tradition declared that the veneration of the calf was a sin whose

---

23. A similar literary pattern attends the story of Solomon's rise to kingship. His claim to the throne is solidified in the very last verse of 1 Kings 2 (1 Kings 2:46b: "So the kingdom was established in the hand of Solomon"), yet the root cause of his kingdom's fall is described in *the very next verse*: "Solomon made a marriage alliance with Pharaoh king of Egypt; he took Pharaoh's daughter and brought her into the city of David" (3:1). According to 1 Kings 11 it was precisely this type of marriage that was the downfall of the united monarchy. The rabbis were sensitive to this matter and saw this first act of intermarriage as the harbinger of far greater tragedies. In *Songs of Songs Rabbah* 1.6, Rabbi Levi declared that the city of Rome—whose armies were destined to destroy the second temple in 70 CE—was founded the very moment Solomon married this daughter of Pharaoh.

24. Of course, there is no evidence in the book of Exodus for such apostasy. Ezekiel clearly wants to imbed Israel's primal sin at the earliest possible point.

consequences were eternal: "No retribution whatsoever comes upon the world which does not contain a slight fraction of the sin of that calf" (*b. Sanhedrin* 102a AT). Had Israel not venerated that calf, their status would have been like that of the angels (*Exodus Rabbah* 32.1 AT): "There would have been no exile, nor would the angel of death have had any power over them." "You were like gods," Ps. 82 asserts, a state that Israel had entered as a result of its pledge to keep the Torah.[25] Having violated that pledge so soon after making it, the penalty of death was laid upon them (*Exodus Rabbah* 32.1, 7): "Nevertheless you shall die like Adam."

Let me summarize. I have argued that a reading of Exod. 19 through Lev. 10 will be deepened if we have some sense of how the previous writings were put in final canonical form. The earliest tradition was a cult-foundation legend that ended with the successful lighting of the sacrificial pyre in Lev. 9:24. This is the legend that Hurowitz claims to find in his study of the ancient Near Eastern materials. Later, the supplementary narrative about Nadab and Abihu's "strange fire" was added. This changed the complexion of this foundation narrative from festal joy to somber reflection on the improper treatment of the altar and its sacrifices. Even later still, when the Torah was being assembled into its final form, the tabernacle narrative was cut in half and the story of the calf was placed in the middle. This move undercut the severity of the priestly error in Lev. 10 but made the moment of original sin more immediate and universal.

Eden and the Fall

The story of Adam and Eve in the J source shows a striking number of parallels to Israel's larger national story. We might say that it is the entire narrative of the Torah in a tersely summarized form. As Joseph Blenkinsopp has observed, the establishment of humans in Eden recalls the experience of "rest," which is very much at home in the stories of conquest as well as in the building of the tabernacle and the enjoyment of the Sabbath. "Permanency in that environment is," Blenkinsopp observes, "contingent on obeying a commandment, and death is threatened as punishment for disobedience."[26] By framing the story of creation in this way, the J writer has "recast the national experience in universal terms by learned use of familiar mythic themes and structures, and placing it at the beginning as a foreshadowing

---

25. On Ps. 82 in rabbinic exegesis, see Joel Kaminsky, "Paradise Regained: Rabbinic Reflections on Sinai," in *Jews, Christians, and the Theology of the Hebrew Scriptures*, ed. A. O. Bellis and J. S. Kaminsky, SBL Symposium Series 8 (Atlanta: Society of Biblical Literature, 2000), 15–43.

26. Blenkinsopp, *Pentateuch*, 66.

of what was to follow."[27] Indeed, it is difficult not to see the influence of a theology very similar to that of Deuteronomy. For in that book God sets life and death before the Israelites and says the choice is theirs: obey my Torah and you shall have life in the land; disobey it and you shall die in exile. Eden is Torah in miniature.

But there is more. By placing the story of Adam and Eve after the creation account of P, the editor of the Torah has said something very profound about the propensity of human nature toward disobedience. The story of Adam and Eve according to our J source stands in a very awkward relationship to the Priestly narrative that precedes it. And this awkwardness is not to be understood simply as the result of poor editorial work on the part of the editor who stitched together these two sources. On the contrary, there is real and evident literary and theological artistry here. In P's story we get a glimpse of the high hopes that attended the creation of the world. All was set in order by a just and orderly God. Humankind, the very image of God, was established as ruler over all. At the conclusion, God took his seat to rest and enjoy the wonders of this cosmos he had set in motion. In J's account things turn sour, and quickly. The first portion of J's account takes us over ground that P has already covered in the first chapter; we watch as man, woman, the beasts, and all the rest of creation take their places upon the earth. The second portion of J's account begins to strike new ground. No sooner is this new territory entered than tragedy occurs. We are not told what happened between the introduction of Eve to Adam (2:21–25) and the approach of the snake (3:1). Adam and Eve had hardly a moment's leisure within the garden of Eden before the snake drew near. If there was a period of time in which Adam and Eve enjoyed the splendors of Eden, we the readers are not privy to it. Adam and Eve fall at the first and only command given to them. And like the nation Israel, the consequence of their disobedience is exile from a land of blessing.

Saint Paul and Original Sin

How then does the idea of original sin get attached to the figures of Adam and Eve rather than to the golden calf? This is the distinctive move made by early Christianity. And the person responsible for this is Paul. Adam is central to his argument for two different but complementary reasons. The first we find in Paul's First Letter to the Corinthians, the second in his Letter to the Romans.

27. Ibid., 66n63.

First Corinthians can be dated to within a couple of decades after the death of Christ (56 or 57 CE), not too long after Paul's own conversion. In the fifteenth chapter he takes up the problem of certain members of the community who lack a clear conviction about the bodily resurrection of Christ. Paul begins his argument by acknowledging that his own teaching is simply a handing on of what he has received. Christ, Paul declares, was buried and "was raised on the third day in accordance with the scriptures, . . . he appeared to Cephas, then to the twelve. Then he appeared to more than five hundred brothers and sisters at one time. . . . Then he appeared to James, then to all the apostles. Last of all, as to one untimely born, he appeared also to me" (vv. 4–8). From this brief résumé we can see that Paul has established the facticity of Christ's resurrection on evidence greater than his own personal authority. The teaching is founded on a tradition for which Paul is merely a conduit, and, more important, Jesus's appearance is an event whose witnesses number in the hundreds.

Paul's interest is not to establish merely the truth of the resurrection. Taken on its own, the event of Jesus's bodily resurrection would seem a wondrous miracle that befell one particular person. For Paul, the event was epoch-making and had cosmic significance. In order to underscore the universal dimensions of this event, Paul introduces the figure of Adam:

> But in fact Christ has been raised from the dead, the first fruits of those who have died. For since death came through a human being, the resurrection of the dead has also come through a human being; for as all die in Adam, so all will be made alive in Christ. But each in his own order: Christ the first fruits, then at his coming those who belong to Christ. (1 Cor. 15:20–23)

Paul was aware, as any Jewish reader of the Bible would be, that the word *Adam* was both the personal name of a literary figure in Genesis and a noun designating humankind more generally. What happened to Adam in Gen. 2–3 was not limited to him alone; by virtue of his name ("humankind") it had ramifications for all persons. If the first (*prōtos*) Adam died, Paul reasoned, then all must die through him. Since Christ was the second or final (*eschatos*) Adam, his death and resurrection must also have had universal dimensions. The resurrection was not an isolated event for one individual in world history, for it involved not one man alone but all humankind.

And it is exactly this type of argumentation that Paul returns to in his Epistle to the Romans. Now, however, his point is slightly different. Rather than arguing for the cosmic significance of the resurrection, he wishes to establish the universal nature of human sin. "Therefore, just as sin came into the world through one man," Paul argues, "and death came through sin, so death spread to all because all have sinned" (Rom. 5:12). Why this desire to make all persons culpable for death? Because the burden of Paul's apostolic office is to show that the benefits of Christ's resurrection extend to all persons, Jew and Gentile. And to do this Paul must show that all are in need of this great benefaction.

If Paul were to look solely at the central Old Testament narratives about Israel's proclivity for sin and rebellion, he would not be able to say much about the state of the gentiles.[28] Paul's turn to the figure of Adam as the prime example of a biblical sinner is not in accord with the basic thrust of the Old Testament itself. The Hebrew Scriptures put their primary focus on the example of Israel.[29] But if the elected nation is so prone to sin, and those sins continue to rebound across generations, then certainly it is not a great leap to extend this insight to humanity at large. What is revealed in microcosm through the nation Israel can be extended, in macrocosm, to all peoples. This, in fact, is the basic thrust of Karl Barth's treatment of original sin in his *Church Dogmatics*. But a full development of that story must await another day.[30]

28. Sadly these stories about Israel's transgressions were mined by many patristic readers solely to score points against Judaism. They regarded the story of the golden calf not as a window into the general human condition but as an example of the exceptional perfidy of the Jews.

29. According to Wayne A. Meeks, Paul was very familiar with the centrality of the golden calf story as an etiology of human sin in the Bible and postbiblical literature. "'And Rose Up to Play': Midrash and Paraenesis in 1 Corinthians 10:1–22," *JSNT* 16 (1982): 64–78.

30. For now, consider Barth's evaluation expressed in his *Church Dogmatics* 4/1, 427 (italics added):

And now—in the light of this—we turn to the breach of the covenant itself in Ex. 32:1–6. In the preceding narrative [the instructions about the tabernacle, Exod. 25–31] there is nothing to prepare us for what is recorded in these verses. In the light of it, it is simply a senseless and causeless act of apostasy. And if the act is presupposed in all its seriousness in the texts which follow, when we have regard to their culmination in the illuminating revelation of the name of God, it seems if anything all the more inconceivable—a refusal in face of these preconditions, an unfaithfulness in face of this faithfulness of *Yahweh*, a withdrawal of Israel from the covenant which He has so securely grounded. The contrast is, if anything, *even more clamant than that of the story of the fall*. It is quite understandable that the tradition which viewed the beginning of the history of Israel in this way—as indelibly blotted in this way—should only be able to view the beginning of the whole race, of history, as it is, in fact, viewed in Gen. 3. Here in Ex. 32 the tradition of Israel speaks from direct knowledge. *Here is the setting of the view of man in relation to God which is attested in Gen. 3, being there projected backwards and referred to the beginning of all peoples*. Here we have a typical picture—a kind of cross-section—for it is against Ex. 32 that we obviously have to see texts like 1 K. 12:28f (the sin of Jeroboam) and corresponding passages in the prophets—of what always takes place in the history of Israel as the counterpart to the faithfulness and grace and mercy of God, the painful contradiction of its whole existence. No wonder that the contours and colours of Gen. 3 seem to be mild compared with what we find here. Here it comes home with a vengeance.

5

Election

The Beloved Son in Genesis and the Gospels

The apostle Paul declares that Christ died "according to the Scriptures." One way to understand this is through the lens of the Isaianic suffering servant. According to the conventional under-standing, a chapter of the Old Testament predicts the coming of a suffering messiah. But the Old Testament can also be understood as a typological pointer to Christ. On this view, Israel's vocation as God's firstborn son is the necessary and nonnegotiable starting point from which to grasp the identity of God's other Beloved Son. As one understands the mystery of Israel, so one understands the mystery of Jesus Christ, and vice versa.

The stories about the patriarchs in Genesis function at two levels simultane-ously. At the simplest level, they are to be read as they appear—that is, as stories about those heroic individuals whom God mysteriously and inscrutably called out of Mesopotamia and brought to the promised land. There in the land of Canaan, Abraham, Isaac, and Jacob had to bide their time. Some four hundred years had to pass before the burden of the sins of the current residents would reach its breaking point and God would drive them out.

> Then the LORD said to Abram, "Know this for certain, that your offspring shall be aliens in a land that is not theirs, and shall be slaves there, and they shall be oppressed for four hundred years; but I will bring judgment on the nation that they serve, and afterward they shall come out with great possessions. As for yourself, you shall go to your ancestors in peace; you shall be buried in a

good old age. And they shall come back here in the fourth generation; for the iniquity of the Amorites is not yet complete." (Gen. 15:13–16)

But at another level, these stories map out a quite different terrain. For what is at stake is hardly the chronicling of those four hundred years as though all that remained in the plot of our story was a restless marking of time. Rather, what we witness in the book of Genesis is the delineation of Israel's character, a character intimately tied to the very identity of God.

The stories thus point beyond themselves and take on, even within the confines of the Jewish Bible, a figural sense.[1] The meaning of the lives of Abraham, Isaac, and Jacob, as well as that of Jacob's most favored son, Joseph, is not exhausted by what happens to them within the narrow contours of Genesis. Part of the narratives' burden is to bequeath the roles played by these individuals to a much larger sodality, the nation Israel.

At the opening of the book of Exodus, when God hears the cries of his people, who have been subjected to cruel servitude in Egypt, he calls forth Moses as his prophet to lead the people to freedom. Having appeared to Moses at the burning bush (Exod. 3:1–6), God proceeds to reveal to Moses some crucial details about himself and about what Moses's mission will entail. At the end of that meeting, God brings the discussion to a close with these words:

> When you return to Egypt, see that you perform before Pharaoh all the marvels that I have put within your power. I, however, will stiffen his heart so that he will not let the people go. Then you shall say to Pharaoh, "Thus says the LORD, *Israel is My first-born son.* I have said to you, 'Let My son go, that he may worship Me,' yet you refuse to let him go. Now I will slay your first-born son." (4:21–23 NJPS, emphasis added)

These remarkable lines telescope the next seven chapters of the book of Exodus into just a couple of sentences. The hardening of Pharaoh's heart will lead to the tenth and last plague, the slaying of all the firstborn of Egypt. By providential design, the story points in this direction so that God may lay claim to his true firstborn, the nation Israel. As God's firstborn son, Israel shares in the identity of the firstborn sons of Genesis; indeed, those patriarchal heroes prefigure Israel.

But for the Christian reader there is even more at stake, for the designation of God's firstborn does not end with the exodus from Egypt. As Paul declares

---

1. For a detailed development of this theological notion, see the aptly titled book by R. W. L. Moberly, *The Old Testament of the Old Testament: Patriarchal Narratives and Mosaic Yahwism,* Overtures to Biblical Theology (Minneapolis: Fortress, 1992).

in the Epistle to the Colossians: "[Christ] is the image of the invisible God, the firstborn of all creation. . . . He is the head of the body, the church; he is the beginning, the firstborn from the dead, so that he might come to have first place in everything" (Col. 1:15, 18). Christ, the firstborn of all creation, bears a familial resemblance to Israel, God's other explicitly designated firstborn son. To understand one, we must understand the other.

Over the course of this essay, I would like to step back into the thought world of the early church—that is, a church not yet in possession of the New Testament. For those early Christians, the claim of Paul that Jesus died and was raised "in accordance with the scriptures" (1 Cor. 15:4) was not just a simple affirmation of faith. It was a challenge to them to pore over the old texts afresh with the goal of laying bare just how and why this is so. If Christ is God's firstborn son, then he must stand in a very tight, figural relationship to God's firstborn son Israel. Jesus does not supplant that earlier figure; rather, Jesus's identity is deepened by attending to the plain sense of Israel's scriptural witness.[2]

Election and the Old Testament

One path the church has consistently trod on its way to understanding the life of Jesus has been the story of Abraham's election and subsequent command to offer Isaac as a sacrifice (the Akedah). The latter text is regularly read during Holy Week and is intended to be heard as a typological foreshadowing of the crucifixion and resurrection. A significant selection of patristic literature and early Christian art interpret the story in precisely this fashion. Nearly every square inch of this sparse narrative has been traced and retraced in an attempt to map out the identity of God's beloved Son.

But to understand the significance of these interpretive moves, we must step back from the dense, forbidding thicket of Gen. 22. We must consider

---

2. There is not sufficient room to develop all that is implied in these brief lines. For now, compare the profound reflection on this matter by Michael Wyschogrod: "If we are prepared to take seriously the implanting of Jesus in his people, if the Israel that gave birth to him and whose boundaries (spiritual, geographic, linguistic, intellectual, etc.) he never left is more than just a backdrop to the drama, a backdrop from which Jesus is to be distinguished rather than into which he is to be integrated, if all this is to change, then what is true of Jesus must in some fundamental way also be true of the Jewish people. And that includes the incarnation." And earlier, in order to draw this particular thesis to a very poignant level, he remarks: "It is told that when the man who was to become Pope John XXIII saw the pictures of the bulldozers pushing Jewish corpses into mass graves at the newly liberated Nazi murder camps, he exclaimed: 'There is the body of Christ.'" Michael Wyschogrod, "A Jewish Perspective on the Incarnation," *Modern Theology* 12 (1996): 207, 205.

the election of Abraham and the subsequent Akedah as a charter story that expresses in quite concentrated form a theological theme that spills over into much of the remainder of Genesis, that is, the election of the beloved son.[3] In the Akedah we have the barest (and most horrifying) narrative outline of its development; in the stories of the other patriarchs, the details emerge in much more elaborate (and temperate) form.

Let's begin with a consideration of how this literary motif works in the stories of Genesis. It will be convenient to unpack the theme through four defining features: surprise, cost, rivalry, and mystery.

The Surprise of Election

In nearly all the stories of Genesis, the designation of the beloved son appears as a *surprise*.[4] For this, we have no better example than the call of Abraham in Gen. 12. The second half of Gen. 11 consists of a genealogy of the descendants of Shem, ending with Abram (Abraham)[5]—significantly, the *tenth* figure in the list. This genealogy looks very much like the one in Gen. 5, which begins with Adam and ends with Noah; both chronicle a succession of righteous descendants that concludes with a climactic flourish at the tenth figure.[6]

3. On these points, see Jon D. Levenson, *The Death and Resurrection of the Beloved Son* (New Haven: Yale University Press, 1993); and R. W. L. Moberly, *The Bible, Theology, and Faith: A Study of Abraham and Jesus* (Cambridge: Cambridge University Press, 2000).

4. See Levenson, *Death and Resurrection*, 70:

To some, these unpredictable acts of choosing will be best described as grace and celebrated as proof of the generosity of God. This is the dominant view within both Judaism and Christianity, though Christianity has generally been more comfortable than Judaism with the utter unpredictability of the choices, that is, with the irrelevance of human worthiness to the intention of God. To others, these unpredictable acts of choosing will be best described as arbitrariness and condemned as unworthy of a God of justice. This view, though rejected by the dominant trends in the Jewish and the Christian traditions, is to be detected behind some biblical narratives. That the justice of the God who chooses is broached at all in the Hebrew Bible is eloquent testimony to the challenge that the theology under discussion posed, the challenge of accepting chosenness as a category of ultimate theological meaning.

5. Abram and his wife Sarai are renamed "Abraham" and "Sarah" by God in Gen. 17. In accordance with the practice of many interpreters, I will refer to them consistently by the latter names except in quotations of the biblical text.

6. Genesis 5: Adam, Seth, Enosh, Kenan, Mahalalel, Jared, Enoch, Methuselah, Lamech, *Noah*. Genesis 11: Shem, Arpachshad, Shelah, Eber, Peleg, Reu, Serug, Nahor, Terah, *Abram*. I will not consider here the problem of the Greek Bible, which inserts another descendant into the list so that Terah becomes the tenth and Abraham is the beginning of a new line. The Greek, in fact, brings Gen. 5 and 11 into stronger alignment. Each ends with a righteous figure in position ten (Noah and Terah) who, in turn, has three sons (Shem, Ham, and Japheth; Haran, Nahor, and Abraham), one of whom will be favored by God (Shem and Abraham).

In Gen. 11, as in the story of Noah, our narrator leaves his habit of revealing just the bare minimum about each of the nine previous descendants and tells us something more about this important tenth figure (Gen. 11:27–32).[7] But we don't learn too much. We are told that Abraham's father, Terah, has three boys: Abraham, Nahor, and Haran. Haran, the father of Lot, has died in Ur of the Chaldeans prior to Terah's migration to Aramea. Abraham and Nahor take wives, and Nahor begets children, but Abraham and Sarah remain childless. The section closes with the genealogical notice that Terah was 205 years old when he died in the city of Haran (11:32).

Then, after the curtain goes down on Gen. 11—and with no proper transition—the reader comes face to face with these amazing lines: "Now the LORD said to Abram, 'Go from your country and your kindred and your father's house to the land that I will show you. I will make of you a great nation'" (12:1–2).

Why Abraham? we must ask, as have many interpreters. The history of the Jewish interpretation of these verses is littered with various midrashim as to what Abraham had done to merit this boon.[8] Consider, for example, the book of *Jubilees,* one of our earliest examples of biblical interpretation (second century BCE). It devotes dozens of verses to filling in the textual gap between Gen. 11 and 12. By its account, God revealed the secret of monotheism to Abraham in Mesopotamia. In that land of polytheism and idolatry, the doctrine proved to be quite controversial. Abraham's courage to affirm God's oneness in the face of physical danger became the occasion for God to reward him with the supreme promise. This interpretive tradition makes for wonderful midrash, but the louder it sounds, the more deafening is the Bible's silence about the same.

The theme of God's unpredictable choices continues throughout the book of Genesis. Consider the preference of God and, in turn, the matriarch Rebecca for Jacob. Esau was the firstborn son, the beloved of his father, Isaac. By the dictates of biblical law, he should have been the heir of his father's blessing and patrimony. But in Genesis the expected course of events is reversed. "I have loved Jacob but I have hated Esau," Malachi observes (see Mal. 1:2–3)—words

7. Compare what is said about Enosh in Gen. 5:9–11. There we learn how old Enosh was at the birth of Kenan, how long he lived afterward, that he fathered other sons and daughters, and the age he was when he died. In 5:32 we learn that Noah was 500 years old when he became the father of Shem, Ham, and Japheth (already a deviation from the established model, in which a man becomes a father at a far younger age and only one son is mentioned by name). The intervening story of the flood breaks apart the genealogical rubric (6:1–9:28); we must wait until the close of chap. 9, where we learn Noah's age at his death (9:29), for the conclusion of the formula.

8. See James Kugel, *The Bible as It Was* (Cambridge, MA: Harvard University Press, 1997), 131–48.

as surprising to him as they were to the hearers of the original story. As will become even clearer through the figure of Joseph, beloved though the youngest of eleven, and later with the choice of Ephraim over the firstborn Manasseh, birth order does not determine divine preference.

The Cost of Election

The natural human response to election is to assume that it represents a very good deal for the person so chosen. In the cases of Isaac and Jacob, the status of favored son means an inheritance that will dwarf that of the other siblings. But there is another aspect to being chosen. Election is not a matter simply of a set of benefits to be claimed and enjoyed: election involves a *cost*. Consider the similarity of these two texts:

Genesis 12	Genesis 22
¹Now the LORD said to Abram, "Go from your country and your kindred and your father's house to the land that I will show you.	²[God] said [to Abraham], "Take your son, your only son whom you love, Isaac, and go to the land of Moriah, and offer him there as a burnt offering on one of the mountains that I shall show you." (NRSV alt.)
	¹⁵The angel of the LORD called to Abraham a second time from heaven, ¹⁶and said, "By myself I have sworn, says the LORD: Because you have done this and have not withheld your son, your only son,
²I will make of you a great nation, and I will bless you, and make your name great, so that you will be a blessing."	¹⁷I will indeed bless you, and I will make your offspring as numerous as the stars of heaven."

The story of the Akedah is told in a way that draws it into comparison with Abraham's original call. Just as Abraham is asked to leave (1) his country, (2) his kindred, and (3) his father's house—each successively signifying a higher degree of personal attachment—so in Gen. 22 Abraham is asked to take (1) his son, (2) his only and beloved son, (3) Isaac by name—each designation marking a higher degree of attachment. And just as Abraham is told to journey to a land unknown that God will show him, so in Gen. 22 he is told to venture forth to a mountain that God will show him. And finally, just as the conclusion of Abraham's journey will result in a glorious promise, so the conclusion of the Akedah results in the reaffirmation of the promise.

But despite these parallels, there is one significant variation. Rather than being simply the recipient of an unmerited divine blessing as he is in Gen. 12, Abraham, through his willingness to sacrifice his only son, becomes the meritorious possessor of that blessing in Gen. 22. What looks like pure gift in Gen. 12 becomes a reward for unparalleled human obedience in Gen. 22. Abraham has to relinquish the very grounds of the promise in order to receive the promise in full. The cost of divine favor is a sacrifice of immeasurable proportion.

A tremendously high cost is to be paid by those whom God favors. For us, God's choice of Abraham in Gen. 12 or Jacob in Gen. 25 may appear as unfair as it did to the biblical characters who were passed over in silence. The burden of the passed-over sibling, such as Esau, is envy. Why Jacob, Esau must wonder, and not me? But the envy that follows naturally from these stories depends on a superficial understanding of election, an understanding our biblical writer wishes to overturn.[9] Election does not mean living a life of unending blessings; it means being chosen to give up one's all for God, even what one holds most dear. For some ten chapters we wait, along with Abraham, for the news that Sarah has become pregnant and will bear a son. Yet almost immediately after the child is born and weaned, Abraham is asked to give that child up. And according to the logic of the Akedah, only by his willingness to give him up does Abraham merit the enjoyment of the benefits the child will bring.

This is the importance of the Akedah, a tale that makes us recoil in horror, in Israel's grand narrative of election. What we find to be most precious must be given up; the Akedah is the ultimate bulwark against any form of spiritual triumphalism. The election of Abraham does not end with his becoming king over the land of Canaan; its literary apogee is Abraham's call to free himself of what he holds most dear. Calvin once said, "Christ . . . is the mirror wherein we must, and without self-deception may, contemplate our own election."[10] In light of the patent parallelism between Abraham's sacrifice and that of Christ, perhaps we could slightly rephrase this dictum of Calvin: "Abraham is the mirror wherein we must, and without self-deception may, contemplate our own election."[11]

---

9. Luther learned from the cross that God reveals himself through opposites. What the world takes as glory, God counts as chaff; what the world takes as ignominy, God esteems as honor. The election of Abraham in Gen. 12, at first blush, calls to mind the randomness of a state lottery: Is the electing hand of God as fickle as the winning number in a game of chance? The author of Genesis, however, takes every opportunity to subvert this understanding.

10. John Calvin, *Institutes of the Christian Religion*, ed. J. T. McNeill, trans. F. L. Battles (Philadelphia: Westminster, 1960), 3.24.5, p. 970.

11. This theme of radical sacrifice adorns the liturgical calendar. Consider the days that are honored immediately after the feast of Christmas: the martyrdom of Saint Stephen, the martyrdom of Thomas à Becket, and the slaughter of the Holy Innocents. Savagery follows on the heels of the birth. Or consider the icons of the nativity among the Orthodox. In a number

The Rivalry between Elect and Non-elect

A third feature of our stories from Genesis concerns the *rivalry* between the elect and the non-elect, a rivalry that seeks and moves toward resolution.[12] The notion is absent from the story of Abraham's election. Though he is one of three brothers, the Bible does not record his family's reaction to his being singled out by God. Instead, the text relates that one brother, Haran, has died prior to that moment and the other brother, Nahor, has evidently been left behind in Ur. Abraham is alone when he hears God's call.[13]

However this might be with Abraham, the situation is quite different with Jacob and Joseph. Both of these sons are clearly favored over their blood brothers, and the act of favoritism becomes a legitimate source of intense anger. Esau schemes to murder Jacob (Gen. 27:41), and only their mother's intervention saves the day (27:42–44). Joseph, on the other hand, is not so lucky: his brothers take steps to rid themselves of him. Only the last-minute interventions of Reuben and Judah preserve him. But these tales of rivalry do not end on notes of rage or vengeance. The Jacob and Joseph cycles have similar denouements: the reconciliation of the brothers. Both Esau's (Gen. 33) and Joseph's brothers (Gen. 45; 50:15–21) come to terms with their rivals.

The Mystery of Election

The fourth feature—and perhaps the most remarkable of all—is the *mystery* of election. Although the subject of most of the fifty chapters of Genesis, election is not fully understood, even by the elect. One of the most stunning stories in all of Genesis is found near the end of the book at Jacob's deathbed (Gen. 48:8–22). Joseph has gathered his two sons, Manasseh and Ephraim, to be blessed by their grandfather. In this act, Joseph lays legal claim to the

of images, Mary lays Jesus out on an altar instead of a crib. No sentimental manger scene, this! Or consider those icons in which Jesus's arms stretch wide across Mary's breast while his head leans backward. Is this the pose of a resistant infant or a cruciform man? It is no surprise that retailers and other merchandisers keep this dimension of Christmastide under wraps. To fall under the spell of that baby born in Bethlehem is not always the charmed moment our secular apostles would wish it to be.

12. On this subject, see Joel S. Kaminsky, *Yet I Loved Jacob: Reclaiming the Biblical Concept of Election* (Nashville: Abingdon, 2007), 15–78.

13. The figure of Lot, son of Haran and hence nephew of Abraham, provides some complication here. Lot accompanies Abraham to Canaan but does not receive a promise like that of Abraham. Abraham, however, is extraordinarily gracious, allowing Lot first choice of where to settle in this promised land. To Lot's consternation—but certainly not outside the umbrella of providence—the land he chooses is rendered uninhabitable by the sins and consequent punishment of Sodom and Gomorrah.

rights of the firstborn even though he is the second-to-last child born to his father. He receives the double portion of his father's blessing through his two sons; his brothers will receive only one blessing each.

Joseph presents the sons to his father, now nearly blind (48:10), in such a fashion that Manasseh, his firstborn, will be blessed by his father's right hand. "Joseph took them both, Ephraim in his right hand toward Israel's left, and Manasseh in his left hand toward Israel's right, and brought them near him" (48:13). Clearly, Joseph, like his brothers before him, expects the paternal blessing to follow the normal rules of primogeniture. Yet as Jacob reaches forward, he undoes Joseph's efforts to orchestrate the blessing: "But Israel stretched out his right hand and laid it on the head of Ephraim, who was the younger, and his left hand on the head of Manasseh, *crossing his hands,* for Manasseh was the firstborn" (48:14, emphasis added).

Although this motif of preferring the younger sibling has been appearing and reappearing in the stories of Genesis—including that of Joseph himself—Joseph reacts with astonishment. "When Joseph saw that his father laid his right hand on the head of Ephraim, it displeased him; so he took his father's hand, to remove it from Ephraim's head to Manasseh's head. Joseph said to his father, 'Not so, my father! Since this one is the firstborn, put your right hand on his head'" (48:17–18). In words that recall those of Isaac to Esau, Jacob tells Joseph that, while the firstborn son will become the progenitor of a numerous and mighty people, "his younger brother shall be greater than he" (48:19).

Joseph as Beloved Son

The central thesis of Jon Levenson's remarkable book on the Akedah is that the near death of Isaac is not some odd, aberrant narrative stuck in the middle of more uplifting tales about the patriarchs. It is, instead, an extremely concentrated précis of Genesis. On Joseph, Levenson writes:

> The story of Joseph in Genesis 37–50 is not only the longest and most intricate Israelite exemplar of the narrative of the death and resurrection of the beloved son, but also the most explicit. In it is concentrated almost every variation of the theme that first appeared in the little tale of Cain and Abel and has been growing and becoming more involved and more complex through the book of Genesis. . . . It is the crescendo to the theme of the beloved son, which it presents in extraordinarily polished form. It is arguably the most sophisticated narrative in the Jewish or Christian Bibles.[14]

14. Levenson, *Death and Resurrection,* 142.

It is in the story of Joseph that we find the theme of election and its high cost set in most brilliant relief. Joseph is elevated over his brothers by his father. This choice is a grand surprise, for Joseph is "the son of [his father's] old age" (37:3). And it is the occasion for a most zealous rivalry, for the choosing of Joseph means the spurning of other, more legitimate claimants. And like the paradigmatic "beloved son" Isaac, Joseph must die as a result of such favor. His death is quite realistic from the perspective of the father; after being sent off to seek his brothers, he comes back in the form of a bloodied garment (37:31–35).

From Joseph's own perspective the death is more metaphorical. He is dropped into a pit, taken down into Egypt, and sold into slavery (37:22–24, 27–28). The Psalter offers good evidence that entrapment in a pit was strongly associated with entering the underworld:

> To you, O Lord, I cried,
>   and to the Lord I made supplication:
> "What profit is there in my death,
>   *if I go down to the Pit?*
> Will the dust praise you?
>   Will it tell of your faithfulness?" (Ps. 30:8–9, emphasis added)[15]

While in Egypt, Joseph undergoes a series of elevations and humiliations only to find himself the provisioner not only of his family in Canaan but of the entire known world.[16] During the first wave of hunger that ripples through Canaan, Jacob sends the ten older brothers to Egypt to buy grain (Gen. 42:1–5). They return with food—from Joseph's hand—but without Simeon, who has been held as surety for Joseph's demand to see their brother Benjamin (42:29–34). When father and brothers again find themselves near death from famine (43:1–10), Jacob is left with a tragic choice. If the brothers stand any chance of securing food, he must surrender Benjamin, his beloved son in place of Joseph, to accompany them into Egypt (43:3–5). In light of Jacob's experience, the surrender of Benjamin to these brothers is tantamount to sacrifice[17]—recalling, once again, the Akedah.

---

15. On this theme, see Gary A. Anderson, *A Time to Mourn, A Time to Dance: The Expression of Grief and Joy in Israelite Religion* (University Park: Pennsylvania State University Press, 1991).

16. He serves as head of the household of Potiphar in Gen. 39, chief assistant to the head jailer in chaps. 39–40, and after successfully interpreting Pharaoh's dreams, ruler of Egypt second only to Pharaoh in chaps. 41–47.

17. Consider what Jacob says after his brothers' first return from Egypt, without Simeon: "I am the one you have bereaved of children: Joseph is no more, and Simeon is no more, and now you would take Benjamin. All this has happened to me!" (42:36).

When his brothers return to Egypt, Joseph greets them happily and provides them with a sumptuous meal in his own home (43:26–34). Later, as the brothers prepare to depart for Canaan with their newly procured food supplies, Joseph arranges to have his prized divining cup placed in Benjamin's belongings. When Joseph's steward subsequently overtakes the brothers and orders a search of all their goods, the cup is "found"—to the brothers' utter horror—in Benjamin's bag (44:6–13). At that moment the brothers are faced with a choice that recalls in a striking way the beginning of the tale. They may once again (this time under external pressure) act to rid themselves of a favored sibling, spurning their father and leaving Benjamin behind in Egypt. But in this case, Judah—who once advocated selling Joseph to the Ishmaelites (37:26–27)—recognizes the grief this will cause his father and chooses an option that requires of him an enormous sacrifice. He pledges his own life in the adored child's stead. Joseph is moved to tears by Judah's love for the son his father dotes on (45:1–2). The envy of his brothers has dissipated, and Joseph can finally reveal his identity. The brothers are sent back to Canaan to tell their father the news.

Consider well the situation of the father. He sent Joseph out to find the brothers, and only a bloodied robe returned. He sent ten brothers out to buy food, and only nine returned. Now he has sent Benjamin out in the care of the brothers, and he holds no hope that this son will return. Yet Benjamin and the brothers do return—"and [the brothers told Jacob], 'Joseph is alive again! What's more, he is ruler over all of the land of Egypt'" (45:26 AT).

To catch the sense of surprise here, consider the reaction of the apostles on Easter Sunday. According to the Gospel of Luke, when told what the women have seen at the tomb, the apostles do not believe them; they reckon it "an idle tale" (Luke 24:11). The loss of Joseph is a type of death; his return, as ruler of Egypt, a type of resurrection in glory. Like the apostles, Jacob is dumbfounded.

A twelfth-century Cistercian homily put it this way:

> What I have placed before you, brethren, is like an egg or a nut; break the shell and you will find the food. Beneath the image of Joseph you will find the Paschal Lamb, Jesus, the one for whom you yearn. The great depth at which he is hidden and the diligence necessary in seeking him and the difficulty you will have in finding him will only make him all the sweeter to your taste. . . . And so here is the explanation in a nutshell. If we think with faith and reverence about the meaning of his name (Gen. 30:24) and go on to consider that he was more handsome and good-looking than the rest of his brothers (Gen. 39:6), that his actions were blameless, that he was prudent in his judgments, that after he had

been sold by his own he redeemed his own from death, that he was humbled even to imprisonment, then elevated to a throne, and was rewarded for his work by being given a new name among the nations—the Savior of the World (Gen. 41:45)[18]—if we think, I say, about all these things reverently and faithfully, we shall surely recognize how truly it was said by the Lord: "Through the Prophets I gave parables" (Hosea 12:10).[19]

The association of Joseph's figural death with the death of Christ is magnificently illustrated in the *Biblia pauperum* (Bible of the Poor) of the thirteenth century.[20] In this image we see Joseph lowered into the pit, Christ's body laid out after his death, and Jonah tossed into the sea. In all these instances, the person facing death will be restored and those who instigated the death will stand to benefit. Consider the plight of Joseph, a man "sold by his own" who "redeemed his own from death." Those who hatefully tried to kill him found their very existence dependent on that rejection.

The Forgiving of the Brothers

And finally, our story takes one more turn and reveals one more denouement. After Jacob dies, the brothers find themselves in a very uncomfortable position. For in giving Joseph up to death, they behaved in a way that is well recognized from the psalms of lament. Our compact text is worth citing in full: "So when Joseph came to his brothers, they stripped him of his robe, the long robe with sleeves that he wore; and they took him and threw him into a pit. The pit was empty; there was no water in it. Then they sat down to eat" (Gen. 37:23–25). The account of the angry act of stripping Joseph of his sign of favor is accompanied by two important details. First is the notice that the pit was empty and without water, a sure indicator that murder was the initial intention. Second is the surprising revelation that the brothers promptly sat down to eat. This seemingly inconsequential detail sets their actions against a much wider canvas. For in the Psalter, to eat and drink in the presence of the demise of another is to put oneself in the role of the "enemy." Psalm 30, which describes the plight of the lamenter as one who has been lowered into a pit likened to Sheol, implores the Lord to release him so that his foes may

18. The Vulgate renders his Egyptian name, Zaphenath-paneah (untranslated in the Hebrew), as *Salvatorem mundi*.

19. Guerric of Igny, *Liturgical Sermons [by] Guerric of Igny*, trans. Monks of Mount Saint Bernard Abbey, 2 vols, CF 32 (Spencer, MA: Cistercian Publications, 1971), 2:81.

20. Emile Mâle, *Religious Art in France*, vol. 3, *The Late Middle Ages* (Princeton: Princeton University Press, 1984), 224. http://iconographic.warburg.sas.ac.uk/vpc/VPC_search/pdf_frame .php?image=00030676.

not "rejoice over" him (Ps. 30:1).[21] Just as Christ is subject to the taunts of the "enemies" while suffering on the cross, so Joseph undergoes a similar fate. If, as the Gospels suggest (Matt. 27:34–35, 39, 46, 48, and parallels), Pss. 22 and 69 accurately portray the indignity of the treatment of Jesus, one could plausibly argue that Ps. 30 does the same for Joseph.

But the invocation of this psalmic category points even deeper. In many of the psalms of lament, the person who is subject to such hatred invokes the deity to take harshest vengeance on the offending enemies. Consider these words (of prayer!) from Ps. 58:

> O God, break the teeth in their mouths;
>> tear out the fangs of the young lions, O LORD!
> Let them vanish like water that runs away;
>> like grass let them be trodden down and wither. . . .
> The righteous will rejoice when they see vengeance done;
>> they will bathe their feet in the blood of the wicked.
> People will say, "Surely there is a reward for the righteous;
>> surely there is a God who judges on earth." (Ps. 58:6–7, 10–11)

Those who are wronged have every right to expect justice in the end. It is not simply a matter of personal revenge; according to the psalmist, the meting out of vengeance is crucial in showing the world that there is a God who judges moral behavior.

And so the brothers have very good reason to be anxious about what Joseph might do. As the psalms of lament attest, Joseph would have good grounds to seek vengeance against those who have treated him so unjustly. Indeed, the brothers themselves give explicit testimony to the fact that such punishment for their behavior is in order. When they first appear before Joseph and are thrown into jail for a few days on the false charge that they are spies (Gen. 42:6–17), they confess, "Alas, we are paying the penalty for what we did to our brother; we saw his anguish when he pleaded with us, but we would not listen. That is why this anguish has come upon us" (42:21). This honest admission of guilt highlights another aspect of the pain the brothers inflicted: Joseph wept for mercy from the waterless pit while they sat by and enjoyed their meal (cf. 37:24–25).

The brothers have every right to wonder just *who* is the Joseph now standing before them. Was Joseph earlier restraining a fierce desire for vengeance solely as a courtesy to his father, Jacob? "What if Joseph still bears a grudge

---

21. On this common trope in the psalms of lament and its relation to eating and drinking, see Anderson, *Time to Mourn.*

against us," the brothers rightly wonder, "and pays us back in full for all the wrong that we did to him?" (50:15). How does Joseph respond? "Do not be afraid!"—words that call to mind the stirring words of consolation and forgiveness that God often speaks through his prophets[22]—"Am I in the place of God? Even though you intended to do harm to me, God intended it for good, in order to preserve a numerous people" (50:19–20).[23]

The brothers' hatred and envy of Joseph is crucial to the story as a whole. The transformation of Judah into one who will die for Benjamin (44:18–34) loses its profundity if his prior rejection of Joseph is not *complete*. And the beneficence of Joseph, his providing for his family and overlooking the sin of his brothers,[24] loses its gravitas if it is not calibrated against the brothers' *expectation of retributive justice*.

Who Are the Betrayers of Jesus?

It is precisely this scenario of a group of men who have callously betrayed their brother and now seem anxious about the price they must pay that warrants a shift in our narrative gaze. Indeed, the story of Joseph and his brothers assumes a new tone when set against the backdrop of the Gospels. For as these books record, the disciples of Jesus also abandoned their Lord at the hour he needed them most. Mark is the bleakest here: Jesus dies alone with just an intimation of the resurrection. Only the centurion gets it right: "Truly this man was God's Son!" (Mark 15:39). The disciples (and the *reader*) are left in a position strikingly similar to that of Joseph's brothers: "[The disciples] went out and fled from the tomb, for terror and amazement had seized them; and they said nothing to anyone, *for they were afraid*" (16:8, emphasis added).

22. Most prominently found in Isaiah; see Isa. 35:4; 40:9; 41:10; passim.
23. The reconciliation between Joseph and his brothers is the subject of a marvelous chapter in Uriel Simon, *Seek Peace and Pursue It* (Tel Aviv: Yediot Aharonot, 2002), 58–85 [in Hebrew]. Especially profound is Simon's sensitive attention to how both the brothers and Joseph mature into their respective roles within the story. An English translation can be found at http://www .lookstein.org/Joseph_booklet.pdf.
24. We would do well, however, not to interpret the scene that closes the tale of Joseph and his brothers (50:15–21) from too sentimental a point of view. It is not at all clear that Joseph and his brothers are fully reconciled. Rather, it seems that Joseph, regardless of whatever personal—and quite human—feelings he may harbor toward his brothers, has determined that any calculated act of vengeance at this time would be an affront to providence. The brothers' intentions notwithstanding, "God intended it for good," Joseph concludes, "in order to preserve a numerous people." In this sense Joseph mediates forgiveness without necessarily owning it. Nevertheless, it is through Joseph, and Joseph alone, that the brothers must seek solace.

As readers, we fill in the gaps of the tale with our post-Easter knowledge from the other Gospels. But let us pause on this bleak Markan moment. If we take our cues from Genesis, we can read these lines in a new light. Just *who* is the Jesus who will meet the disciples who spurned him in his most trying hour? The psalms of lament that fill out the events of Good Friday bear elegant witness to the dejection and humiliation of Jesus. But for those who have betrayed him, these psalms could hint at an even darker reality. The prayer of Ps. 69 (see Mark 15:36 and parallels) says not only "For my thirst they gave me vinegar to drink" (69:21) but also "Add guilt to their guilt; may they have no acquittal from you. Let them be blotted out of the book of the living" (69:27–28). The disciples must wonder, who is this Jesus who awaits them? Will the encounter be one of wrath or of mercy?

Mark is not alone in the harsh indictment passed on the very men Jesus called to follow him. Matthew, Luke, and John are just as insistent about their perfidy. At the foot of the cross—while Jesus suffers—they are absent. And so, may I suggest, are we. "The chain of these handings-over is forged theologically," Hans Urs von Balthasar concludes. "All of humanity's representatives, considered theologically, are integrated from the outset into guilty responsibility for Jesus' death."[25]

For this insight von Balthasar is indebted to Luther. In Luther's theology of the cross, none of us is innocent. "You must get this through your head," Luther advised his congregants in his understated way,

> and not doubt that you are the one who is torturing Christ thus, for your sins have surely wrought this. In Acts 2[:36–37] St. Peter frightened the Jews like a peal of thunder when he said to all of them, "You crucified him." Consequently three thousand alarmed and terrified Jews asked the apostles on that one day, "O dear brethren, what shall we do now?" Therefore, when you see the nails piercing Christ's hands, you can be certain that it is your work.[26]

This insight was not lost on Paul Gerhardt, the author of the the words of the eleventh movement of Bach's *St. John Passion*:

25. Hans Urs von Balthasar, *Mysterium Paschale: The Mystery of Easter*, trans. Aidan Nichols (Edinburgh: T&T Clark, 1990), 113–14.

26. Martin Luther, "A Meditation on the Passion," in *Devotional Writings 1*, ed. Helmut T. Lehmann and Martin O. Dietrich, vol. 42 of *Luther's Works*, ed. Jaroslav Pelikan et al. (Philadelphia: Fortress, 1971), 9. Of course, this is not to deny the highly vituperative character of Luther's anti-Semitism as witnessed in other parts of his writings. But it is worth noting that precisely here at the crucifixion, where a diatribe against the Jews would seem most natural, Luther holds back. His theological understanding of the cross requires him to focus the blame on contemporary Christian congregants; as a result, the Jews of the first century as well as of the sixteenth are not condemned for Christ's death.

The second stanza of no. 11, the Lutheran chorale with its remarkable disso-
nance on the first syllable of *Sünden* (sins), spells things out the most clearly
and forcefully of all, its "I, I" referring to the Lutheran congregants:

> I, I and my sins,
> which are as numerous as the grains
> of sand on the seashore,
> they have caused you
> the sorrow that strikes you
> and the grievous host of pain.[27]

Gerhardt makes it quite clear that no benefit is gained from reflecting on the
question of culpability from a purely *historical* frame of reference. Whether
Jew or Roman or both actually slew Christ is not of prime significance. The
death of Jesus must be grasped *theologically*. From a theological frame of
reference, Jesus's death was made necessary by *our* sin. Through the disciples
whom Jesus called, we have spurned his loving advances.[28]

At Passiontide we are absent. We have abandoned Jesus in his most demanding hour. At the foot of the cross, we do not kneel. If we kneel now, in the
liturgy, it is only in view of our post-Easter knowledge that he has forgiven us
in spite of our spurning him. A hymn of Luther furnishes us our only prayer:

> Our great sin and sore misdeed Jesus, the true Son of God, to the cross has
> nailed. Thus you, poor Judas, as well as the host of Jews, we may not inimically
> upbraid; guilt is truly ours. Lord, have mercy.[29]

And this is the key to the passion: like the brothers of Joseph, we reject the
Elect One of Israel, but the Elect One does not reject us. And strikingly, it is
precisely the *culpability* of the brothers or the disciples that allows them to
experience and ponder the miracle of their forgiveness. As Robert Jenson so
aptly puts it: "To the question 'Who crucified Jesus?' only the church is able
to say, 'We did.' The [human] race in general must, in justice, say, 'We were
not there,' and just so go its way."[30]

27. Michael Marissen, *Lutheranism, Anti-Judaism, and Bach's "St. John Passion"* (New
York: Oxford University Press, 1998), 34.
28. It is worth noting that the midrash makes a similar move regarding the culpability for
Joseph's "death." The guilt continues to haunt Israel, even after the actual brothers have died
and vanished from the scene. According to the early Tannaitic midrash, the *Sifra* (at Lev. 9:3),
Israel must bring a goat offering at the inauguration of the public cult in order to atone for the
sin of selling Joseph into slavery.
29. From the Wittenberg hymnal of 1544, cited in Marissen, *Lutheranism*, 26.
30. Robert W. Jenson, *Systematic Theology*, vol. 1, *The Triune God* (Oxford: Oxford University Press, 1997), 192. The irony here is how the classic smear of the Jews as Christ-killers

A Precursor to the *Felix Culpa*?

If we pause again on the story of Joseph, we may uncover a darker irony. Had the brothers of Joseph not "slain" their brother, would they have survived the famine? And what of the rest of humanity? Their fate as well seems to have depended on what occurred between the brothers: "*All the world* came to Joseph in Egypt to buy grain, because the famine became severe throughout the world" (Gen. 41:57, emphasis added). In other words, is the story of God's people dependent on an act of betrayal? By raising such a question, we call to mind the theme of the *felix culpa* as well as the age-old question whether Christ would have become human apart from the Fall. How profoundly the story of Joseph illumines what Luther called the supreme saving act of the cross. God's works are "hidden under the form of their opposite" (*abscondita sub contrario*). The brothers thought they were putting Joseph to death, but what they really were doing was assuring their own salvation. The brothers, even at the end, worried that such an act would merit harshest vengeance. But Joseph knew differently: "Even though you intended to do harm to me, God intended it for good, in order to preserve a numerous people" (50:20).

I have often thought that the story of Joseph should be read on one's knees. Or, to borrow an image from how some perform the creed—that is, bowing at the moment we come to the mystery of the incarnation—perhaps we should bow periodically during the reading of this story. Let us bow when the brothers lower Joseph into the pit, when Judah offers to give up his life for Benjamin, when Jacob surrenders Benjamin to his other sons, when Jacob hears that Joseph is alive and of royal stature. And let us reserve our deepest and longest bow for when we hear Joseph's words of forgiveness to his brothers: "Do not be afraid!" We are those brothers, and only the Elect One of Israel can speak the words of absolution.

---

is disarmed. The act of laying the blame outside oneself places one outside the very bounds of grace that the story seeks to establish. Those who have hated the Jews have not been good Christian theologians.

PART 3

"The Word Became Flesh"

6

Christology

The Incarnation and the Temple

The debates about the nature of the person of Christ are generally treated in a strictly historical fashion. The evidence from the various New Testament documents is sifted for whatever hints it might provide, and then the various controversies that the church faced during the first few centuries are added in sequence to the equation. One begins with the gnostics, who questioned the humanity of Jesus; followed by Arius, who worried about Christ's divine nature; and finally Nestorius and his school, who struggled with the relationship of the divine and human natures in the person of Christ. Left out in such an analysis is any serious investigation of how the Old Testament was employed in these debates. As we know from the Gospel of John, God's indwelling of Jesus of Nazareth was thought to stand in a tight figural relationship with the way God indwelt the temple. By pursuing the church's thinking on this score, we will not only learn a great deal about Christ's person, but we will be pushed to take more seriously the significance of the tabernacle-cum-temple in the Old Testament.

This chapter and the next will treat the way in which the texts about the tabernacle (and, by extension, the temple) in the Old Testament were employed in the New Testament and the early church to treat issues of Christology and Mariology. That the tabernacle plays such a role has long been realized, but discussion has often been limited to the role it plays in a particular New Testament book or in the evolution of patristic theology. The next two chapters will consider how the per se voice of the Jewish Scriptures has functioned within the Christian tradition as it reflected on the identities of Jesus and Mary. Thus I will make the perhaps surprising claim that reading the Old

Testament from a christological vantage point does not efface a Jewish reading but deeply respects it. The best way to approach this particular challenge is to follow the mode of canonical reading first marked out by Brevard Childs and then deepened and extended by his student Christopher Seitz. Let us begin with some general remarks about the essential lineaments of this method.

The Deference of the New Testament to the Old

Seitz has thought long and hard about the relationship of the Old and New Testaments. And the test case that animates much of his writing is the book of Isaiah. This book has long been dear to Christian readers, so dear in fact that Ambrose was known to refer to this venerable prophet as "the First Apostle" and instructed the newly converted Augustine to read it carefully in order to learn about the gospel.[1] Yet for all this, in an essay on the usage of Isaiah in the New Testament, Seitz makes a startling observation. "What is striking," he concludes about all these citations, "is that none of them pick up Isaiah's royal texts for their own sake to show that Jesus is the messiah promised of old by God's prophets."[2] One might presume that this conclusion would be hard to maintain in light of Matthew's first citation of Isaiah, the announcement about the coming figure of Immanuel in 7:14. Yet even in this quotation, Matthew shows more interest in the virginal birth of Jesus and his divine origins than in establishing the fact that he fulfills the full array of hopes attached to Israel's messianic faith.

Though it would be impossible to enter the minds of the various New Testament writers and know exactly what concerns dictated their use of the Old Testament, this reluctance to engage the powerful royal promises in Isaiah in favor of other themes, such as God's intention to incorporate the gentiles, is striking. For Seitz there are a number of answers that could be offered. Perhaps these promises of Isaiah were not compatible with the predominant interests of the early New Testament community. In this case, the most important point to be established was rather the authorization of the mission to the gentiles. Or maybe these promises, because they are so focused on glory, were not seen as fit instruments for rendering the unique picture of Israel's *suffering* Messiah. Seitz expresses some unease with explanations such as these because they configure the picture as though the usage of the Old Testament in the early church was governed solely by the interests of the kerygmatic needs of the

---

1. Christopher Seitz, *Word without End: The Old Testament as Abiding Theological Witness* (Grand Rapids: Eerdmans, 1998), 281.
    2. Ibid., 216.

first apostles. In Christ all the answers were to be found; the Old Testament was simply mined for appropriate prooftexts. But what if we consider the matter from a quite different vantage point? What if Isaiah's own voice had not been lost from view but still continued to resound within the gathering halls of early Christian assemblies? What if the eschatological royal promises found in Isaiah—promises that seem to be so "over the top," promises that tell of all the nations streaming to Zion to hear God's Torah, promises of the coming reign of Israel's king, which will usher in a day when the wolf will dwell with the lamb, the leopard lie down with the kid, and neither sun nor moon be required because God's own light will shine over all—continued to function as they did in Isaiah, as promises of what Christ's coming rule will bring to fulfillment?

Though it may be impossible to make any conclusive decisions about the intentions of the writers of the New Testament themselves, there can be no doubt that the early church heard eschatological texts such as these in precisely this fashion. Origen, for example, specifically says that the promise regarding Israel's Messiah entering Jerusalem on an ass found in Zech. 9:9 and fulfilled in Matt. 21:5 cannot be understood in a simple historical manner as though the events of Palm Sunday constituted the complete fulfillment of this messianic vision. As Origen's Jewish interlocutors made clear, the literary context of Zechariah makes such a reading impossible.[3] For in the verse immediately following the prediction of the Palm Sunday entrance, Zechariah writes: "And he will destroy the chariots out of Ephraim, and the horse out of Jerusalem, and the bow for war will be destroyed, and a multitude and peace from the gentiles, and he will rule the waters to the sea and the springs of the rivers of the earth."[4] Yet nothing of the sort occurred during the last week of Jesus's earthly life. A simple promise-fulfillment reading, Origen concludes, cannot make sense of the narrative sequencing of Zechariah's own voice. And in this meeting of the two Testaments, Origen will not allow the voice of the Old to be eviscerated in favor of its reception in the New.

The complex manner in which the church has heard the Old Testament's eschatological royal promises is perhaps best illustrated in the liturgical celebration of Advent. For the church's celebration of Christ's advent contained two parts: the proclamation that the hope of Israel's restoration had appeared, but

3. Origen's discussion of the problem can be found in book 10 of his commentary on the Gospel of John. A convenient translation and discussion of the text can be found in Joseph Wilson Trigg, *Biblical Interpretation*, Message of the Fathers of the Church 9 (Wilmington, DE: Michael Glazier, 1988), 105–6.

4. The translation here, reflecting Origen's practice, is from the Greek version. There are some small but important differences.

that the full scope of the kingdom he wished to inaugurate was yet to come. In short, the first advent of Israel's Messiah does not result in fulfillment of the full array of Israel's messianic hopes. God's intentions for his people and the world have not been brought to completion. In this fashion a document issued by the Pontifical Biblical Commission strikes exactly the right note:

> What has already been accomplished in Christ must yet be accomplished in us and in the world. The definitive fulfillment will be at the end with the resurrection of the dead, a new heaven and a new earth. Jewish messianic expectation is not in vain. It can become for us Christians a powerful stimulant to keep alive the eschatological dimension of our faith. Like them, we too live in expectation. The difference is that for us the One who is to come will have the traits of the Jesus who has already come and is already present and active among us.[5]

So in Advent we are put in the peculiar position of celebrating one advent while awaiting another. The readings of the first few Sundays are most explicit here, for their apocalyptic tenor clearly puts most of the emphasis on the second coming. Paradoxically, it is in the celebration of the birth of Israel's Messiah that Jews and Christians come together in the closest possible way. The Old Testament is not simply a pointer to the New—even in regard to the Messiah—but an independent witness whose integrity must still be respected.

And what is the rub for us?—that Isaiah's full eschatological horizon is not exhausted by the appearance of the earthly Jesus. In the church's elaboration of its eschatological hopes it *defers* to the larger *scopus* of Isaiah's eschatological horizon. Seitz writes:

> But the larger point is that the horizon of Isaiah in respect of royal promises is not a past fulfillment in Jesus that validates Christian hopes and invalidates those of the Jews. In Advent we do not just look back nostalgically on a perfect fit between the prophet's longings and their absolute fulfillment in Christ: like arrows hitting a bull's-eye. Instead, Isaiah's horizon remains the final horizon for Jew and Christian and Gentile: Christ's coming, Christ's advent in glory and in judgment. This is absolutely consistent with the New Testament's own *per se* witness to Isaiah, as we have seen by tracking how Isaiah is heard *in novo receptum*, where Isaiah's promises are not explicitly referred to as fulfilled but *deferred* to as *per se* promises yet to be fulfilled.[6]

5. Pontifical Biblical Commission, *The Jewish People and Their Sacred Scriptures in the Christian Bible* (Boston: Pauline Books and Media, 2002). Also available on the Vatican website: http://www.vatican.va/roman_curia/congregations/cfaith/pcb_documents/rc_con_cfaith_doc_20020212_popolo-ebraico_en.html.
6. Seitz, *Word without End*, 227.

Israel's hope has not been superseded. Rather, the church's true frame for construing the role of the earthly Jesus in ushering in the kingdom has been interpreted so as to conform to the larger horizon of Old Testament expectation. The Old Testament is not simply *background* to the gospel; it is part of the very fabric of the Gospel whose full meaning can only be articulated by a conversation between the two Testaments.

The Word Became Flesh

One of the most often cited texts from the Gospel of John is the line from the prologue that reads, "The Word became flesh and lived among us." Though many Christian readers of this verse will presume instantly that they know what it is all about, it must be said that this exegetical confidence comes not so much from the simple sense of John's Gospel as from the influence of the rule of faith or creed on what is at stake. One meaning, however, is ruled out, even among the most ardent supporters of Chalcedon: the flesh of Jesus is not wholly convertible with the being of God. The *logos* does not become the physical body of Jesus without remainder. But, on the other hand, the flesh cannot be a purely accidental feature unrelated to the task of identifying the second person of the Trinity.

The German New Testament scholar Klaus Berger has provided sufficient grounds for seeing why this text has been such a controverted problem in early Christianity.[7] For Berger, following in part the lead of Käsemann, the prologue of John is still a long way from what will become the standard christological teaching of the church. That the Word becomes flesh does not imply any sort of intrinsic relation between flesh and the Godhead. Rather, the flesh and bones of this first-century Jew are merely the accidental occasion for a momentary epiphany of the *logos* or divine word. As proof for his thesis, Berger points to a text in the *Paraleipomena Jeremiou* (also known as *4 Baruch*) wherein an eagle is sent by Baruch to Jeremiah and his exiled brethren in Babylonia.[8] At precisely the moment of the eagle's arrival, Jeremiah and a coterie of exiled Judeans are making their way outside the city to bury a corpse. The eagle suddenly takes voice and says, "I say to you Jeremiah, the chosen one of God, go and gather together the people and come here so that they may hear a letter which I have brought to you from

---

7. Berger, "Zu 'Das Wort ward Fleisch' Joh. 1 14a," *Novum Testamentum* 16 (1974): 161–66.

8. See the bilingual edition of Robert Kraft and Ann-Elizabeth Purintun, *Paraleipomena Jeremiou*, Texts and Translations 1 (Missoula, MT: Scholars Press, 1972). The section that tells the story about the eagle can be found in 7.1–23.

Baruch and Abimelech" (7.16). As the eagle begins to descend, it alights upon the corpse, which is miraculously revived. The narrator then remarks that all "this took place so that they might believe." Then the people rose up and solemnly acclaimed: "Is this not God who appeared to our fathers in the wilderness through Moses and now in the form of an eagle he has appeared to us" (7.20).[9] Berger remarks: "As in the first chapter of John, there is found here a statement of identification (the eagle is God) and a statement as to how it came to this identity. From the manner of its coming to this identity it is clear that we are not talking about a transformation but a [momentary] becoming immanent [Immanent-Werden]."[10]

My point is not to claim that Berger is correct in finding this text an apt parallel to the Christology of the Johannine prologue. Other New Testament scholars, such as the doyen of Johannine studies Raymond Brown, would not have found this thesis compelling. But it should also be added that even Brown recognized a certain cogency to Käsemann's position, which is closely related to that of Berger. Brown writes that Käsemann

> insists that the scandal of the incarnation consists in the presence of God among men and not the becoming flesh—not the how, but the fact. For Käsemann [v.] 14a ["the word became flesh"] says no more than [v.] 10a, "He was in the world." The parallelism between [v.] 14a and [v.] 14b ["and made his dwelling among us"] gives support to Käsemann's contention.[11]

The point I would like to emphasize here is that identifying Jesus as "the Word made flesh" does not inexorably point to the high Christology of Chalcedon. In brief, to repeat a line found in many handbooks on patristic theology, there

9. I have slightly adjusted the translation given by Kraft and Purintun.

10. Berger, "Zu 'Das Wort ward Fleisch,'" 163. Berger's essay is a response to G. Richter, "Die Fleischwerdung des Logos im Johannesevangelium," *Novum Testamentum* 13 (1971): 81–126; 14 (1972): 257–76, who argues that John 1:14 declares that the Word truly became flesh. For Berger, the meaning of the Greek is the opposite of what Richter maintains: the Word "appeared in a form without becoming it" ("Erscheinen in einer Gestalt, ohne damit diese zu 'werden'"). He compares this extrinsic connection of *logos* to flesh to the way God inhabits a temple (at 164): "The appearance of Christ in the flesh and the dwelling in the community does not mean that the Lord has become identical with these human beings but that he dwelt among them as if in a temple (just as one speaks of the spirit)." ("Das Erscheinen des Christus im Fleisch und das Wohnen unter/in der Gemeinde bedeutet also nicht, daß der Kyrios mit diesen Menschen identisch wird, sondern daß er in ihnen als in einem heiligen Tempel wohnt [so wie man es sonst vom Pneuma sagt].") This precise question, whether God appeared in the flesh or became that very flesh, was the subject of enormous disagreement in the fourth- and fifth-century christological controversies.

11. Raymond Brown, *The Gospel according to John I–XII*, AB 29 (Garden City, NY: Doubleday, 1966), 31.

were good exegetical grounds for many of the positions that the church would eventually deem heretical.

What is striking, however, when one turns to patristic attempts to sort out the various exegetical options for "the Word became flesh," is the fact that these writers operate in a manner quite different from the guild of modern New Testament studies. They do not marshal their arguments solely within the ambit of the New Testament documents and their near historical relations. Rather, the Old Testament functions as an equally powerful source for rebutting the views of those professing a low Christology. Childs has summarized this principle well:

> Although it is obviously true that the Old Testament was interpreted in the light of the gospel, it is equally important to recognize that the New Testament tradition was fundamentally shaped from the side of the Old. The Old Testament was not simply a collage of texts to be manipulated, but the Jewish scriptures were held as the authoritative voice of God, exerting a major coercion on the early church's understanding of Jesus' mission. In fact, the Jewish scriptures were the church's only scripture well into the second century. As H. von Campenhausen has forcefully stated, the problem of the early church was not what to do with the Old Testament in light of the gospel, which was Luther's concern, but rather the reverse. In the light of the Jewish scriptures which were acknowledged to be the true oracles of God, how were Christians to understand the good news of Jesus Christ?[12]

In the case of the incarnation, one common point of reference in the Old Testament was that of God's dwelling within the temple or tabernacle of Israel. And indeed that very symbol is explicitly alluded to in the Johannine prologue. For John declares not only that the Word has become flesh but that it "dwelled among us, and we have seen its glory, the glory of a father's only son" (1:14 AT). The key clause in establishing that this text speaks to the matter of the temple is "he dwelled among us." The Greek verb *skēnoō* is clearly borrowed from the story of the tabernacle in Exodus and serves to translate the Hebrew word *šākan/miškan*. As Raymond Brown remarks, "We are being told that the flesh of Jesus Christ is the new localization of God's presence on earth, and that Jesus is the replacement of the ancient tabernacle."[13] And

---

12. Brevard S. Childs, *Biblical Theology of the Old and New Testaments: Theological Reflection on the Christian Bible* (Minneapolis: Fortress, 1992), 225–26.

13. Brown, *Gospel according to John*, 33. Three works that have treated this theme at great length are Craig Evans, *Words and Glory: On the Exegetical Background of John's Prologue* (Sheffield: Sheffield Academic, 1993), 77–113; A. Kerr, *The Temple of Jesus' Body: The Temple Theme in the Gospel of John*, JSNTSup 220 (Sheffield: Sheffield Academic, 2002); and Craig

as such this idea nicely dovetails with another major feature of this Gospel, which is that Jesus is "the replacement of the temple (2:19–22)," which, Brown adds, is simply "a variation of the same theme."

Brown also notes the very important linkage between the "tenting" of the Word and its becoming visible to the naked eye. "In the OT," he observes, "the *glory* of God (Heb. *kābôd*; Gr. *doxa*) implies a visible and powerful manifestation of God to men." Then, having reviewed several biblical texts that describe the appearance of God at the site of a temple, he concludes that "it is quite appropriate that, after the description of how the Word set up a tabernacle among men in the flesh of Jesus, the prologue should mention that his *glory* became visible."[14]

To borrow the terminology of Seitz, we could say that the author of the Gospel of John does not elaborate this point of how Jesus and the temple are similar because he presumes that his readers will bring to this text a knowledge of how God had dwelled in the temple within Israel itself. (And this is precisely the value of Brown's commentary on John that I cited above; he locates those sections within the Old Testament that cast light on the terse formulation in John.) Reading the Gospel of John in terms of its present canonical placement within a two-part Bible, one could say that this Gospel defers to the Old Testament. The very form of the Christian Bible asks the reader to look backward to Exod. 25–40 and in effect says, "If you want to know more, compare these two moments of divine indwelling."

So with these compass points in mind, let us turn back to these foundational chapters in the book of Exodus with an eye toward discerning what they can say about how God indwells a particular physical space.

The Instructions for the Tabernacle

Even the most casual reader will note that the commands concerning the construction of the tabernacle exceed the bounds of what would ordinarily be expected. The sheer volume of detail lavished on this building is uncommon even for the ritually-minded Priestly writer. Generally, he is prolix only when introducing a theme for the first time; should a return to the theme be warranted, he is more than capable of abbreviation.[15]

Koester, *The Dwelling of God: The Tabernacle in the Old Testament, Intertestamental Jewish Literature, and the New Testament*, CBQMS 22 (Washington, DC: Catholic Biblical Association, 1989), 100–115.

14. Brown, *Gospel according to John*, 34.

15. Compare, e.g., the law regarding how to offer the sin and holocaust offerings in Lev. 5:8–9, 10a; the former law is long and detailed because none of the previous chapters have

This general pattern of composition is not followed in regard to the tabernacle. Especially striking is the tendency to repeat the list of appurtenances that are found within the tabernacle (Exod. 30:26–30; 31:7–11; 35:11–19; 39:33–41; 40:2–15; 40:18–33). Six times these items are listed; the final three are perhaps most striking because they occur one right after the other. Indeed, one could say that the account of the tabernacle ends with a concatenation of three lists of the materials for the tabernacle and includes only enough extraneous material to keep the thread of a narrative from disappearing altogether.

As Menahem Haran has remarked, "The priestly writers find [this] subject so fascinating that . . . [they are] prompted to recapitulate the list of its appurtenances time and again. Their tendency to indulge in technicalities and stereotyped repetitions has here reached its furthest limits."[16] I suggest that this is because the tabernacle furniture was understood as possessing something of the very being of the God of Israel. As such, it bears careful and detailed repetition whenever the occasion arises, not unlike the piling up of divine epithets in a psalm of praise or descriptions of the beloved that flow from the pen of a lover. While Mesopotamian scribes could mark temple accessories as divine by using the cuneiform *dingir* sign, the Bible could only indicate this by way of repetition.[17]

I cannot consider all the evidence from the biblical period, though some background will be necessary. This chapter concerns the role that the temple and its furniture assume in the Second Temple period (roughly 520 BCE to 70 CE) and beyond. I hope to show the following: (1) that the furniture of the temple was treated as quasi-divine in both literary and iconographic sources during the Second Temple period; (2) that the exalted estimation of these pieces of furniture made them dangerous to look at but at the same time, quite paradoxically, desirable or even compulsory to contemplate; (3) that the impossibility of dividing with precision the house of God from the being of God led the early Christians to adopt this Jewish theologoumenon as a means of clarifying how it was that Jesus could be both God and man.

The Ark and the Realism of the Bible's Liturgical Language

Anyone who has worked on the problem of the cult in the Bible knows that there is a highly realistic quality to the liturgical language used therein. The

dealt with this type of offering; the latter is abbreviated because a law already exists to which it can refer (Lev. 1:14–17).

16. Menahem Haran, *Temples and Temple-Service in Ancient Israel: An Inquiry into Biblical Cult Phenomena and the Historical Setting of the Priestly School* (Winona Lake, IN: Eisenbrauns, 1985), 149.

17. On the Mesopotamian evidence, see below.

temple is God's home and hence the spot where he dwells among humans. In order to breathe life into this belief, the Bible provides legislation for how to prepare the home for God's dramatic entrance, for how to provide God with food in a way that befits his dignity, and finally how to keep his home clean so that he will remain there and offer his blessings to the worshipers and pilgrims who desire to revere him.[18] Not unlike kings portrayed in other ancient Near Eastern literatures, the biblical King of kings will from time to time make a personal appearance. And, like other devout subjects of the imperial realm, Israelites are urged to appear before him periodically to demonstrate their fealty (Exod. 23:17 and parallels).[19]

This theophanic aspect is most vividly brought to light in the laws for the pilgrimage festivals. According to Exod. 23:17 and its parallels, Israelites must appear three times a year at the temple in order to "see the face of the LORD." As noted already by Samuel David Luzzatto in his commentary on Isaiah, and seconded by Abraham Geiger, August Dillman, and most modern interpreters, the decision of the Masoretes to vocalize the verbal stem *ra'â* as a Niphal ("to present oneself [before the face of the LORD]") is not likely the original reading.[20]

18. The best account of the "real presence" of God in the tabernacle is that of Haran, *Temples and Temple-Service*. For a fine treatment of the theme in Mesopotamia, see the classic essay of A. Leo Oppenheim, "The Care and Feeding of the Gods," in *Ancient Mesopotamia: Portrait of a Dead Civilization* (Chicago: University of Chicago Press, 1964), 183–98. On the statue itself, Elko Matsushima writes: "These statues played a central role in many important rituals and religious ceremonies in the temple area and sometimes even outside the temple. The cult statue of the god was fully identified with the god in question and was considered by the worshippers to be actually a living being, able to do whatever a human being does, for example, sleep, wake, or eat, even though the statue was always motionless and dumb." Matsushima, "Divine Statues in Ancient Mesopotamia: Their Fashioning and Clothing and Their Interaction with the Society," in *Official Cult and Popular Religion in the Ancient Near East: Papers of the First Colloquium on the Ancient Near East—The City and Its Life, Held at the Middle Eastern Culture Center in Japan (Mitaka, Tokyo), March 20–22, 1992*, ed. Elko Matsushima (Heidelberg: Universitätsverlag C. Winter, 1993), 209.

19. An appearance before a king was a sign of beatitude and favor. This point is driven home in the story of Absalom's banishment from the court of his father, King David. Begrudgingly, David accedes to Joab's plea to normalize relations and allows Absalom to return. Nevertheless, David lets Absalom know that things are still not well by telling Joab: "Let Absalom return to his house; but *my face let him not see*. So Absalom returned to his house, but the face of the king he did not see" (2 Sam. 14:24 AT). "My face let him not see" uses the exact same idiom as that found in Exod. 23:17. In Akkadian texts as well, the idiom *amaru pani* "to see the face of" means to encounter either the king or the god in a face-to-face fashion (see *CAD* 1/2:21–22). In the case of an audience with the god, the idiom refers to beholding the cult statue.

20. See Luzzatto, *Sefer Yeshayahu* (Padua, 1855) on Isa. 1:12; Geiger, *Ha-Miqra' we-turgemav* (Jerusalem: Mosad Bialik, 1949), 218–19; A. Dillmann, *Das Bücher Exodus und Leviticus* (Leipzig: S. Hirzel, 1897), 276. Luzzato notes the following problems: First, nowhere in the Bible

The most likely reading of this verse is that the Israelites must come "to see the face of the Sovereign, YHWH" three times a year. But having made the case for such a reading we have created a new problem. If the command demands that Israel "see the face of God," how was that command fulfilled? The dramatic theophany that Israel witnessed at the completion of the tabernacle (Exod. 40:34–35) was certainly not standard fare at every pilgrimage festival. What exactly did later pilgrims see when they ascended the mountain of the Lord?

The most obvious answer would be the ark. As scholars have long noted, the ark is regularly identified with the Lord's presence and at one time in its history was the subject of ceremonial processions. This is certainly implied by the liturgical refrain of Num. 10:35–36:

Whenever the ark set out, Moses would say,

"Arise, O Lord, let your enemies be scattered,
  and your foes flee before you."

And whenever it came to rest, he would say,

"Return, O Lord of the ten thousand thousands of Israel."

A similar identification of the ark with the being of God is presumed by the entrance liturgy of Ps. 24:7–10, "Lift up your heads, O gates! And be lifted up, O ancient doors! that the King of glory may come in." According to Frank Moore Cross, this portion of Ps. 24 is "an antiphonal liturgy used in the autumn festival . . . [and it] had its origin in the procession of the ark to the sanctuary at its founding, celebrated annually in the cult of Solomon and perhaps even of David. On this there can be little disagreement."[21]

The close nexus between God and this piece of cultic furniture is nicely illustrated in the story of the battle with the Philistines that would eventually

---

do we find the expected combination of the passive stem "to appear" with an indirect object (*lipnê YHWH*); rather this passive stem is somewhat anomalously conjoined to a direct object (*'et panê YHWH* or *panê YHWH*). And, more significantly, in every text where the context is some sort of personal appearance—with the exception of those involving God—we invariably find the infinitival form of the N-stem "to appear" spelled with a *heh* after the *lamed* (e.g., in 2 Sam. 17:17 or 1 Kings 18:2). But in Isa. 1:12, Exod. 34:24, and Deut. 31:11—texts that concern coming to the temple—we find the infinitive spelled without the *heh*. Since the infinitive of N-stem is regularly spelled in a *plene* fashion in biblical texts, and only in rabbinic Hebrew do we find regular elision of the intervocalic *heh*, the simplest solution is to assume that the Masoretes have wrongly vocalized these texts. And if these texts have been wrongly vocalized, then there is a high probability that Exod. 23:17 has been as well.

21. See his *Canaanite Myth and Hebrew Epic: Essays in the History of the Religion of Israel* (Cambridge, MA: Harvard University Press, 1973), 93.

lead to the ark's capture. Having been routed badly in an initial exchange of hostilities, the Israelite militia regrouped to prepare a new strategy. "Let us bring the ark of the covenant of the LORD here from Shiloh," they decided, "so that he may come among us and save us from the power of our enemies" (1 Sam. 4:3). The response to the ark's entry into the Israelite war camp reveals how close was the attachment of God's being to this piece of furniture.

> When the ark of the covenant of the LORD came into the camp, all Israel gave a mighty shout, so that the earth resounded. When the Philistines heard the noise of the shouting, they said, "What does this great shouting in the camp of the Hebrews mean?" When they learned that the ark of the LORD had come to the camp, the Philistines were afraid; for they said, "*Gods have come into the camp.*" They also said, "Woe to us! For nothing like this has happened before. Woe to us! Who can deliver us from the power of these mighty gods? (1 Sam. 4:5–8, emphasis added)

The highly realistic tenor of the language here must not be overlooked. Though God is not fully reducible to or coterminous with the ark, his presence is nevertheless so closely interwoven with it that one can point to the ark as it approaches in military processions and say, "Here comes God."[22]

This entire scene—which demonstrates the rash and ill-considered efforts of the Israelites to misuse this divine image—must be contrasted with the story of David's ignominious retreat from Jerusalem in the wake of Absalom's revolt. As David departs, Zadok appeared along with a group of Levites bearing the ark. Given that the odds in favor of David's reclaiming his kingdom

---

22. It may be worth pointing out that in *CAD* the entry *ilu* or "god" has as its seventh meaning "image of the deity." One might note the important and widespread theme in Second Temple Judaism that the most valuable temple furniture (most notably the ark; the other items vary across the different traditions) was hidden prior to the Babylonian destruction and will be revealed at the eschaton. There is not space in this chapter to go into any of the details, but clearly implied here is the notion that just as God himself was not as fully present in the second temple, neither was his full array of furniture. The two are inextricably related. The classic examples of this tradition are to be found in 2 Macc. 2:4–8; *Life of Jeremiah* 11–19; *2 Bar.* 6.5–9; *4 Bar.* (*Paraleipomena Jeremiou*) 3.1–9; and Pseudo-Philo, *LAB* 26.112–15; numerous rabbinic texts give evidence of a similar understanding. Strikingly, the Temple Scroll from Qumran includes instructions for assembling almost all the furniture in the glory of their original condition. See the essay by Lawrence H. Schiffman, "The Furnishings of the Temple according to the Temple Scroll," in *The Madrid Qumran Congress: Proceedings of the International Congress on the Dead Sea Scrolls, Madrid 18–21 March, 1991*, ed. Luis Vegas Montaner and Julio Trebolle Barrera, STDJ (Leiden: Brill, 1992), 621–34. He does not discuss the relationship of the instructions to build this furniture with parallel traditions about the revelation of where they were hidden at the end of time.

did not seem high, Zadok drew the only possible conclusion: David's future would depend on divine assistance and the easiest way to assure this would be to bring God along for the departure.[23] David, however, will have none of this, but not because he views such a stratagem as rooted in a "magical" concept of the ark. Quite the reverse. David believes himself to be in the process of paying the price for past sins (2 Sam. 12:7–15) and willingly takes upon himself this period of exile from his city and his God. His own words are most revealing: "Carry the ark of God back into the city. If I find favor in the eyes of the LORD, he will bring me back and *let me see both it* and his habitation" (2 Sam. 15:25 NRSV alt.). Favor with the deity will be symbolized not only by David's restoration to his kingdom but by being granted the privilege of *seeing* the ark.

"Seeing" the Deity

This high valuation on seeing the representation of the deity should not surprise anyone familiar with ancient Near Eastern practice. As early as 1924 and even before, Friedrich Nötscher argued[24] that references to seeing God in pilgrimage laws and the Psalter were to be understood against the background of the act of displaying the statue of the god or goddess in non-Israelite cultures. Although Israel's cultic life was without a direct and immediate representation of God himself, the ark and other pieces of the tabernacle furniture supplied an almost exact parallel.

No better witness to the close nexus between temple appurtenance and the presence of God could be seen than in the priestly rules about how to disassemble the tabernacle prior to the Israelite camp moving to a new destination in the wilderness. The rules are carefully laid out with one goal in mind: the prevention of inappropriate Levitical groups from laying eyes on the holiest parts of the structure. "But the Kohathites must not go in to look on the holy things even for a moment," the writer warns, "otherwise they will die" (Num. 4:20).[25]

23. On the theological and political importance of the cult-image to the identity of a people, see Patrick D. Miller and J. J. M. Roberts, *The Hand of the Lord: A Reassessment of the "Ark Narrative" of 1 Samuel*, Johns Hopkins Near Eastern Studies (Baltimore: Johns Hopkins University Press, 1977).

24. In his book *"Das Angesicht Gottes Schauen": Nach Biblischer und Babylonischer Auffassung* (Würzburg: Becker, 1924).

25. In a first-century CE representation of a procession from Palmyra, Syria, a portable sanctuary is borne by a camel covered by a piece of red cloth. The worshipers greet the artifact with upraised arms as though the deity himself sat astride the camel. See Othmar Keel, *The Symbolism of the Biblical World: Ancient Near Eastern Iconography and the Book of Psalms* (Winona Lake, IN: Eisenbrauns, 1997), 326.

In this text, seeing the furniture is analogous to seeing the very being of God, which likewise would result in death.[26]

Finally, I might mention Ps. 48, a text that describes in considerable detail the circumambulation of the city of Jerusalem after the destruction of enemy forces that foolishly attempted to overtake it. Having exhorted the inhabitants of Zion and the surrounding province of Judah to stream forth in pilgrimage to celebrate this event, the psalmist urges them to make a close visual inspection of the architecture of the city.

> Walk about Zion, go round about it,
>   number its towers,
> consider well its ramparts;
>   go through its citadels,
> that you may tell the next generation
>   that *this is God,*
> our God forever and ever. (Ps. 48:13–15 AT [48:12–14 Eng.])

It is the last two lines here that should occasion some surprise. Here our author seems to take his paean of praise to unimaginable heights. He claims that these buildings testify to the very being of God. Amos Hacham puts his finger directly on the pulse of this text when he writes, "[Regarding the phrase] 'this is God,' the word 'this' [*zeh*] is similar in meaning to 'look here.' It is an expression of palpable excitement, and its point is that the one who sees the temple in its splendor and glory feels within himself as if he saw, face-to-face, the glory [*kābôd*] of the Lord. He cries, 'this [this building] is God, our God.'"[27]

I suggest that this language is not solely a result of the excess or hyperbole that often characterizes the genre of praise (although obviously this is a factor). Rather, these texts exhibit ancient Israel's deeply held view that God really dwelled in the temple and that all the pieces of that building shared, in some fashion, in his tangible and visible presence. To use a modern metaphor, one might imagine the temple as a giant, electric-generating plant that powered the land of Israel. In its core was a nuclear reactor in which the radioactive rods emitted divine energy that was absorbed by the entire structure. Though the glow was brightest at the center, even the periphery had to be entered with caution. Not even the thickest cement wall or lead surface could prevent the

---

26. See, e.g., Exod. 33:20. In one rabbinic tradition, this law was promulgated because the Kohathite clan was in the habit of "feasting their eyes on the *Šəkînâ*," who dwelled among the furniture (*Numbers Rabbah* 5.9). This illustrates nicely the attraction that the temple appurtenances were felt to possess, as well as the attendant danger.

27. *Sefer Tehillim*, Daat Ha-Miqra (Jerusalem: Rav Kook, 1990), 278.

divine energies from overwhelming their boundaries and radiating divinity upon whatever stood in their vicinity.

The Angelic Host and the Aura of God in His Temple

In understanding this biblical motif, Mesopotamian texts provide a very close parallel. "The aura of a god in his temple," W. G. Lambert writes, "could so attach itself to the temple, or architectural parts of it in particular, also to the implements he used, and to the city which housed the temple, in such a way that these various things also became gods and received offerings as a mark of the fact."[28]

Not only was the statue of the god imbued with the veritable presence of the god it represented, but more remarkably, the divine aura was shared even by the furniture and other accessories dedicated to the temple.[29] The whole building pulsated with the presence of the god—the structure of the temple itself literally shared in the presence of the divine.[30]

As we will see, this deeply rooted ancient Near Eastern tendency to link the appurtenances of the building to the central cultic image had a vibrant afterlife in post-biblical Judaism. But perhaps even at this point some examples would be in order. In the *Songs of the Sabbath Sacrifice* from Qumran there is regularly some confusion as to whether a particular title identifies the Holy One, the God of Israel, or one of his angelic host.[31] Such syntactic difficulties are regular enough that one has a hard time imagining that it is the gulf of

28. W. G. Lambert, "Ancient Mesopotamian Gods: Superstition, Philosophy, Theology," *Revue de l'Histoire des Religions* 207 (1990): 115–30, here 129.

29. Note the concluding observations of Gebhard Selz's remarkable essay, "The Holy Drum, the Spear, and the Harp: Towards an Understanding of the Problems of Deification in the Third Millennium Mesopotamia," in *Gods and Their Representations*, ed. Irving L. Finkel and Markham J. Geller, Cuneiform Monographs 7 (Gröningen: Styx, 1997), 184: "A statue of a god was an independent entity, because it stood on a holy place, and had the name of a god, the appearance of a god, and so on. It was these qualities of a statue, including its partaking in certain rituals, which left no doubt that it was the god himself. *The same holds true for the 'cultic objects'; it is their function and their special attributes, including their participation in holy rites, which made them god-like*" (emphasis added). Compare also the essay of K. van der Toorn, "Worshipping Stones: On the Deification of Cult Symbols," *Journal of Northwest Semitic Languages* 23 (1997): 1–14.

30. These Mesopotamian texts had a decisive semiotic advantage over their biblical brethren; they could mark the overflow of the divine energies by attaching a *dingir* sign to lists of temple furniture. See Selz, "The Holy Drum, the Spear, and the Harp," 176–79.

31. The text from Qumran includes a portrayal of a heavenly throne room and a liturgy of angels. See in particular the commentary of Carol Newsom on the seventh Sabbath Song in her *Songs of Sabbath Sacrifice: A Critical Edition*, HSS 27 (Atlanta: Scholars Press, 1985), 213–25. Note also her comment on 24: "Many occurrences of *elohim* in the Shirot are ambiguous and might refer to God or to the angels."

many centuries between composition and commentary that is creating the problem. The text itself seems to enjoy the confusion it creates, from time to time, between the two categories.

The most likely explanation for this is to be found in the Bible itself. As James Kugel has explained, in the course of a theophany the angel of the Lord will frequently fade into the person of God himself.

> The fact that [this confusion occurs] in text after text (even if, after a time, it became conventional) suggests that there was something essential about this confusion. It represents the biblical authors' most realistic sense of the way things actually are. The spiritual is not something tidy and distinct, another order of being. Instead, it is perfectly capable of intruding into everyday reality, as if part of this world.[32]

But it is not only the case that angels bleed into God and vice versa; the same syntactic difficulties attend the sanctuary as well. As Carol Newsom has argued, the thirteen *Songs of the Sabbath Sacrifice* are organized around the important seventh song.[33] And, as in the two songs that flank this centerpiece (the sixth and the eighth), the number seven is itself crucial to the compositional structure. The song opens with seven highly ornate exhortations to the angelic priesthood to commence their praise. Then we move from voices of the angelic host to the sanctuary itself bursting into song:

> [and along with the seven groups of angels who were exhorted to sing praise][34] let all the [foundations of the hol]y of holies offer praise, the uplifting pillars of the supremely exalted abode, and all the corners of its structure. Sin[g praise] to Go[d who is dr]eadful in power[, all you spirits of knowledge and light] in order to [exa]lt together the splendidly shining firmament of [His] holy sanctuary. [Give praise to Hi]m, O god-[like] spirits, in order to pr[aise for ever and e]ver the firmament of the upper[m]ost heaven, all [its] b[eams] and its walls, a[l]l its [for]m, the work of [its] struc[ture. The spir]its of holie[st] holiness, living god-like beings[, spir]its of [eter]nal holi[ness] above all the hol[y ones.][35]

The building itself breaks into song, dramatically eclipsing the difference between the angelic host and the building in which they serve.

32. James L. Kugel, *The God of Old: Inside the Lost World of the Bible* (New York: Free Press, 2003), 36.

33. Newsom, *Songs of Sabbath Sacrifice*, 13–17.

34. The use of *hǎllēlû* as an imperative call to praise marks the beginning, middle, and end of the seventh song. See *4QSongs of the Sabbath Sacrifice^d* (4Q403), 1.30, 41; 2.15. First the angels are called to offer praise, then the temple itself, and finally the chariots of the inner sanctum.

35. 4Q403 1.41–45.

Even more striking is how the text vacillates over just what precisely is the object of praise. With the angels, one is never in doubt that they are the ones who must offer praise. However, the divinized temple not only offers praise, but itself becomes the object of praise. "Give praise to Him, O god-like spirits," the text exhorts, "in order to praise/confess (*le-hôdôt*) . . . the firmament of the uppermost heaven, all its beams and walls." Indeed the last sentence quoted above ("The spirits of holiest holiness . . .") is difficult to parse grammatically. How exactly is it related to its immediate antecedent, that is, to the list of architectural features of the temple? Newsom's commentary is revealing:

> The expression *ruhey qodesh qodashim* may mean either "most holy spirits" . . . or "spirits of the holy of holies." However the title is construed, these angelic spirits are in some way associated with the heavenly sanctuary which has just been described, either as attendants or as the *animate spiritual substance of the heavenly Temple itself.*[36]

No matter which way we go with these two options, we reach essentially the same destination. Either the temple is such an overpoweringly holy structure that angelic spirits literally ooze from its various surfaces, or those surfaces themselves slip into the realm of divine being itself. Hebrew constructions such as *'ĕlōhîm ḥayyîm* ("the living God") that one would normally construe as divine titles now become attributes of the supernal temple ("a living pulsating godlike [building]").

Although the end of the seventh song is fragmentary, enough remains for Newsom to conclude that the praise moves from the outer parts of the heavenly sanctuary to its inner sanctum and its furnishings. As such, the structure of this crucial middle song anticipates "to a certain extent the structure and content of the ninth through the thirteenth songs."[37] And not surprisingly, in these latter songs the structural edifice of the supernal temple again comes to life to voice its praise. It is striking, Newsom notes, that the thirteenth and final song appears to conclude with a systematic list of the contents and structures of the heavenly temple.

That the Sabbath songs seem to feel no embarrassment about ascribing divine qualities to the temple provides a striking piece of data against which we can contextualize how the Samaritan version of the Pentateuch and the Septuagint handle several texts in Exodus that speak of "seeing" God. We have already mentioned the command to visit Jerusalem during

---

36. Newsom, *Songs of Sabbath Sacrifice*, 233 (emphasis added).
37. Ibid., 9.

the three pilgrimage festivals in order to fulfill the obligation of "seeing the face of the Sovereign, YHWH" (Exod. 23:17). The Masoretes smoothed over this arresting phrase by rendering "to see" in the passive "to be seen / appear."

The Samaritan version found another way around the problem. Building on the common confusion of the Hebrew letters *dalet* and *reš*, it reads the line as "to see the presence of the ark [reading *'ărôn* in place of *'ādôn*] of the Lord." Though correctly dismissed by text-critics as a secondary reading, it is an invaluable piece of information for the scholar of early biblical exegesis.[38] Minimally, this reading demonstrates that for at least one strand of ancient Judaism, seeing the ark was a close substitute for seeing God himself. Maximally, it may provide us with a piece of indirect evidence that, in the Second Temple period, pieces of the temple furniture were taken out of the building and displayed before the eyes of earnest pilgrims.[39]

Though the Septuagint anticipates what the Masoretes will do with this verse by rendering "to see" in the passive form, in a couple of other places it replaces the difficult construction of "seeing God" with the notion of beholding the structure in which he dwells. Compare, for example, Exod. 25:8, where Moses is told that the entire purpose of building the tabernacle is "so that I may dwell among [the Israelites]." The Septuagint replaces the idiom of dwelling with a reference to vision: build the sanctuary, Israel is exhorted, "so that I may *be visible* among you."

Similarly, in Exod. 24:10, where the MT declares that Moses and the select group that ascended to the top of Mount Sinai "saw the God of Israel," the Septuagint introduces a rather significant qualification: "They saw *the place where* the God of Israel stood."

If we skip ahead to the book of Revelation, it is perhaps significant that when the kingdom of God is to be revealed at the end of time and the appearance of God in his full glory would seem to be at hand, what is described is something not unlike what Moses must have beheld at Sinai:

Then the seventh angel blew his trumpet, and there were loud voices in heaven, saying,

> "The kingdom of the world has become the kingdom of our Lord
>   and of his Messiah,
> and he will reign forever and ever."

---

38. The importance of this textual variant for the practices of Second Temple Judaism has already been noted by Israel Knohl, "Post-biblical Sectarianism and the Priestly Schools," *Tarbiz* 60 (1991): 139–46, esp. 140–41.

39. On this, see the suggestive arguments of Knohl, "Post-biblical Sectarianism."

Then the twenty-four elders who sit on their thrones before God fell on their
faces and worshiped God, singing,

> "We give you thanks, Lord God Almighty,
>   who are and who were,
> for you have taken your great power
>   and begun to reign.
> The nations raged,
>   but your wrath has come,
>   and the time for judging the dead,
> for rewarding your servants, the prophets
>   and saints and all who fear your name,
>   both small and great,
> and for destroying those who destroy the earth."

*Then God's temple in heaven was opened, and the ark of his covenant was
seen within his temple*; and there were flashes of lightning, rumblings, peals
of thunder, an earthquake, and heavy hail. (Rev. 11:15–19, emphasis added)

The common denominator that binds all these examples together is that of
gazing upon the architecture of the sanctuary as a fit replacement for seeing
the face of God.

God Tabernacled among Us

Scholars have long been aware that the New Testament and early Christianity
thought of the person of Jesus Christ and the community that he founded in
terms of the temple. As to the former, no text could be clearer than the Gospel of
John. Early in his ministry when Jesus is asked for a sign to authorize his teaching and actions he declares: "Destroy this temple, and in three days I will raise it
up" (John 2:19). His interlocutors puzzle over this declaration and wonder how
a building that has been under construction for some forty-six years could be so
quickly reestablished. At this point the narrator intervenes with an important
clarification: "But [Jesus] was speaking of the temple of his body. After he was
raised from the dead, his disciples remembered that he had said this; and they
believed the scripture and the word that Jesus had spoken" (2:21–22).[40]

The early New Testament community was viewed as an eschatological
temple that represents the perduring body of Christ after his resurrection

---

40. For a recent survey of the issue, see Alan R. Kerr, *The Temple of Jesus' Body*. Still very
useful is the magisterial survey of Yves Congar, *The Mystery of the Temple* (London: Burns
& Oates, 1962).

and ascension. This can be seen in Paul's declaration, "Do you not know that you are God's temple and that God's Spirit dwells in you? If anyone destroys God's temple, God will destroy that person. For God's temple is holy, and you are that temple (1 Cor. 3:16–17)."[41]

But my purpose is not to survey the literature about how the temple serves as a metaphor for Jesus's person or of the community he founded. Rather, I would like to limit myself to how the metaphor of the temple is associated with the notion of sight—such that looking at the physical body of Jesus becomes tantamount to beholding the very person of God. And for these purposes there is no better text than John 1:14: "And the word became flesh and lived among us and we have seen his glory, the glory as of a father's only Son, full of grace and truth."

The Johannine theme that God became visible in the flesh of Jesus had an extraordinary influence in early Christianity. For Irenaeus, writing about 180, the primary reason for God becoming human was that the world could see him.[42] To see God was to be drawn into the divine realm.

Tertullian (d. ca. 225) reaches the same destination but via a slightly different path.[43] He was bothered that God regularly makes himself visible to Israel in the Old Testament yet also says that anyone who gazes upon his face will die (Exod. 33:20). How can these two things be reconciled? For Tertullian, the Gospel of John provides the key; for while it affirms that no human being has seen the Father (John 1:18), it concedes that human beings can see the Word (1:14). When one reads, then, in the Old Testament of appearances of God to various holy individuals, these are to be understood as nothing other than appearances of the Word of God prior to his full incarnation. Like Irenaeus, Tertullian thinks the purpose of the incarnation is to make God visible to human eyes.

Perhaps even more emphatic about this theme was Gregory of Nyssa (d. 395). He writes that

If everyone had the ability to come, as Moses did, inside the cloud, where Moses saw what may not be seen; or to be raised above three heavens as Paul

41. See also 2 Cor. 6:16; Eph. 2:20–22; Heb. 13:15–16; 1 Pet. 2:5; 4:17; and Rev. 3:12; 11:1–2. The literature on this matter is considerable. For a brief review, see Richard Bauckham, "James and the Gentiles (Acts 15:13–21)," in History, Literature, and Society in the Book of Acts, ed. Ben Witherington III (Cambridge: Cambridge University Press, 1996), 165–68. An older survey of the problem can be found in Bertil E. Gärtner, The Temple and the Community in Qumran and the New Testament: A Comparative Study in the Temple Symbolism of the Qumran Texts and the New Testament (Cambridge: Cambridge University Press, 1965).
42. Irenaeus, Against Heresies 4.20.
43. Tertullian, Against Praxeas 14–16.

was and to be instructed in Paradise about ineffable things that lie above reason; or to be taken up in fire to the ethereal region, as zealous Elijah was, and not be weighed down by the body's baggage; or to see on the throne of glory, as Ezekiel and Isaiah did, the one who is raised above the cherubim and glorified by the Seraphim—then surely if all were like this, there would be no need for the appearance of our God in flesh.[44]

Why then did Jesus become flesh according to John 1:14? For Nyssa the answer resides in what he saw as the progressive decline of the world. Because of a deepening weakness of spiritual sight within the human race, folks in Jesus's day had lost the ability to see as Moses saw. Therefore, like a physician matching his cure to the infirmity of the patient, God took dramatic measures and became visible in human flesh.

There is one more twist in the story worth attending to. If Jesus inhabits flesh the way God will inhabit the temple, just how might we understand the relationship of the Godhead to the building in which it rests? Is the relationship an intrinsic one? By this I mean: Is the entire body of Jesus, in all its carnality, divinized by this indwelling? Or to use the Jewish metaphors we have followed: Is the body of Jesus like the temple walls in the Sabbath Songs, that is, so infused with the divine energies that they come to life (and are called *'ĕlōhîm ḥayyîm*, "*the living God*" or "*living divine beings*") during moments of angelic praise? Or is it like the table of presence presented before the pilgrims in order to fulfill their obligation to see God; or, like the veil that separates the visible portions of the temple from the invisible? All of these Jewish metaphors bespeak an intrinsic relation inasmuch as it is not possible to divide or separate fully the being of God from the objects he inhabits.

The other option is to consider the relationship of the Word to Jesus as more extrinsic in nature. The carnal flesh of Jesus, on this view, is a dispensable vehicle through which the divine medicine has been administered; as such, it can and indeed must be ignored by spiritual adepts in order to attend to the true source of divinity, namely, the *logos* that resides within. This, of course, is not an idle matter; the question of how to render John 1:14 became one of the major forks in the road for early Christianity.[45]

44. *To Theophilus, against the Apollinarians.* See Friedrich Müller, ed., *Gregorii Nysseni Opera Dogmatica Minora, Pars 1* [Gregory of Nyssa, Minor Dogmatic Works, Part 1] (Leiden: Brill, 1958), 123–24. The English translation is courtesy of my colleague Brian Daley, SJ, and is used with his permission.

45. In one direction was the docetic option, which claimed that the Word did not so much become flesh as it was made manifest in the flesh. For the problem of rendering the Greek, see note 10 above.

For Athanasius, writing in the fourth century, there was only one answer to that question: the flesh of Jesus *participates* in the divinity of the indwelling *logos*. In order to drive home this point, Christian thought would declare that what was predicated of the fleshly person of Christ could also be predicated of God, as well as the reverse (the so-called communication of properties, or *communicatio idiomatum*).

The manner by which Athanasius arrives at this conclusion depends on a construal of the biblical temple as a structure that *physically* participates in the life of the God who inhabits it. Athanasius is concerned about the readiness of the Arians to "divide" the person of Christ into two, his human side and his divine side. To do so, Athanasius argues, is idolatrous, because when Christians prostrate themselves before Jesus they do so before the whole person—that is, the Word and the flesh.

If the two are divisible, then the act of venerating the person Jesus results in worship of a creature. "We do not worship a creature," Athanasius declares. "And we neither divide the body . . . from the Word, and worship it by itself; nor when we wish to worship the Word do we set Him far apart from the Flesh, but knowing . . . that 'the Word was made flesh' [John 1:14], we recognise Him as God also, after having come in the flesh."[46]

How does Athanasius justify his argument from the standpoint of Scripture? By attending to the practice of the Jewish pilgrimage feasts.

> But we should like your piety to ask [the Arians] this question. When Israel was ordered to go up to Jerusalem to worship at the temple of the Lord, where the ark was, "and above it the cherubim of glory overshadowing the mercy-seat" [Heb. 9:5], did they do well or not? If they were in error, how is it that those who despised this law became liable for punishment? For it is written that "if a man make light of this command and not go up, he shall perish from among his people" [Num. 9:13]. But if they were correct in this practice and so proved themselves well-pleasing to God, then are not the Arians abominable and the most shameful of any heresy, even many times more worthy of destruction?
>
> For they approve the former people [the Jews] for the honor paid by them to the temple, but they will not worship the Lord who is in the flesh as a God indwelling a temple. . . . And [the Jews] did not, when they saw the temple of stones, suppose that the Lord who spoke in the temple was a creature; nor did they set the temple at nought and retire far off to worship. But they came to it according to the Law, and worshipped the God who uttered his oracles from the temple. Since this was so, how can it be other than right to worship the body of the Lord, all-holy and all-reverend as it is, announced by the Holy

46. *Letter* 60.3 ("To Adelphius, against the Arians," *NPNF²* 4:575).

Spirit and made the vestment of the Word. . . . Therefore, he that dishonors the temple dishonors the Lord in the temple; and he that separates the Word from the Body sets at nought the grace given to us in him.[47]

Athanasius's point is crystal clear. Just as the Jews had complete justification in prostrating themselves before a building of stone and not dividing God from the house in which he dwelled—for though they knew God was not limited to the stones or the furniture, at the same time they used that limitation as license for not going up to Jerusalem—so Christians have complete justification in prostrating themselves before Jesus and not dividing the indwelling God from the flesh that contains him.

Seeing God in the Temple: A Summary of the Evidence

It has often been stated that because of Israel's radically anti-iconic stance, it came to prefer forms of revelation that were mediated by Word rather than sight. This assertion, like all such truisms, is to some extent accurate. Nevertheless, as we have seen in this essay, it should not be assumed that because Israel rejected the representation of God in statuary form in the temple, it thereby rejected all linkages of God to a specific physical domain.

As Haran has pointed out with such clarity, the realistic language of the cult—that is, the providing of the Deity with light, a pleasing aroma, and food—presumes that some aspect of the Deity has actually taken up residence within the confines of the tabernacle. Moreover, according to the Priestly narrative, he sits astride the ark of the covenant and is veiled from view by both the darkness of his inner cella and the outstretched wings of the cherubim that stand in front of him.

Because his presence was thought to be localized in this specific place, the effect of this theologoumenon on the entire tabernacle compound was almost exactly that of what we find in other ancient Near Eastern settings. The aura of the Deity's presence was so overwhelming that all parts of the temple compound came to share in its effulgence. There is ample biblical proof that this was believed to be the case: First, the injunction one finds in the psalms "to gaze" upon the temple or the presence of God within the temple; second, the original form of the pilgrimage laws which most certainly commanded that Israelites "see the face of the Lord"; and third, the Priestly fascination with the architectural detail of the tabernacle, a fascination that leads this source to repeat the list of its appurtenances whenever the narrative will allow it.

47. *Letter* 60.7–8 (PG 26:1080–82; *NPNF*[2] 4:577 alt.).

And again, as we have seen, this evidence is greatly extended when we move into the Second Temple period. In the *Song of the Sabbath Sacrifice* from Qumran there is an intentional ambiguity as to the nature of the praise being made. The texts could be read as describing either an anthropomorphic temple offering praise or the temple itself receiving praise as a quasi-divinized being. The high theology of the temple building is also attested in the Samaritan and Septuagint versions of the Bible. Both versions alter the MT at several points to inform the reader that seeing God means seeing either the place where he dwells (the structure of the tabernacle itself) or the ark itself.

Michael Wyschogrod has argued that the temple provides a close, though not exact, analogy to what Christianity means by the doctrine of incarnation: "The God of Israel is a God who enters the world of humanity and in so doing does not shun the parameters of human existence that include spatiality."[48] Indeed, when God assumes residence in the tabernacle, he so ties his personal identity to that building that praise of the building can come close to praise of God himself.

This close continuity of God and temple would seem to be radically compromised by its destruction in 587 BCE and (again) in 70 CE. Some Christian apologists were certainly alert to this fact and used the temple's destruction as a basic building block in their argument that God had permanently abandoned the Jews. But, in fact, just the opposite occurs. As the temple vessels are removed from the building just prior to this catastrophic end, God's presence and future promise of restoration become tied to where these vessels are interred and when they shall be revealed. The attachment of God to his home continues even after that home is destroyed.

This analogy of the temple to the incarnation was not lost on early Christianity. Beginning with John 1:14 we see an attempt to describe the tabernacling presence as God's becoming present in Jesus such that he can be "seen" among men and women. For decades after the appearance of John's Gospel, debate raged, however on just how God was attached to this person.

Did he actually become the (now divinized) flesh of Jesus Christ, the claim of nascent orthodoxy, or did he simply make use of the ordinary human flesh as the occasion to manifest himself in a way that only those with the proper esoteric knowledge could ascertain, as the gnostics claimed? To answer this question, Athanasius turned to a set of logical relations that would have been most at home in Second Temple Judaism. He asked whether the pilgrims to Jerusalem, when they prostrated themselves in veneration before the building, distinguished between the invisible God who dwelled there and the very brick-work that enclosed him. At some theoretical level, of course, a distinction could and must be made, but the manner in which the Deity overtook the space in which he was housed was so overwhelming that any distinction at the phenomenological level of human experience was not possible. As God became one with his furniture, so God became one with flesh.

The Tabernacle and the Mystical Turn

But the story of Christian exegesis is not exhausted by this specific christo-logical turn. The narratives about the tabernacle, narratives so beholden to technical detail that they nearly become unintelligible to modern readers, became a favorite site for mystic contemplation for many spiritual writers.

John of Ruusbroec, a fourteenth-century Flemish mystic, wrote an extensive commentary on this portion of the Bible, *The Spiritual Tabernacle*. "Although its heavily allegorical character may not be attractive to modern readers," a commentator remarks, "it seems to have been very popular in Ruusbroec's own day, at least if we deduce this from the fact that more manuscripts of this treatise are extant than those of any other of his writings."[49]

The impetus to accord such importance to the biblical material on the tab-ernacle begins with Gregory of Nyssa's *Life of Moses*. In this work, the ascent of Moses to the top of Mount Sinai to contemplate the heavenly tabernacle became the very model for the life of serious prayer and contemplation. Moses, as the first mystic adept, has paved the way for the rest of humanity to follow.

But more important than Gregory was the influence of Pseudo-Dionysius the Areopagite, active in the fifth and sixth centuries and the undisputed father of the Western mystical tradition.

> It is not for nothing that the blessed Moses is commanded to submit first to purification and then to be separated from those who have not undergone this (Exod. 24:15–18). When every purification is complete (his forty days of fasting) he hears the many-voiced trumpets (Exod. 20:18). He sees the many lights, pure and with rays streaming abundantly. Then, standing apart from the crowds and accompanied by chosen priests, he pushes ahead to the summit of the divine ascents. *And yet he does not meet God Himself, but contemplates, not him who is invisible, but rather where he dwells* (Exod. 25). This means, I presume, that the holiest and highest of things perceived with the eye of the body or the mind are but the rationale which presupposes all that lies below the Transcendent

49. *John Ruusbroec: The Spiritual Espousals and Other Works*, trans. James A. Wiseman, Classics of Western Spirituality (New York: Paulist, 1985), 24.

One. *Through them* (that is, the *physical* appurtenances of the Tabernacle in
Exod. 25), however, his unimaginable presence is shown, walking the heights
of those holy places to which the mind at least can rise.[50]

The striking line here is how Dionysius understands the function of all the
textual detail in Exod. 25–40. Moses is called to the top of Mount Sinai for
an intimate audience with God, yet the direct vision of God is something that
no human person is able to withstand.

How was God to mediate his presence to this budding novice of the religious
life? According to Dionysius, who is clearly following the lead of the biblical text, Moses does not see God himself but rather confronts the next best
thing. He is allowed to contemplate the invisible God in the visible form of
his domestic furniture. For, as he argues, it is through this furniture that "his
unimaginable presence is shown." To paraphrase Dionysius, we cannot see
God face to face, but he has graciously consented to let us see where he dwells.[51]

50. This translation is from Paul Rorem, "Moses as Paradigm for the Liturgical Spirituality
of Pseudo-Dionysius," in *Studia Patristica* 18/2, ed. Elizabeth A. Livingstone (Kalamazoo, MI:
Cistercian Publications, 1989), 275–79.

51. Before closing I should adduce one modern parallel that might make this abstract concept more concrete. Two of the most heavily visited tourist sites in the United States are the
Oval Office and Graceland Mansion—the office of the president of the United States and the
home of Elvis Presley. Now even in this visual age, where photographs and film clips of these
two people are readily available on youtube.com, it is striking to hear what tourists say when
they can lay their physical eyes on the furniture used by them. Numerous persons report an
intimacy that overwhelms the senses. It is as though an unimagined part of that person came
vividly to life. Somehow the possessions themselves and the way they are configured in a room
convey something crucial about the person's being. An explanation for this is not difficult to
find. If the identity of a person we love and admire is always elusive, no matter how often
we see them, then our best chance to achieve a fuller knowledge is to avail ourselves of every
possible clue to their identity. Nonverbal cues are often as good as and sometimes even better
than verbal ones. There is much to be learned from how people dress and comport themselves.
Equally revealing are decisions about one's domicile and how one has organized the domestic
space. For individuals such as the president or Elvis, where there is little or no opportunity for
face-to-face contact, perhaps one of the best ways of learning about who they are is seeing how
they arrange their most intimate living spaces. If I have been successful in this chapter, I will
have advanced the thesis that the same holds true for God himself.

7

Mariology

The Mother of God and the Temple

This chapter continues the discussion that began in the previous chapter and extends the subject of the temple to cover the figure of Mary as well. Since she held the second person of the holy Trinity in her womb, everything that could be said about the temple as a "house for God" could be transferred to her. The development of Mariology is not simply grounded in developments internal to the church in the first several centuries of its existence but is also a result of a careful investigation of the figural relationship within the church's two-Testament Bible.

> What is this flesh . . . [that]
> . . . strikes a sudden chill into my bones
> And bids my hair stand up?
>   "The Mother of God,"
>   William Butler Yeats[1]

The figure of Mary has provided a considerable challenge for ecumenical relations between Catholics and Protestants. Historically, the grounds for this suspicion rest largely on the Protestant fear that Catholics commit idolatry when they venerate the person of Mary. In an article on the subject of Mary, the evangelical scholar Timothy George makes this point quite clear in an amusing vignette from the life of the famous Scottish Reformer John Knox. George recounts the incident thus:

1. Here Yeats captures Mary's shock that she was capable of holding the Creator of the universe within her womb.

Having been delivered from "the puddle of papistry," as he called it, he was taken to be a prisoner in the French galleys where he remained for nineteen months. On one occasion, he tells us, while he was serving in the galleys, the Catholic chaplain of Knox's ship held forth a beautifully painted wooden statue of the Blessed Virgin Mary and encouraged Knox and the other prisoners to genuflect and show proper reverence. When the statue of Mary was forcibly placed in Knox's hand, he grabbed it and immediately threw it overboard into the sea. "Let our Lady now save herself," he said. "She is light enough; let her learn to swim!" Never again, Knox adds, was he forced to commit "idolatry" by kissing and bowing to an image of the virgin Mary.[2]

The charge of idolatry has a long pedigree, going back ultimately to the reforms of King Josiah (2 Kings 22:12–23:24) and the legislation of Moses on Mount Sinai. Catholics (and the Orthodox) have not been deaf to these worries and typically distinguish between an act of worship (*latreia*) that can be offered to God alone and an act of veneration (*douleia*) that befits an icon or the Blessed Mother. But in the heat of fervent religious polemic a distinction such as this appears too clever by half. Any sort of compromise, many of the later Reformers reasoned, would be tantamount to apostasy. The official sanctioning of idol-smashing by King Josiah became the model for the iconoclasts.[3]

In the context of his article, Timothy George does not address the substance of Knox's criticism. Accordingly, it should be no surprise that the veneration of an image of Mary—be it icon or statue—does not find a position of respect within his otherwise revisionary program. Mary, to the degree that she has a special role to play in the tradition, is to be revered as the Mother of the church. This appellation is grounded in the "yes" she voices to the angel Gabriel at the annunciation and her faithfulness to Christ that extends even to the depth of his passion. Though the disciples—including even Peter—fled from Christ at the advent of his passion, Mary remained steadfast in her devotion. "Her fidelity under the cross," George observes, "showed that the true faith could be preserved in one sole individual, and thus Mary became the mother of the (true remnant) church."[4]

In this chapter I wish to revisit the relationship between Mary's representation in the tradition and in the Bible with the goal of proposing a characterization of the Mother of God that would go beyond the admittedly admirable

2. Timothy George, "The Blessed Virgin Mary in Evangelical Perspective," in *Mary Mother of God*, ed. C. Braaten and R. Jenson (Grand Rapids: Eerdmans, 2004), 100–101.

3. See the masterful treatment of Carlos Eire, *The War against the Idols: The Reformation of Worship from Erasmus to Calvin* (Cambridge: Cambridge University Press, 1986).

4. George, "Blessed Virgin Mary," 119.

but narrow contours drawn by George. To do so, I propose to follow a quite unlikely path: the witness to Mary that is to be found in the Old Testament. This approach will certainly strike most as startling—as well it should. For the figure of Mary is referred to in no explicit fashion in the Old Testament. But as a hint toward the direction my argument will go, let me say that my point of departure derives from the liturgy of the Angelus.[5] Here the moment of the incarnation is the subject of great praise. At one point, while recounting the drama of the annunciation, John's Gospel is cited: *verbum caro factum est et habitavit in nobis*. The key phrase for my purpose is *habitavit in nobis*, for these words recall that momentous occasion in the Old Testament when God took up residence with his people in the tabernacle (Exod. 29:38–46) and stands in a tight figural relationship to it. Accordingly, one can only respond as did the Israelites of old: with bended knee and full-throated praise. The words of the Angelus are altogether apt: *Ave Maria, gratia plena, Dominus te cum, et benedictus fructus ventris tui, Iesus*.

The Temple and the Incarnation among the Antiochenes

As we saw in our previous chapter, texts such as John 1:14 compelled early Christian thinkers to ponder the mystery of the incarnation against the background of God's indwelling of the tabernacle that Moses constructed at the foot of Mount Sinai. Given the importance of this christological theme in the Bible and the early church as we have traced it, one might have expected that this "temple theology" would have had a long afterlife itself. But in fact it does not go much further than Athanasius himself. This is because of what happens within the school of Antiochene Christianity. There, already with the figure of Theodore of Mopsuestia, it is propounded that God abandons Jesus at his passion and lets the man suffer on his own. Though the scriptural justification is grounded in a textually problematic verse from Hebrews,[6] the larger thematic argument comes from the metaphor of a temple. For though God can indwell a temple such that his presence infuses even the furniture

---

5. A particular source of inspiration has been the soaring vocal rendition of the same by Franz Bieble (1906–2001).

6. Theodore grounded this remarkable assertion in a textual variant of Heb. 2:9. "And in order to teach us why He suffered and became 'a little lower [than the angels]' he said: '*Apart from God* [in place of, 'by the grace of God'] He tasted death for every man.' In this he shows that the Divine nature willed that He should taste death for the benefit of every man, and also that the Godhead was separated from the one who was suffering in the trial of death, because it was impossible for Him to taste the trial of death if (the Godhead) were not cautiously remote from Him."

and masonry, *he can also depart from a temple and go into exile*. Ezekiel is the best witness to this theologoumenon. For in a famous section of his book, he articulates in considerable detail how God mounted his chariot-throne in the holy of holies and departed the temple, making it completely vulnerable to the assaults of the Babylonian invaders (Ezek. 8–11).

Pursuing this aspect of temple theology to its logical end, Theodore, and later most notoriously Nestorius (early fifth century), argued that the indwelling of God in Jesus's body, like a temple, is a *wholly extrinsic* affair. There was no intrinsic relationship between the temple and the deity who resided within. God was free to come and go at his leisure. And such was the method of reading the Gospels evidenced by Nestorius and his circle. In some parts of the gospel story we see only the weak human body that Jesus inhabits; in others the deity bursts onto the scene. At the crucifixion God literally departs from his temple and leaves the man Jesus to die on his own.

Theodore's position is well illustrated in his *Commentary on the Nicene Creed*.[7] Throughout this text Theodore distinguishes what happened to the man Jesus—here described as the material framework of the temple—in contrast to God who resided within him—here understood to be like the glory of the Lord that sits atop the ark and is free to come and go as it pleases. As a result, Theodore could not countenance any sort of "strong reading" of John 1:14; the Word appears in the flesh but does not in any way become flesh.[8]

It is not Divine nature that received death, but it is clear that it was that man who was assumed as a temple to God the Word which was dissolved and then raised by the one who had assumed it. And after the Crucifixion it was not Divine nature that was raised but the temple which was assumed, which rose from the dead, ascended to heaven and sat at the right hand of God; nor is it to Divine nature—the cause of everything—that it was given that every one should worship it and every knee should bow, but worship was granted to the form of a servant which did not in its nature possess (the right to be worshipped). While all these things are clearly and obviously said of human nature he referred them successively to Divine nature so that his sentence might be strengthened and be

7. A. Mingana, ed. and trans., *Commentary of Theodore of Mopsuestia on the Nicene Creed*, Woodbrook Studies 5 (Cambridge: Heffer, 1932).

8. See the good discussion by F. Young, *From Nicaea to Chalcedon: A Guide to the Literature and Its Background* (London: SCM, 1983), 209: "The Logos could not move from place to place, nor 'become' flesh except *kata to dokein*—he meant 'metaphorically' rather than 'docetically' because he continued: 'In appearance, not in the sense that he did not take real flesh, but in the sense that he did not *become* flesh.' For Theodore truer expressions are to be found in the phrases 'he tabernacled among us' or 'he assumed flesh'—'flesh' being a term which he explicitly takes to mean human nature in its entirety. So the incarnation could not imply any change in the essential Godhead any more than it could undermine the autonomy of the manhood."

acceptable to hearers. Indeed, since it is above human nature that it should be worshipped by all, it is with justice that all this has been said as of one, so that the belief in a close union between the natures might be strengthened, because he clearly showed that the one who was assumed did not receive all this great honor except from the Divine nature which assumed Him and dwelt in Him.[9]

If this text is read side by side with that of Athanasius, one can see significant points of continuity. And this should occasion no surprise, for Theodore thought of himself as a vigorous defender of Nicene orthodoxy. Athanasius's opponents were his own opponents. Most important in this regard is his claim that, because God indwelled Jesus as he had the temple, one can worship and bend the knee toward Jesus. Theodore, however, goes one step further. He takes special pains to emphasize the division between the body and the God who indwelled it. The relationship between the two bespeaks, to be sure, "a *close union* between the natures," but a union that remains sufficiently divisible that God can abandon this temple and three days later raise it up. Proper Gospel interpretation, by extension, requires the ability to divide the human figure from the divine being who indwells him. This propensity to divide the person of Christ met extreme resistance in the person of Cyril of Alexandria and the controversy that erupted between him and Nestorius.

Mary and the Temple

In the aftermath of the Nestorian controversy, the temple metaphor as a means of understanding the incarnation was categorically rejected. Leo the Great's homilies on the Nativity make this clear,

> For this wondrous child-bearing of the holy Virgin produced in her offspring one person which was truly human and truly Divine, because neither substance so retained their properties that there could be any division of persons in them; *nor was the creature taken into partnership with its Creator in such a way that the One was the in-dweller, and the other the dwelling*; but so that the one nature was blended with the other.[10]

9. Mingana, *Theodore of Mopsuestia on the Nicene Creed*, 66.

10. Leo the Great, *Sermon* 23.1 [3.1] (*NPNF*[2] 12:132, emphasis added). For Leo it is crucial that there be no division between God and man in the person of Jesus Christ. As a result, the temple metaphor as used by the Antiochene school is allowed no place at the table. In Leo's mind, Nestorius had effectively divided the in-dweller (God the Son) from the dwelling (Jesus as man) and hence ruled out any direct comparison of Jesus to the temple. For the Latin original, see Léon le Grand, *Sermons*, SC 22, 2nd ed. (Paris: Cerf, 1964), 94–99. The note appended by Dom René Dolle, the editor of the text, is worth citing (97n3): "C'était là, en effet, une expression

In this text Leo desires to make clear that the concept of a "close union" between deity and humanity that Theodore favored was not adequate for defining the christological mystery. What was needed was a form of expression that allowed the two natures to interpenetrate one another so fully that such a separation would be very difficult. For these purposes the doctrine of *communicatio idiomatum* (what can be predicated of the divine can also be said of the human and vice versa) provided far better service. In this vein, the metaphor of the temple would no longer be appropriate because Ezekiel's depiction of the exile allowed one to construe the relation of the indweller to the dwelling in a far too casual manner.

But then what became of the rich temple language of the Old Testament once it lost its natural connection to the person of Christ? It was far too central a witness to be passed over in silence. If the integrity of the character of God across the two Testaments was to be preserved, the metaphor of the temple could not be ignored. The logical place to turn was the womb of the Virgin Mary. That person who would be identified in the iconographic tradition as "the container of the uncontainable"—an unmistakable allusion to the God of Israel, whose being could not be contained even in the highest of the heavens (1 Kings 8:27) yet who nevertheless deigned to dwell in Jerusalem—proved a fit dwelling wherein the creator of the universe could find habitation. Leo writes,

> For the uncorrupt nature of Him that was born had to guard the primal virginity of the Mother, and the infused power of the *Divine Spirit had to preserve intact the chamber of chastity and the dwelling place of holiness that it had chosen for itself*: that Spirit (I say) who had determined to raise the fallen, to restore the broken, and by overcoming the allurements of the flesh to bestow on us in abundant measure the power of chastity: in order that the virginity which in others cannot be retained in child-bearing, might be attained by them at their second birth.[11]

employée par Nestorius pour caractériser l'union du Verbe divin avec l'homme Jésus. Dans une letter à S. Cyrille, il écrivait: 'Il est exact et conforme à la tradition évangélique, d'affirmer que le corps du Christ est le temple de la divinité' (PG 77,49), texte qui pouvait certes s'entendre dans un sens orthodoxe mais qui prenait un sens très particulier dans le contexte de pensée nestorienne." ([The temple metaphor] was, in effect, an expression employed by Nestorius for characterizing the union of the divine Word with the human Jesus. In a letter to Saint Cyril, he wrote: "It conforms exactly to the gospel tradition to affirm that the body of Christ is the temple of Divinity" (PG 77:49), a text that can be heard in an orthodox fashion but that assumes a very peculiar sense in the context of Nestorius's thought.)

11. *Sermon* 22.2, NPNF² 12:130. For the Latin, see Léon le Grand, *Sermons*, 80–81. I have slightly altered the English translation. My thanks to Brian Daley for assisting me with the Latin.

Mary does not become God, of course, but she does "house" God in the most intimate way imaginable. The extrinsic manner of relating God to temple is put to good use: Mary both receives the divine son and gives birth to him. God both enters and exits her womb. But according to the logic of the incarnation, this moment is transformational. Her body remains holy forever thereafter because it has housed the Holy One of Israel. And as the temple could be revered and praised on its own terms without any worry of committing some form of idolatrous apostasy, so Mary could be revered and adored. Not as a god(dess), but as the one who housed God. If one could turn to the temple and say "how lovely is thy dwelling place" and attend to its every architectural detail, why would one not do the same with the Theotokos?

In late Byzantine hymns to Mary, the temple imagery reaches new heights. Indeed, even a brief glance at the patristic homilies that Brian Daley has collected and edited in his volume on the Assumption of the Blessed Virgin reveals how important the Old Testament stories about the tabernacle and temple were for the construction of her character.[12] Almost anything that was said about this Old Testament precursor became fair game for depicting the life of the Virgin Mary, of which the New Testament authors in their great modesty "neglected" to tell us. Consider this sample from John of Damascus:

> And so your holy, spotless body is committed to a reverent burial, as angels go before you and stand around you and follow after, doing all the things by which it is fitting to serve the mother of their Lord. The Apostles, too, are there, and all the full membership of the Church, crying out divine hymns to the music of the harp of the Spirit: "holy is your temple, wonderful because of God's salvation" (Ps. 64:5) and again, "the most High has made his tabernacle holy" (Ps. 45:5), and "God's mountain is a mountain of plenty, the mountain where God is pleased to dwell" (Ps. 67:16). The company of the Apostles lift you up on their shoulders, the true ark of the Lord God, as once the priests lifted up the typological ark that pointed the way to you. Your immaculate, completely spotless body was not left on earth, but you have been transported to the royal dwelling-place of heaven as queen, as lady, as mistress, as Mother of God, as the one who truly gave birth to God.[13]

Or in turn, consider the description of the procession of Mary's bier from Mount Zion to Gethsemane found in the writings of Theoteknos of Livias. It is created, in large part, from stories about the procession of the ark in the Old Testament.

---

12. Brian E. Daley, *On the Dormition of Mary: Early Patristic Homilies* (Crestwood: St. Vladimir's Seminary Press, 1998).

13. Ibid., 197–98.

[6] The all-blessed body, then, of the holy one was being carried towards the place I have mentioned, accompanied by angels' songs of praise; and the unbelieving Jews, who had killed the Lord, looking down the valley, saw her remains lying on the bier and went towards it, intending to do violence in that very spot to the body which God had honored; his temple, his lampstand, his vessel containing the pure oil, his altar of holocausts, appearing in splendor within the Holy of Holies.

All those who meant to attack her and to burn her body were struck with blindness; and one of them, who touched her bier with his own hands, was deprived of them—they were cut off! (cf. 2 Sam. 6) So that immaculate flesh was glorified; all of them came to believe and confessed her Mother of God, and the one whom they had vilified as a seductress they now praised in song as God's own mother. And those who had lost their sight saw the wonders worked by God toward his mother. . . . For a wonderful thing happened: the hands of the one who had lost them [were restored to him.] And all believed in Christ, who was before her and from her and with her, "the Son of David according to the flesh" (Rom. 1:3).

Let no one think that the miracle worked by the all-holy body of the Mother of God was something impossible—for she had remained a virgin incorrupt. It was, after all, fitting for the spiritual ark, which contained the vessel of manna and the blooming rod of Aaron (Num. 17:23), for she blossomed and bore the fruit that can never be consumed. The former ark defeated the hostile foreigners, who wanted to do it violence; how much more, then should the spiritual ark defeat those who from the beginning have fought against God and against the beautiful name "that is invoked over us" (Jer. 14:9).

[7] For she is ark and vase and throne and heaven. She was judged worthy to be entrusted with ineffable mysteries; she was judged worthy to reveal things hidden and sealed in the Book of Daniel, and through her "all of us, with faces unveiled, will gaze on the glory of the Lord (2 Cor. 3:18). Through her, the veil on Moses' face has been lifted.[14]

The cult of Mary in the medieval period is greatly indebted to this development. But it would be a grave error to leave the story in this simple developmental sequence. To be sure, temple images for Jesus became difficult to sustain after Chalcedon, and their logical referent was transferred to the Virgin Mary. But it would not be accurate to say that Mary's character subsequently developed in an unprecedented way. For the connection of Mary to the temple has a long pedigree that antedates Chalcedon. Already in *Protevangelium of James*, Mary is imaged as something like a living, breathing temple into which the creator of the universe has taken up residence. What we witness in the developments

14. Ibid., 75–76.

after Chalcedon is a marked amplification of a pre-existing theme in light of
its restriction to Mary.

Mary in the Old Testament: A Methodological Reprise

The development of the temple metaphor in relationship to the incarnation
sheds considerable light on how the early church conceived the relationship
between the two Testaments. The relationship between the two is not simply
predictive, but figural. What I mean by this is that the Old Testament is more
than simply a set of prophecies about the coming Messiah. It also provides
the Christian reader with a set of theological premises that retain their per
se voice even after the advent of Israel's Messiah. Indeed, we could state the
matter more strongly: certain theological subjects raised in the New Testament necessitate a return to the Old Testament in order for their contents to
be understood. Consequently, we can say that the Old Testament does more
than simply anticipate the New; rather, it fills in areas that the New merely
gestures toward.

This is perhaps best illustrated in Augustine's reading of the book of Psalms
through the figure of the *totus Christus*. Since Christ adopts Israel's persona
on the cross by expressing his grief through the opening words of Ps. 22
("My God, my God, why have you forsaken me?"), Augustine reasoned that
the rest of the Psalter could be understood in a similar fashion. This opened
up a dramatic new vista into the person of Jesus Christ that forever altered
how the book of Psalms would be read. The Psalter became a resource for
christological reflection that amplified and broadened the picture one derives
from the Gospels. A similar hermeneutical move was made by the church
fathers in regard to the temple and the figure of Mary. Once the figural link
was established, the character of Mary grew well beyond what little the New
Testament had said about her. While the New Testament may be very laconic
in what it says about her person, if we turn to the texts about the tabernacle
and temple, our source material expands exponentially.

The loss of a deep figural sensibility about the two Testaments can be seen
in Timothy George's otherwise excellent article on Mary. At one point in his
discussion he notes that Luther, Calvin, and Zwingli were all in agreement
about the perpetual virginity of Mary even though Scripture makes no explicit
judgment on this matter. "Strangely enough," George observes, "Zwingli
attempted to argue for this teaching on the basis of Scripture alone, against
the idea that it could only be held on the basis of the teaching authority of
the church. His key proof text is Ezekiel 44:2: 'This gate shall remain shut. It

shall not be opened, and no one shall enter by it. For the LORD, the God of Israel, has entered by it.'"[15] But this is not nearly as strange as George believes. Zwingli is simply articulating the results of a figural reading of the Bible that goes back to the patristic period. For the fathers of the church, the prediction of a new temple in Ezek. 40–48 had to be understood in light of Mary's obedient response of "yes" to the angel Gabriel. What is most remarkable about this example is how unintelligible figural exegesis has become over the past few centuries.

But let me make one important clarification. A figural reading of these Old Testament texts about the tabernacle does not result in a simple, univocal prediction of Mary's role in the incarnation. Here the model of the *totus Christus* is of considerable value. All the Psalms, even in the Augustinian register, retain their—historically primary—Israelite voice.[16] Indeed they must retain their original voice because it is that specific voice that Jesus wishes to assume. Jesus cannot speak in *persona Israel* if there is no *vox Israel* to assume! When Ezekiel spoke of Israel's eager hope for the rebuilding of the temple and the return of God's presence to dwell within it, Christian homilists almost uniformly assumed that the ultimate referent was that of the person of Mary. Indeed, in the icons used during the Marian feasts in the Eastern Church, Ezekiel is almost always shown holding his temple, a figure for the person of Mary. But this does not obliterate the primary historical reference the text has in the prophet's own self-consciousness and within the subsequent living tradition of Judaism. To illustrate this, consider the rendering of Ezekiel in Michelangelo's Sistine Chapel.[17] The prophet stands just below the fifth and central panel of the Genesis cycle that adorns the ceiling. In this panel Eve comes forth from Adam's rib, a painting that can also be read as the church (i.e., Mary) issuing forth from the rib of Christ.[18] Loren Partridge catches the drama well:

15. George, "Blessed Virgin Mary," 109.
16. Christopher Seitz has made a very similar argument with respect to the role of the Isaianic prophecies about Israel's Messiah. See Seitz's excellent essay, "Isaiah in New Testament, Lectionary, Pulpit," in his *Word without End: The Old Testament as Abiding Theological Witness* (Grand Rapids: Eerdmans, 1998), 213–28.
17. http://uploads7.wikiart.org/images/michelangelo/the-prophet-ezekiel-1510.jpg.
18. On the relationship of Eve to Mary on the ceiling of the Sistine Chapel, see the extended discussion in Gary Anderson, *The Genesis of Perfection* (Louisville: Westminster John Knox, 2002), 1–20 and esp. 4–7. For a brief review of the pertinent data, consider these comments of Loren Partridge, who argues that this panel's
    pivotal role was both deliberate and appropriate, for it was a common symbol of the founding of the Church, embodied by the Virgin, the second Eve, just as the Virgin's Assumption, to which the chapel was dedicated, symbolized the Church's triumph. Eve's importance is underlined by the mighty figure of God, cramped within the pictorial field,

Ezekiel has just spun around from one genius—his scarf and scroll still rippling from the sudden movement—to carry on an intense polemic with the other angelically beautiful genius who points heavenward with both hands while Ezekiel's open-palm gesture equivocates between accepting and questioning. His extraordinary physical and rhetorical energy [. . .] is heightened by the parallel diagonals of bull neck, thick torso, titanic limbs and broad lavender drapery falling across his orange tunic and between his splayed knees.[19]

Why such excitement and surprise? I would suggest that Michelangelo knows that what the prophet is made to say within the Christian tradition is not what the prophet himself had in mind. His scroll in his left hand points in one direction—to *terra firma*—while the angelic figure to his right points upward. As Eric Auerbach had argued so well, the Christian figural tradition attempted to retain an integral voice for the Jewish Scriptures while at the same time reconfiguring its various compass points to point beyond themselves.[20]

But this process of development should not be left solely within the plane of hermeneutics, as if all we are talking about are rules of literary growth. What allows the church fathers to proceed in the direction they do is a profound appreciation of what the subject matter or *res* of Scripture consists of. Both the Old and New Testaments are chock-full of references to how God takes up residence amid his people. And these texts are not simply symbolic, for—to paraphrase and domesticate the fiery tongue of Flannery O'Connor—if they were merely literary devices then their relationship is endlessly fungible. And could one confidently declare that God was present in any of them? Certainly the poetic idiom of Yeats found at the beginning of this chapter turns on precisely this point. What could be the cause of the sudden chill in Mary's bones that bids her hair stand on end?

The challenge to the reader is to see how these references to God's *real* presence—both in Israel and within the church—relate to one another. On

---

who appears for the first time standing on the earth. Born from the side of Adam, Eve also alludes to the Church's principal sacraments of baptism and Eucharist, for both water and blood flowed from the side of Christ, the second Adam. And indeed, Adam is intended to suggest the sacrificial Christ by his crumpled sleeping figure leaning awkwardly against a dead, cross-like stump. (*Michelangelo: The Sistine Ceiling, Rome* [New York: George Braziller, 1996], 50)

19. Partridge, *Michelangelo*, 80.

20. As is well known, Auerbach exerted a strong influence on the work of Hans Frei and many of the "narrative theologians" who came to make up the Yale school. In this instance, Michelangelo's understanding of Ezekiel allows the prophet to retain his historical voice within the community of ancient Israel. Ezekiel thought that Israel's restoration would require the rebuilding of the actual temple in Jerusalem. The angel, however, alerts the prophet that God's providential ordering of his words will result in an interpretation that is very different from what he had intended.

the one hand, Scripture witnesses to the deeply transformational quality of these moments of indwelling. As the biblical author makes very clear, God wants the tabernacle built not simply as a place for him to dwell, but so that he can dwell among his chosen people, Israel (Exod. 25:8). As a result of this indwelling, Israel is obligated to live a life that befits such holiness (e.g., Lev. 11:44–45). All the moral and sacral legislation of Leviticus and Numbers depends on this crucial point. But on the other hand the object of this incarnation—be it tabernacle, temple, or womb—becomes worthy of veneration in its own right. This is not a vestige of paganism or a form of idolatry; it is the reverent admission that any part of creation brought that close to the presence of God is overwhelmed by his power and sanctity. The liturgy of the Angelus allows one to recall *and adore* this event afresh. Here the witness of the Old Testament is absolutely crucial in order to counter the charges brought against the Catholic Church in the wake of the Reformation. The Holy One of Israel cannot indwell a space and leave it unchanged. Venerating Mary as Mother of God (*Ave Maria, gratia plena*) does not detract from the doctrine of the incarnation; it safeguards it. (On this point, consider the acts of veneration that Jews bestow on sacred texts that hold the veritable name of God.)

My own approach to the development of Mary's person has gone in a somewhat different direction from that of the Lutheran-Roman Catholic commission that produced the very influential and stimulating volume, *Mary in the New Testament*.[21] The interests expressed in that volume were necessarily quite different from mine. A vigorous scholarly attempt was made to read each New Testament author on his own and not to allow later church doctrines to be read back into the original voices of the text anachronistically. The results of this study were clear, sober, and unassailable. But the end result of the volume was unsatisfying for me because the implication was that the growth of Marian doctrine was conceived to be a slow and careful outgrowth of what the New Testament had only hinted at. One would not have gathered from this volume that the elaboration of Mary in the church was just as much an attempt to understand her in light of the church's two-part Bible.

But I should concede that the two-Testament witness of the Christian Bible is not the whole story. In addition, one must reckon with the influence of the vicissitudes of history. Had Theodore of Mopsuestia not brought to light the fact that the deity seems free to enter and leave the temple as witnessed in Ezek. 8–11, the wholesale transfer of the temple form to Mary might not have happened. (Though texts like the *Protevangelium of James* were already

---

21. Raymond Brown et al., eds., *Mary in the New Testament: A Collaborative Assessment by Protestant and Roman Catholic Scholars* (Philadelphia: Fortress; New York: Paulist Press, 1978).

moving far in that direction, most patristic writers up to Chalcedon seemed to be most comfortable using the image of the temple as a metaphor for the indwelling of the Godhead within the person of Jesus.) In addition, the rising importance of the Marian feasts within the liturgical life of the church in the wake of Chalcedon should not be underemphasized. These feasts quickened the need for and the development of icons and innumerable homilies dedicated to the Virgin. The icons and the homilies, in turn, provided the fertile soil in which the veneration of Mary's temple-like being could emerge. Given the paucity of material about Mary in the New Testament, it can hardly be surprising that the homilies on the Dormition that Brian Daley has collected devote such an extraordinary amount of space to the metaphor of Mary as temple.

In sum, one can see that the doctrine of the incarnation was not understood in patristic tradition as solely an affair of the New Testament. In some very important ways, the New Testament was thought to defer to the Old. The task of the Catholic reader of the Old Testament is perhaps best illustrated by Michelangelo's portrayal of Ezekiel. In keeping with the historical sense it is absolutely crucial that we allow this Old Testament prophet his own voice. Otherwise, whence will come his surprise? The Old Testament, with complete theological integrity, imagines that all world history points toward God's rebuilding of Zion. We cannot compromise this perspective. In the New Testament, on the other hand, that hope takes a radical and unexpected turn, but not one that renders null and void the subject matter of Ezekiel's hopes. As Michelangelo indicates, God has dwelled in a virgin, and the task of the Christian reader is to explore how Ezekiel's words and imagery take new shape in light of the mystery of Christ. The Angelus is one such means the tradition has offered for adoring the moment of incarnation. For when Mary responds "*fiat mihi*," her body becomes a fit vessel (*gratia plena*) to contain the uncontainable. Just as the Israelites of old fell on their faces in adoration when they witnessed the descent of God to earth to inhabit his tabernacle, so for the church when she reflects on the mystery of the incarnation (*ave maria . . . dominus tecum*). In this fashion a high doctrine of Mary both ensures and safeguards the doctrine of the incarnation.

8

Christology

Tobit as Righteous Sufferer

This final treatment of Christology continues a theme from the previous few chapters. The plot of the book of Tobit, I suggest, follows a pattern very similar to the way the Gospels present the life of Jesus. But the point here is not simply that Tobit anticipates the mystery of Christ but that the identity of Christ can, in turn, be better understood by calibrating it against its exemplars in the Old Testament. The point is made once more that a christological focus on Old Testament exegesis need not be supersessionist, as many presuppose. When done properly, the result should be a deeper respect for Judaism.

A few years ago one of my colleagues read my essay "Mary in the Old Testament" and was surprised to see that a typological reading of the Old Testament need not efface either the simple sense of the biblical text nor its place within the Jewish canon. Though he had been educated in a Catholic context, he had never thought that one could read the Old Testament in light of the New. Only by keeping the two Testaments completely separate could one avoid the admittedly horrible sin of supersessionism. Catholic education, understandably perhaps, but also lamentably, had taught him to read the two Testaments as two wholly different worlds.

In this chapter I wish to come at the problem of how to read our two-Testament Bible from the perspective of the book of Tobit.[1] Though this book

---

1. The best work on the theological challenge of reading the Christian Bible is that of B. Childs and C. Seitz. For the former, see his *Biblical Theology of the Old and New Testaments*

was written in either Hebrew or Aramaic by a Jew in either the third or second
century BCE, it is not found in the Jewish Bible. It was translated into Greek,
however, and became part of the Greek Jewish Bible (LXX) and from there
came into the Christian Bible, where it remained until the sixteenth century,
when some Protestant groups removed it.[2] It will be my thesis that imbedded
in the plotline of this Jewish book is a profound christological pattern. But in
order to approach this problem, I will need to survey the way the story unfolds.

Tobit's Devotion to the Temple in Jerusalem

The first point to be made is that Tobit was a righteous sufferer within the
people Israel. As the book opens we learn that he was in the habit of going
to Jerusalem to offer sacrifices (1:6–8). This behavior is quite striking because Tobit hails from the northern kingdom of Israel, where there were
two competing worship centers, Dan and Bethel. King Jeroboam, the first
king of Israel after its separation from Judah, had established these cult sites
to provide alternative centers for worship to discourage pilgrimage to the
southern city of Jerusalem (1 Kings 12:25–33). Yet it is also important to note
that the biblical author condemns in the harshest terms possible this decision
of the king. Though the prophet Ahijah had offered Jeroboam the promise
of an eternal kingdom like that of David (11:38), after Jeroboam's act of
apostasy his dynastic house was condemned to ruin (13:33–34). Given that
all the power of the state was invested in the cult sites of Dan and Bethel, it
is quite impressive that Tobit chose to deliver his gifts to the temple in Jerusalem in conformity with the laws of the Torah (see Deut. 12:1–28). All the
more impressive is the fact that Tobit was from Naphtali (Tob. 1:1), a tribe
located in the far northern reaches of the kingdom. That made the trek to
Jerusalem all the more arduous and taxing. His devotion to Jerusalem must
have depended on a very deep and abiding faith.

Sadly for Tobit, he was a unique individual within the northern kingdom. Everyone else had chosen to follow the lead of King Jeroboam (1:5–6).

(Minneapolis: Fortress, 1992); for the latter, see his *Word without End: The Old Testament
as Abiding Theological Witness* (Grand Rapids: Eerdmans, 1998); and *Figured Out: Ty-
pology and Providence in Christian Scripture* (Louisville: Westminster John Knox, 2001).
Also important is the Pontifical Biblical Commission's *The Jewish People and Their Sacred
Scriptures in the Christian Bible* (Boston: Pauline Books and Media, 2002). Available on the
Vatican website: http://www.vatican.va/roman_curia/congregations/cfaith/pcb_documents
/rc_con_cfaith_doc_20020212_popolo-ebraico_en.html.

2. For general introductory matters of the book, such as date, language of composition,
and canonicity, see the excellent discussion in J. Fitzmyer, *Tobit*, Commentaries on Early Jewish
Literature (Berlin: de Gruyter, 2003), 3–57.

According to the book of Kings, this placed the entire nation in the position of apostasy and would eventually lead to the destruction of that nation at the hand of the Assyrian Empire (2 Kings 17). Tobit, it should be noted, was among those unfortunate individuals whom the Assyrians forcibly exiled.

The poignancy of Tobit's plight cannot be understood without a careful consideration of the prominence of Jeroboam's sin in the book of Kings. This work emphasizes that each and every king in the northern kingdom followed the path of apostasy that Jeroboam had laid down. To recall the words of the apostle Paul, not one was found righteous; all were guilty of grievous sin. In light of this background, the character of Tobit as a just and righteous man shines through all the more brilliantly. He alone was obedient to the divine commands. Yet he did not profit in any observable way from his courageous display of piety; he was forced to suffer the fate of his nation in spite of his innocence.

Tobit Buries the Dead and Gives Alms While in Exile

While in exile, Tobit continued to practice his piety. He refused to consume food that did not conform to Levitical strictures (1:10–11). But just as important, he replaced his obedience to the temple in Jerusalem with the practice of various acts of charity (1:16–17), of which pride of place goes to the giving of alms and the burying of the dead (1:18). It is worth noting that in Second Temple Judaism, the giving of alms became a suitable substitution for animal sacrifice.[3] Rabbinic Judaism went even further: the giving of alms was equated with fulfilling all the commandments in the Torah. It is important to note this because it allows us to see the continuity in Tobit's character before and after the exile. Wherever Tobit finds himself, his consummate devotion to the God of Israel is always manifest. In the land of Israel he excelled in devotion to the temple, in the Diaspora in works of loving kindness to the poor and disadvantaged.

But just as Tobit suffered in spite of his devotion to the temple in Jerusalem, so his acts of kindness put his life in mortal danger. At one point in the story, King Sennacherib wished to punish the Jews by putting some of them to death and then leaving their corpses exposed to the elements of nature. In spite of the force of this royal edict, Tobit continued to bury the dead. Tobit's efforts

---

3. On the importance of alms in Second Temple Judaism (and early Christianity), see my essay, "Redeem Your Sins by the Giving of Alms: Sin, Debt, and the 'Treasury of Merit' in Early Judaism and Christianity," *Letter & Spirit* 3 (2007): 37–67. This theme is dealt with much more extensively in my book, *Sin: A History* (New Haven: Yale University Press, 2009).

to frustrate the edict of the king were not looked upon with favor. With the death penalty attached to his head, he was forced to flee into a second exile. As in the first, he lost everything (1:18–20).

But when that king had died, Tobit was granted a reprieve and allowed to return home (1:21–22). Not surprisingly, he picked up where he left off: he continued to bury the dead. But his troubles did not come to an end. His fellow Israelites found his behavior to be ill-advised and taunted him for his piety. "Is he still not afraid?" they asked in disbelief. "He has already been hunted down to be put to death for doing this, and he ran away; yet here he is again burying the dead!" (2:8). But this was hardly the end of the matter. Tobit was not only forced to endure these taunts from his neighbors (and here one is reminded of the frequent theme of the Psalms in which the righteous Israelite suffers at the hands of his enemies), but he was forced to endure even greater suffering by his God. Adding insult to injury, at the end of this episode Tobit became blind (2:9–10). Tobit is truly a Joban figure: his piety was not only unrewarded, it had become the occasion for a considerable trial.[4]

Tobit's Prayer

In despair over his plight, Tobit turns to God in prayer and begs to die (3:1–6). This prayer, in my estimation, is one of the most moving texts in all of Scripture. For what one would have expected is a moving and tearful lament, a prayer that would have underscored the righteousness of Tobit and implored God to visit the sins of his enemies. Psalm 26:1–5 would have been an excellent candidate:

> Vindicate me, O LORD,
>> for I have walked in my integrity,
>> and I have trusted in the LORD without wavering.
> Prove me, O LORD, and try me;
>> test my heart and mind.
> For your steadfast love is before my eyes,
>> and I walk in faithfulness to you.
> I do not sit with the worthless,
>> nor do I consort with hypocrites;
> I hate the company of evildoers,
>> and will not sit with the wicked.

4. On the relationship of Tobit to Job, see the essay of A. Portier-Young, "Eyes to the Blind: A Dialogue between Tobit and Job," in *Intertextual Studies in Ben Sira and Tobit: Essays in Honor of Alexander A. Di Lella, OFM*, ed. J. Corley and V. Skemp, CBQMS 38 (Washington, DC: Catholic Biblical Association, 2005), 14–27.

But instead of words like these, let us listen to what Tobit actually says in his prayer:

> You are righteous, O Lord,
>   and all your deeds are just;
> all your ways are mercy and truth;
>   you judge the world.
> And now, O Lord, remember me
>   and look favorably upon me.
> Do not punish me for my sins
>   and for my unwitting offenses
>   and those that my ancestors committed before you.
> They sinned against you,
>   and disobeyed your commandments.
> So you gave us over to plunder, exile, and death,
>   to become the talk, the byword, and an object of reproach
>   among all the nations among whom you have dispersed us.
> And now your many judgments are true
>   in exacting penalty from me for my sins.
> For we have not kept your commandments
>   and have not walked in accordance with truth before you.
> So now deal with me as you will;
>   command my spirit to be taken from me,
>   so that I may be released from the face of the earth and become
>   dust.
> For it is better for me to die than to live,
>   because I have had to listen to undeserved insults,
>   and great is the sorrow within me.
> Command, O Lord, that I be released from this distress;
>   release me to go to the eternal home,
>   and do not, O Lord, turn your face away from me.
> For it is better for me to die
>   than to see so much distress in my life
>   and to listen to insults.

Two features of this prayer are, in my mind, quite striking. The first is Tobit's open acknowledgment that the ways of God are righteous and just. This is an audacious claim given the fact that God's ways appear to be less than just in the case of Tobit's own life. I mentioned above that Tobit was something of a Joban character. This is true insofar as he suffers in spite of his innocence.[5]

---

5. Of course it must be conceded that once he becomes blind, he does sharply rebuke his wife in a quite unflattering and uncivil way. This leads to a harsh rebuke on her part: "Where

What separates Tobit from Job is his tenacious adherence to his faith. God, Tobit declares, remains righteous and just in his guidance of the world.

The second striking feature is the way Tobit understands his relationship to his fellow Israelites. Though he has ample opportunity to trumpet his own innocence in the face of great apostasy (see Ps. 26:1–5), he does not march down that path. Instead, when he catalogues the sins of Israel that have led the nation to its current predicament, he does not distinguish his own behavior from that of his peers. He asserts quite remarkably in 3:5:

> And now your many judgments are true
>   in exacting penalty *from me* for my sins.
> For *we* have not kept your commandments
>   and have not walked in accordance with truth before you. (emphasis added)

For Tobit, the present predicament of Israel is not simply the result of the sin of others; *he identifies himself among the guilty.*[6]

Tobit's Request to Die

The prayer of Tobit ends with a request that he die (3:6). In a wonderfully ironic turn, we learn that Tobit's prayer is in fact answered, but not in the way that he expects (3:16–17). For as soon as Tobit concludes his prayer, he summons his son Tobias so that he can instruct him in Torah one more time before he dies (4:3–21). His speech is prompted by the memory that he had once

---

are your acts of charity? Where are your righteous deeds? These things are known about you" (2:14). There can be no question that the two difficult questions that Anna poses focus the problems of Tobit in such a fashion that his prayer for an early death in the very next set of verses (3:1–6) makes perfect sense. But I think it would be a gross misreading to think that the error in judgment that Tobit makes in this episode of his life could lead one to think that he is no longer a righteous sufferer. Anna's rebuke seems to highlight the fact that it is his virtue that has gone unrewarded, and this is, no doubt, the cause of his terrible despair.

6. Many modern readers of the Gospels have been puzzled about why Jesus consented to John's baptism, which was explicitly said to be given for the purpose of forgiving sins (see Mark 1:4 and parallels). Some interpreters have taken this as unassailable evidence that the "historical" Jesus saw himself as a sinner—something that the Gospel writers did their best to cover up. Yet as John Meier has shown (*A Marginal Jew: Rethinking the Historical Jesus*, vol. 2, *Mentor, Message, and Miracles* [New York: Doubleday, 1994], 106–16) such accusations are hard to square with contemporary Jewry, which frequently understood the need for forgiveness in corporate terms. The point of emphasis for Jesus would have been "our" rather than "my" sin. Tobit's prayer would be an outstanding example of this. Though innocent of the sins that led to Israel's exile, he continues to see himself as organically linked to the fate of his people, even to the point of identifying with their sin.

left money on deposit during his travels to Media (4:1, 20; cf. 1:14–15). These funds, Tobit reasons, will be necessary for Tobias to maintain his mother and to continue to give alms. Unknown to Tobit, however, is the larger providential plan that this journey sets in motion. For during his journey Tobias secures two things that prove far more valuable than the money: a proper wife and an unguent that heals his father's blindness.

The book ends with Tobit living to the ripe old age of one hundred and twelve (14:2). Given that he was sixty-two when he was struck blind, his life expectancy was nearly double what he had initially imagined. In the end, his life of charity was fully rewarded. In what he thought would be his last words to his son, he asserted, "Almsgiving delivers from death" (4:10). In their original setting the words were quite ironical, for Tobit made this gnomic assertion against the background of his own personal despair. In the context of his life up to that point, it would have been more accurate to say that almsgiving had been the cause of death!

Resurrection in Its Old Testament Inflection

Here it is absolutely important to recall what the concepts of "death" and "life" mean within the cultural world of the Old Testament. Prior to the advent of an idea of bodily resurrection, the Bible imagines the descent into Sheol—a place bereft of any contact with God or kin—as the plight of all those who fall terribly ill, as well as those who die prematurely and without a family of any significance. For the former consider the first three verses of Ps. 30:

> I will extol you, O LORD, for you have drawn me up,
>   and did not let my foes rejoice over me.
> O LORD my God, I cried to you for help,
>   and you have healed me.
> O LORD, you brought up my soul from Sheol,
>   restored me to life from among those gone down to the Pit.

It is crucial to note that the reference to God's raising this person from the underworld concerns not a postmortem resurrection, as one might be inclined to think. Instead, being brought back from Sheol refers to God's miraculous act of healing a person who felt himself slipping into the netherworld. Being dead in the Hebrew Bible encompasses more than what we identify with physical death.

Though many handbooks will say that because there was no doctrine of physical resurrection in the Hebrew Bible all were doomed, eventually, to enter and dwell in Sheol, this is not quite accurate.[7] Indeed, Philip Johnson has noticed that the distribution of the term Sheol in the Old Testament is quite different from the distribution of the term for death. Whereas the root for death can be found nearly a thousand times in the Bible, the word Sheol occurs less than seventy times. How should one account for the paucity of references to the underworld? Johnson writes,

> The term [Sheol] occurs mostly in psalmodic, reflective and prophetic literature, where authors are personally involved in their work. By contrast it appears only rarely in descriptive narratives, and then almost entirely in direct speech. In particular, "Sheol" never occurs in the many narrative accounts of death, whether of patriarchs, kings, prophets, priests or ordinary people, whether of Israelite or foreigner, of righteous or wicked. Also, "Sheol" is entirely absent from legal material, including the many laws which prescribe capital punishment or proscribe necromancy. This means that "Sheol" is very clearly a term of personal engagement.[8]

It seems that the Bible keeps the terms for the grave and Sheol distinctly separated. What then would be the reason for an author to make special reference to the domain of Sheol? As Jon Levenson has persuasively argued, Sheol is an appropriate location for those who live incomplete lives, that is, those who die young and without a family to continue their legacy.[9] It is for this reason that Jacob refuses the comfort of his sons upon learning of Joseph's demise: "No, I shall go down to Sheol to my son, mourning" (Gen. 37:35). Yet when he hears that Joseph has not only not died but become second in command over all Egypt, he exclaims: "Enough! My son Joseph is still alive. I must go and see him before I die" (45:28). Significantly, he does not say "I must go and see him before I die and descend to Sheol." The Hebrew Bible, strikingly, does not use the term Sheol as a matter-of-fact "address" for the place where all the dead reside.

If there is an equivalent to the beatific vision in the Old Testament, it is the opportunity to live to a ripe old age and be given the privilege of seeing one's extended family gathered around at the point of death. Abraham, Jacob, and Job are three figures who merit such a benefaction. And in each case the

7. Consider the statement of J. Pederson that "everyone who dies goes to Sheol," found in his classic work, *Israel: Its Life and Culture*, SFSHJ 28 (Atlanta: Scholars Press, 1991; originally published 1926–40), 461.

8. P. Johnson, *Shades of Sheol: Death and Afterlife in the Old Testament* (Downers Grove, IL: InterVarsity, 2002), 72.

9. J. Levenson, *Resurrection and the Restoration of Israel: The Ultimate Victory of the God of Life* (New Haven: Yale University Press, 2006), 67–81.

blessing of many children at the end of life was completely unexpected. As Jon Levenson has written,

> [The] biblical Sheol is the prolongation of the unfulfilled life. There is no equivalent prolongation of the fulfilled life precisely because it is fulfilled. The prolongation of those who die fulfilled comes, rather, not in the form of residence in a place, the joyful antipode to the miserable Sheol, but in the form of descendants, such as those three or four generations that Jacob, Joseph, and Job are privileged to behold just before they die.[10]

I wish to argue that we could include Tobit in that list as well. There are, indeed, many parallels between his life and those of Jacob and Job. After being rescued from what appeared to be an abrupt and tragic end, he was granted a full and prosperous life. Like Jacob and Job, he was fortunate enough to lay his eyes on his children and grandchildren as he prepared himself to die (Tob. 14). Thus, when Tobit declares in his song of thanksgiving that "[God] afflicts, and he shows mercy; *he leads down to Hades* in the lowest regions of the earth, and *he brings up from the great abyss*" (13:2, emphasis added), he is not only echoing Ps. 30:1–3, he is describing his own *earthly* life. God did afflict him with blindness and left him and his wife with only a single child. His premature death prior to the chance to see any grandchildren was tantamount to being led to the realm of Sheol. The dramatic, if not miraculous, restoration he experienced (from blindness to sight, from one child to a large extended family, from little money to wealth of great proportions) was an unexpected miracle, an event that he can honestly identify as resurrection from the dead.

The final scene of the book gives clear testimony to a scriptural truth that Tobit uttered many decades earlier: "Almsgiving delivers from death." Though his citation of this teaching was originally tinged with a considerable degree of irony, the reader learns at the end that this apothegm is a trustworthy piece of wisdom. It cannot be accidental that Tobit's last words return to the need for living a life characterized by charity: "So now, my children, I command you, serve God faithfully and do what is pleasing in his sight. Your children are also to be commanded to do what is right and to give alms" (14:8).

Tobit's Plea for Israel within His Prayer of Thanksgiving

But the resurrection of Tobit is the occasion for another surprise. Just as Tobit refused to see himself as superior to his fellow Israelites in regard to their

10. Ibid., 78.

exilic plight, so now in his hymn of praise he uses the occasion of his own restoration to life not to beat his own drum but to exhort Israel to a similar sort of hope.[11] Tobit asks Israel to:

> Acknowledge [God] before the nations, O children of Israel;
>   for he has scattered you among them.
>   He has shown you his greatness even there.
> Exalt him in the presence of every living being,
>   because he is our Lord and he is our God;
>   he is our Father and he is God forever.
> He will afflict you for your iniquities,
>   but he will again show mercy on all of you.[12]
> He will gather you from all the nations
>   among whom you have been scattered.
> . . . .
> O Jerusalem, the holy city,
>   he afflicted you for the deeds of your hands,
>   but will again have mercy on the children of the righteous.
> Acknowledge the Lord, for he is good,
>   and bless the King of the ages,
>   so that his tent may be rebuilt in you in joy.
> May he cheer all those within you who are captives,
>   and love all those within you who are distressed,
>   to all generations forever. (Tob. 13:3–5, 9–10)

George Nickelsberg has noted that Tobit's life runs parallel to that of the nation Israel.[13] The book of Tobit, it turns out, is really the pairing of two

11. It should be noted that many of the individual laments in the Psalms end not simply with thanksgiving over what God has done or will do for the supplicant but with a word of exhortation to God to do the same for the nation at large. Two outstanding examples can be found in Pss. 25 and 34, where the redemption of the nation (25:22; 34:23) concludes both psalms yet falls outside the acrostic sequence. This late redactional move within the Psalter anticipates, in my view, the move Augustine makes to understand the Psalms within the framework of the *totus Christus*. (The "whole Christ" refers to the complete "body of Christ": head [Christ] and members [the church]. When Christ takes up the voice of Israel in praying the Psalms, the voice of Israel becomes one with his.) Here would be the analogy: the redeemed Israelite is to the nation Israel as the head of the church (Christ) is to his members (the church at large). This famous patristic insight, we can conclude, has deep biblical roots.

12. Note the parallelism of vv. 2 and 5. In verse 2 Tobit had declared that God had afflicted him and shown him mercy. Now he affirms the same for Israel. Whereas God had "raised Tobit from Hades" (13:2), now he promises to "gather [Israel] from all the nations." That sounds a lot like the promise of national restoration expressed by the concept of resurrection in Ezek. 37, the famous vision of the valley of dry bones.

13. In Nickelsberg's short commentary on the book (*The HarperCollins Bible Commentary*, ed. James Mays, [San Francisco: HarperCollins, 2000], 719), he writes: "Parallel to the story

stories: we see at one level the suffering of Tobit and his eventual resurrection, but at another level is the suffering of the nation and its hope for restoration. The key difference between the two stories is also the point of tension that probably led to the composition of the book itself: while the resurrection of Tobit was an accomplished fact, the restoration of Israel remained a living but fragile hope. This very fragility is no doubt why the angel Raphael's last piece of advice to Tobit is to tell the story of what God has done to him to everyone he meets. "Bless God and acknowledge him," Raphael exhorts, "in the presence of all the living for the good things he has done for you" (12:6). For though it is proper to keep the counsel of a human king to oneself, the exact opposite is true for the works of God. They are to be revealed and acknowledged to anyone who wishes to hear.[14] The underlying logic of Raphael's advice is clear: from your own personal story, Tobit, the faith of the nation Israel can be nourished. For the miraculous resurrection that you have undergone is what God has in store for the people he loves so dearly. Tobit proves himself obedient to the words of Raphael. He makes haste to offer his words of thanksgiving but expresses his gratitude in a manner that would put the spotlight not on what God has done for him alone but on what God wishes to do for the people of whom Tobit is a part.

Tobit as Imitator of Christ

Let us step back a second and take stock of where we have come. We have followed the story of a righteous Israelite, a man in whom there were no egregious faults.[15] Indeed we can say more than that: we have followed the life of a man who fulfilled the mandates of the law in the deepest way imaginable,

of Tobit is the uncompleted story of Israel. Tobit's situation is paradigmatic for the exiled nation. As God has chastised Tobit, so Israel, suffering in exile, is being chastised. But God's mercy on Tobit and his family guarantees that this mercy will bring the Israelites back to their land. Since this event, described only in predictions, awaits fulfillment, one level of the double story is incomplete."

14. Raphael is simply giving voice to standard protocol for those who would offer words of thanksgiving beside the sacrificial altar after an experience of deliverance. The Psalms are full of such testimony. For a particularly robust example, see Ps. 22:25–31. On the sacrificial character of such acts of praise, see G. Anderson, "The Praise of God as a Cultic Event," in *Priesthood and Cult in Ancient Israel*, ed. G. Anderson and S. Olyan, JSOTSup 125 (Sheffield: Sheffield Academic, 1991), 15–33.

15. Let me reiterate what I mentioned earlier: Tobit, though innocent, is not without fault. His accusation that his wife had stolen a young goat that was in fact a gift from her employer (see 2:11–14) is a low point for him and his marriage. Yet at the major structural pieces of the plot—Tobit's actions within the body Israel—he is emphatically innocent. Nay even more, he is heroically obedient to the will of God even when he knows it will cost him dearly.

even at the risk of his own life. His faith in and obedience to the God of Israel became the occasion for his conflict with the pagan elite as well as with his own people, a conflict that led to what Tobit thought was his own premature death. Yet, in spite of all this, Tobit never condemned his Israelite brethren; quite remarkably, he identified with them. And at the midnight hour, when all hope had vanished and Tobit felt himself slipping into the domain of Sheol, God intervened and restored him to life. Tobit, in turn, was prompt to praise God for this marvelous act of mercy, but he was not satisfied with viewing this saving act solely within the confines of his own life. God's work would not be complete until it was realized in Israel at large. This righteous sufferer cannot be disarticulated from the nation he served.

Does this not sound like the message of the gospel in miniature? Can it be accidental that if we replace the name of Tobit with that of Jesus the basic narrative plot of Jesus's own life emerges? For Jesus too was a righteous Israelite who kept the law of the God of Israel (as he understood it) in the deepest way imaginable. It was precisely his obedience to the law that brought him into conflict with both the pagan rulers of his day and many of his coreligionists.[16] At the midnight hour it looked as though Jesus's life would come to ruin and rest on the shoals of bitter disappointment. Yet he did not use the occasion of his own demise to trumpet his innocence over against the depraved mores of those he traveled with and met. Rather he identified himself with them.[17] When God miraculously intervenes to raise Jesus from the dead on the third day, this also is not the occasion of a simple vindication of the innocent. For the early church the raising of Jesus was an initial pledge on a much larger act of restoration that God had in mind for the nation he loved so dearly (1 Cor. 15). God's action in the man Jesus of Nazareth was at the same time a foretaste of an action-to-come within the nation Israel.

Let me summarize. Many interpreters of Israel's Scripture rightly worry that any move to correlate the two Testaments will result in a measurable loss to the integrity of the Old Testament witness. Although I sympathize with these concerns to a considerable degree, there is a danger of isolating the figure of Jesus from the Old Testament. First of all, we will miss the way in which the narrative shape of the life of Jesus evolves from the nature of Jewish

16. The relationship of Jesus to Jewish law has been a very problematic subject in New Testament scholarship, often generating much more heat than light. For a sober view of the whole question, see J. Meier, *A Marginal Jew: Rethinking the Historical Jesus*, vol. 4, *Law and Love* (New Haven: Yale University Press, 2009).

17. A point made most emphatically in Luke wherein Jesus says, "Father forgive them; for they do not know what they are doing" (23:34). The saying is not in all manuscripts and may have originated with Stephen's similar cry in Acts 7:60. In any event, at the very least it reflects how the early church understood the identity of Jesus.

Scriptures themselves. Though Jewish readers will naturally have reservations about specific claims Christians make about Jesus (in specific, that he is God incarnate), this should not blind us to the fact that the cruciform shape of his life conforms to an important segment of the Old Testament witness. Jews are skeptical about a suffering Messiah for good reasons, but I do not think they would reject the claim that a righteous sufferer might have a role in the redemption of Israel.[18] The book of Tobit is a case in point that this aspect of Jesus's identity emerges quite naturally from Second Temple Judaism.

But just as importantly, and somewhat paradoxically, I would claim that this move to integrate Jesus into the Old Testament has considerable benefits for Jewish-Christian relations. What we see, if we tell the story the way I have, is that Jesus also dies and rises in *unity* with his people Israel. The redemption that Christ has wrought must be grasped, at first, as an event within the history of God's relationship to the people he chose over all others. As Michael Wyschogrod has so aptly put the matter:

> If we are prepared to take seriously the implanting of Jesus in his people, if the Israel that gave birth to him and whose boundaries (spiritual, geographical, linguistic, intellectual, etc.) he never left, is more than just a backdrop to the drama, a backdrop from which Jesus is to be distinguished rather than into which he is to be integrated, if all this is to change, then what is true of Jesus must in some fundamental way also be true of the Jewish people.[19]

In other words, attention to the Old Testament type—exemplified in the person of Tobit—provides a check on the all too common tendency of Christian readers to extract Jesus from the Jewish world in which he lived and taught and from which he derived his identity.

As biblical scholars have come to emphasize, the universalism of the New Testament derives from the universalism that is already present in the great eschatological promises of Israel's prophets. When redemption comes to the nation Israel, it will be of such magnitude that it will redound to the nations round about. Tobit himself makes this a point of emphasis when he says:

18. The association of chosenness with suffering is basic to the narratives of Genesis and much of the remainder of the Old Testament. On this subject, see J. Levenson, *Death and Resurrection of the Beloved Son: The Transformation of Child Sacrifice in Judaism and Christianity* (New Haven: Yale University Press, 1993). To some degree it is also part and parcel of the story of David (consider the suffering he undergoes while Saul is alive). But the passages that speak to the restoration of Israel and the coming Messiah (e.g., Isa. 9:1–6) do not foreground this theme. Isaiah 53 is not an exception, because this text does not claim that the suffering servant has a *messianic* identity.

19. M. Wyschogrod, "A Jewish Perspective on Incarnation," *Modern Theology* 12 (1996): 207.

> A bright light will shine to all the ends of the earth;
>   many nations will come to you from far away,
> the inhabitants of the remotest parts of the earth to your holy name,
>   bearing gifts in their hands for the King of heaven. (13:11)

The mission to the gentiles is a clear interest of Tobit (derived, of course, from Isa. 60), but it does not compromise in any way Israel's favored place in the eyes of God. Only when Israel is freed from captivity and restored to Jerusalem shall the nations come to recognize the sovereignty of Israel's God.

As Robert Jenson once remarked, it is important to attend carefully to what Jesus says in Acts 1:6–11, the narrative of the ascension.[20] As the disciples prepare to take their leave they sound a note of puzzlement over the fact that the resurrection of Jesus has left one terribly important matter unsolved: "Lord," they asked, "is this the time when you will restore the kingdom to Israel?" And note how Jesus responds. He does not wave it off as some might expect: "Oh are you still so ignorant! My kingdom was solely spiritual in nature. Look within; there you will find it." Rather, Jesus says, "It is not for you to know the times or periods that the Father has set by his own authority." The Pontifical Biblical Commission picked up this theme quite nicely when it declared that in the present both Jews and Christians pray for the coming of the Messiah. For the work of the Messiah is not finished; as in the case of Tobit, what we see in the resurrection of Jesus is a pledge toward a much larger redemption that is to come. On this point let me cite the Pontifical Biblical Commission document *The Jewish People and Their Sacred Scriptures in the Christian Bible*:

> Insistence on discontinuity between both Testaments . . . should not lead to one-sided spiritualization. What has already been accomplished in Christ must yet be accomplished in us and in the world. The definite fulfillment will be at the end with the resurrection of the dead, a new heaven and a new earth. Jewish messianic expectation is not in vain. It can become for us Christians a powerful stimulant to keep alive the eschatological dimension of faith. Like them, we too live in expectation. The difference is that for us the One who is to come will have the traits of the Jesus who has already come and is already present and active among us.[21]

Just as the book of Tobit revolves around two poles, the character of Tobit and the nation Israel, so it is for the person of Jesus and the people from

---

20. Robert Jenson, "Toward a Christian Theology of Israel," *Pro Ecclesia* 9 (2000): 43–56.
21. The Pontifical Biblical Commission, *The Jewish People and Their Sacred Scriptures in the Christian Bible* (Boston: Pauline Books and Media, 2002), 60.

whom he came. Just as the redemption of Israel, in Tobit's eyes, will be of such magnitude that even the nations will be transformed, so it is for the kingdom that Jesus initiates. Though the nations have streamed to Zion, Christians who ignore the Jewish roots of this idea do so at their own peril.

PART 4

"Conformed to the Image of His Son"

9

The Treasury of Merits

Faith and Works in the Biblical Tradition

The concept of meritorious deeds constitutes something of a third rail in biblical studies. In a book on the subject of the heavenly treasury, Peter Brown remarked that the concept is "surrounded by a loud silence. Neither in the Catholic Dictionnaire de la Spiritualité *nor in the Protestant* Theologische Realenzyklopedie *is there an entry on* trésor *or* Schatz. . . . Even the few articles devoted to the theme . . . have approached it with ill-disguised embarrassment."[1] In this chapter I will try to show what the biblical background for this Jewish-cum-Catholic doctrine is and why Protestant exegetes need not be worried about it. Though I write as a Catholic, my intentions are deeply ecumenical. A careful review of the secondary literature will show that doctrinal concerns about the status of "good works" have made a number of biblical texts subjects of great controversy. Only an adequate understanding of how human merit is to be grasped theologically can help us read these texts in the way their authors intended.*

As scholars have long known, there was a dramatic shift in the Hebrew language during the Second Temple period, roughly 520 BCE to 70 CE.[2] The language of the Mishnah, the compilation of the Jewish oral law, for example, is so different from that of the Bible that most students of Biblical Hebrew have a very difficult time making sense of it. Yet the vocabulary and idiom of

1. Peter Brown, *The Ransom of the Soul: Afterlife and Wealth in Early Western Christianity* (Cambridge, MA: Harvard University Press, 2015), 28.
2. This chapter treats in short compass a number of themes that are given a more leisurely exposition in my *Sin: A History* (New Haven: Yale University Press, 2009). The interested reader may wish to consult that book for a deeper pursuit of the arguments made here.

this dialect are more important for understanding the imagery of the New Testament than those of Biblical Hebrew. Why? The explanation is quite simple: Jesus was a Jew living in the Second Temple period who spoke the local language.

One area where the difference between Biblical and Second Temple Hebrew is rather dramatic is that of sin. During the Second Temple period it became common to refer to the sins of an individual or a nation as the accrual of a debt.[3] This explains the diction of the Our Father, "forgive us our debts" (Matt. 6:12).[4] The metaphor of sin as a debt is rarely attested in the bulk of the Hebrew Bible. But as soon as it became a commonplace to view a sin as a debt—and this took place early in the Second Temple period—it became natural to conceive of virtuous activity as a merit or credit.

This logical move was advanced significantly in rabbinic literature by the fact that the words for debt and credit (ḥôb and zəkût) are logical antonyms. It should come as no surprise that the rabbis were fond of telling stories in which a person's credits (zəkūyôt) were weighed against debits.[5] It was as though the heavenly courts were outfitted with a set of scales. When God needed to determine the future fate of a person, he would put the accumulated bonds of indebtedness in one pan of the scale and the credits in the other. In a rabbinic court of law, if the debits were heavier, then one would be required to make up the difference. For some crimes the offender would owe a sin offering (ḥayyāb ḥattā'ṭ)—that is, the sin offering would generate the currency needed to make good on the debt. For others a set of lashes might be owed (ḥayyāb makkôt); for truly serious crimes the penalty was death (ḥayyāb mîtâ). These graded penalties served to raise sufficient currency so as to satisfy the debt owed. As the apostle Paul, himself a good Second Temple Jew, put it, "the wages of sin is death" (Rom. 6:23). For every sin there was a cost.

3. See Gary A. Anderson, "From Israel's Burden to Israel's Debt: Towards a Theology of Sin in Biblical and Early Second Temple Sources," in *Reworking the Bible: Apocryphal and Related Texts at Qumran*, ed. Esther G. Chazon, Devorah Dimant, and Ruth Clements, Studies on the Texts of the Desert of Judah 58 (Leiden: Brill, 2005), 1–30.

4. The prayer would have sounded odd in Greek because the forgiving of debts was not thought of as a religious image.

5. Though the two words are standard in rabbinic Hebrew, it is most likely the case that both came into Hebrew as loanwords from Aramaic. The basic meaning of the verb ḥāb is "to lose either in battle, or in the courtroom." Because a person who loses is generally obligated to pay (either a fine in the courtroom or tribute on the battlefield), the nominal form ḥôb identified the payment that was owed. The verb zākâ, on the other hand, means "to win." It is a bit more difficult to see how this root produces a nominal form, "merit" or "credit"—and in Syriac it does not—but perhaps it is because the victor in battle can lay claim to the spoils while the winner in a court case is often entitled to claim damages. These spoils or damages become, in turn, the "credits" due the innocent or virtuous person.

But the God of Israel was not always so exacting in his standard of justice. Rabbi Yose ben Hanina taught in the late first century that when the scales of judgment were evenly balanced with bonds of debt on one side and acts of merit on the other, God would snatch away one of the bonds so that he could forgive the sinner.[6] In a more striking midrashic narrative, Moses was able to avert the hand of God, which was bent on destroying Israel after it venerated the golden calf, by recalling the merits that had accrued to the patriarchs (*zəkût 'ābôt*), among which pride of place would go to Isaac's willingness to offer himself as a sacrifice (Gen. 22).[7] In his consent to being sacrificed Isaac had done a work of supererogation that yielded an immeasurable outpouring of merit. And so it was altogether logical, the midrash reasoned, for Moses to ask God to draw from this "treasury of merits" so as to pay down the debt that had accrued to Israel's account.[8]

Yet it is important to note that the linkage of debt and credit is not driven by the unique semantic situation (*ḥôb* and *zəkût*) that exists in rabbinic Hebrew or Aramaic. For in early Syriac Christianity a similar construal of debits and merits exists—even though Syriac lacks the noun *zəkût* meaning "credit" or

---

6. See tractate *Pe'ah* 5a, in *The Jerusalem Talmud, First Order, Zeraim: Tractates Peah and Demay*, ed. Heinrich W. Guggenheimer, Studia Judaica 19 (Berlin: de Gruyter, 2000).

7. Isaac's own role in the Akedah is never highlighted in the Bible. However, the importance of Isaac's participation is a familiar subject in rabbinic literature, which transforms him into a willing participant who consents to his father's bidding. *Exodus Rabbah* (44.5), which dates to the eleventh or twelfth century, comments on Moses's demand that God remember Abraham, Isaac, and Israel so as not to destroy the nation Israel after it worshiped the golden calf (Exod. 32:13): "Why are the three patriarchs here mentioned? Because, said the sages, Moses argued: (A) 'If it is burning that they deserve, then remember, O Lord, Abraham who jeopardized his life in the fiery furnace in order to be burnt for thy name and let his burning cancel the burning of his children. (B) If it is decapitation that they deserve, then remember their father Isaac who stretched forth his neck on the altar ready to be slaughtered for thy name and let now his immolation cancel the immolation of his children. (C) And if it is banishment that they deserve, then remember their father Jacob who was banished from his father's house to Haran. In summary, let all those acts [of the patriarchs] now atone for their act [in making the calf]'; this is why he said: '*remember Abraham, Isaac, and Israel*.'" See generally, H. Freedman and Maurice Simon, *Midrash Rabbah*, 10 vols. (London: Soncino, 1939). For a full exposition of the merit of the patriarchs in rabbinic literature, see S. Schechter, *Aspects of Rabbinic Theology* (New York: Macmillan, 1909), 171–89; and Arthur Marmorstein, *The Doctrine of Merits in Old Rabbinic Literature* (1920; repr., New York: Ktav, 1968).

8. It should be noted that the "treasury of merits" was subject to considerable theological reflection, and it was not the case that this treasury could be invoked by just anyone at any time. Nor were the merits inexhaustible. Some rabbis, in fact, rejected the value of the treasury altogether and put the full onus of moral responsibility on the individual. Others argued that the treasury had been exhausted by Israel's past sins and that now Israel was dependent solely on the covenantal fealty of God alone. For details on this, see the discussion in Schechter, *Aspects of Rabbinic Theology*, 171–89.

"merit."[9] This can be seen from the way in which Saint Ephrem, in the fourth century, characterizes the victory won by Christ.

> Blessed is [Christ] who endured, withstood, and triumphed [*zākyâ'*];
> his head is held high with its crown.
> He is like a creditor [*mārē ḥawbâ'*]
> who demands his payment with a bold voice.
> He is not like me, too weak to fast, too weary for the vigil,
> The first to succumb [*ḥāb*]. My enemy is skillful.
> When he overcomes me, he lets me rise
> only to throw me down once more.
> O Sea of Mercies, give me a handful of mercy,
> so I can wipe out the note of my debt [*'eštar ḥawbāty*]. (*Hymns on
>   Fasting* 1.13 AT)[10]

The picture drawn here is that of Christ's encounter with Satan in the wilderness just after Jesus's baptism. There he is tempted by Satan and emerges as the victor (*zākyâ'*). In Ephrem's view, both his fast and his obedience in the face of temptation allow Christ to accrue enormous credit. He becomes, in Ephrem's terms, a creditor, or more literally, "a possessor of a bond [*mārē ḥawbâ'*]," who can boldly demand payment. Ephrem, however, laments his own condition. Unlike Christ, he is so weak that he would be the first to succumb in such a test (*ḥāb*). His only hope is that Christ will have mercy on him so as to wipe out his bill of indebtedness ('*eštar ḥawbaty*).[11] Ephrem must rely on the merits that his redeemer has secured.

The parallels to rabbinic Judaism are patent. As Isaac's self-sacrifice generates a credit upon which Israel can subsequently draw, so Ephrem prays that he might benefit from the victory of Christ, who, as possessor of a bond, can demand payment and distribute the proceeds as he pleases. The underlying concept of a "treasury of merits" is deeply embedded in the language and culture of Second Temple Judaism and two of its natural heirs, rabbinic Judaism and early Christianity.

But here I get a little ahead of myself. I want to begin my account of the role of merits in the Old Testament itself. For already in the book of Daniel we can see the firstfruits of an idea that comes to full harvest in later rabbinic and Christian thought. Indeed, much of the structure of how both Jews and

---

9. It should be noted that Syriac does possess the two roots *ḥāb* and *zkâ'*, but in this dialect of Aramaic they mean "to lose" and hence "to owe" and "to win" respectively.

10. For the Syriac text, see Edmund Beck, ed., *Des Heiligen Ephraem des Syrers: Hymnen de Ieiunio*, CSCO 246 (Louvain: Secrétariat du Corpus SCO, 1964).

11. For the source of this idea, see Col. 2:14.

Christians came to understand the process of forgiving sins follows from what we find in the book of Daniel.

King Nebuchadnezzar's "Debt"

In Dan. 4 King Nebuchadnezzar has a terrifying dream and summons Daniel to his court to lay bare its meaning. The dream consists of two parts. At first, the king sees a tree of great stature whose top literally reaches the heavens. Underneath its vast foliage, the animals of the field congregate to enjoy its shade and to consume its abundant fruit. Then the scene changes abruptly as an angel descends from heaven and orders that the tree be cut down, its foliage stripped and its fruit scattered. The stump, however, is to be left in the ground. The curious image of the tree transforms itself into the person of the king.

> But leave its stump and roots in the ground,
>   with a band of iron and bronze,
>   in the tender grass of the field.
> Let [Nebuchadnezzar] be bathed with the dew of heaven,
>   and let his lot be with the animals of the field
>   in the grass of the earth.
> Let his mind be changed from that of a human,
>   and let the mind of an animal be given to him.
>   And let seven times pass over him. (4:15–16)

The dream concludes with the observation that this sentence has been decreed by the angelic host so that all creatures will come to know that God Most High "is sovereign over the kingdom of mortals; he gives it to whom he will and sets over it the lowliest of human beings" (4:17).

Daniel realizes the ominous future this dream portends and hesitates to reveal its obvious meaning. But Nebuchadnezzar presses him, so Daniel must declare that the king himself is the gigantic tree that will be cut down and stripped of foliage and fruit. Because of the king's arrogance, he will be reduced to a near animal state until he comes to know that his grandeur comes solely from God.

There is a certain family resemblance between the king's dream and Pharaoh's dreams in Gen. 41. The dreams of both rulers portend a terrible future (seven consecutive years of severe famine or eviction from the throne), and both dreams require a righteous Israelite (Joseph or Daniel) to interpret them. But Pharaoh's dreams curiously occur as a *pair*. In one he sees seven gaunt and sickly cows emerge from the Nile and consume seven sleek and fat ones (Gen. 41:2–4). In the second he sees seven thin ears of grain blighted by the hot east wind. Joseph concludes that "the doubling of Pharaoh's dream means that the thing is [*firmly*] *fixed* by God, and God will shortly bring it about" (Gen. 41:32).

Nebuchadnezzar's one dream led Daniel to conclude that it could not possess the same degree of certainty of its fulfillment. In other words, there must be a way to avert or at least ameliorate what was coming. So Daniel concludes his interpretation of the dream with a short piece of advice. "Therefore, O king, may my advice be acceptable to you: redeem your sins by almsgiving (*ṣidqâ*) and your iniquities by generosity to the poor (*miḥan ʿănāyîn*); then your serenity may be extended" (Dan. 4:24 [4:27 Eng.]).[12]

Let us pause for a moment to consider the theological logic that informs the thinking of our biblical prophet. Daniel's advice to the king to redeem himself through almsgiving accords nicely with the debt imagery that we have been tracing. King Nebuchadnezzar is treated as though his sins have put him in terrible arrears. In order to be forgiven he must redeem himself by purchasing his way out of debt.[13] The Aramaic verb for "redeem" is *praq*,[14] the term that normally translates the Hebrew verb *gaʾāl* when it refers to redeeming a person who has been reduced to slavery by his creditors. In Lev. 25, a chapter that dedicates a considerable amount of space to the topic of debt slavery, we encounter a situation that is analogous to that of King Nebuchadnezzar.

> If resident aliens among you prosper, and if any of your kin fall into difficulty with one of them and sell themselves to an alien . . . he shall retain his right to be *redeemed* even after he has been sold [into slavery]. One of their brothers may *redeem* them . . . or, if they prosper, they may *redeem* themselves. (Lev. 25:47–49 NRSV alt.)

12. The translation is my own. The conventional translations vary considerably for reasons that will become clear below.

13. Compare the *Mekhilta of Rabbi Ishmael*, a third- or fourth-century commentary, on Exod. 21:30. Ishmael says: "Come and see how merciful he by whose word the world came into being is to flesh and blood. For a man can redeem himself from the heavenly judgment by paying money, as it is said . . . 'therefore, O king, may my advice be acceptable to you: Redeem your sins by almsgiving' [Dan. 4:24 (4:27 Eng.)]." For the text, see Jacob Lauterbach, *Mekilta de-Rabbi Ishmael*, 3 vols. (Philadelphia: Jewish Publication Society, 1935), 3:86–87.

14. Some would translate the term "to break off." Originally it meant "to untie, dismantle" or even "to take apart." It was often used to describe the action of removing a yoke from an animal or a slave. From there it assumed the secondary sense of "to redeem," since redemption of a slave is the removal of a type of "yoke" that binds him to his master. Because of the financial imagery of giving alms, it seems wisest to assume that *praq* is to be translated "redeem."

All instances of "redeem" here represent the Hebrew root *ga'āl*. All the Aramaic translations use *praq*, the same root used in the text from Daniel.[15] In Levitical law, when a family member falls into terrible debt and is sold into slavery,[16] one of two things can happen. A family member can intervene and redeem him (*ga'āl, praq*) or pay off his debt. Alternately, the debtor himself, should he prosper and raise the necessary funds, can redeem himself. If we understand King Nebuchadnezzar's plight according to the analogy of Lev. 25, we would say that his sins have left him in considerable debt. As Israel was once sold into slavery in Babylon,[17] Nebuchadnezzar is about to be sold as a slave so that he can begin repaying his debt through the currency of bodily suffering. But as in the case of the Israelite debt slave, he can purchase his way out of this state if his fortune changes and he prospers.

How can Nebuchadnezzar raise the currency to buy his way out of this predicament? Daniel's advice is that he redeem his sins by almsgiving (Dan. 4:24 [4:27 Eng.]). This verse is something of a watershed in the history of biblical thought, because here for the first time we have a clear and unambiguous reference to almsgiving as a penitential act. Precisely because of the seemingly high valuation Daniel places on a human work, this verse became a veritable battleground in the wake of the Reformation.[18] In rabbinic Judaism and early Christianity, Daniel's advice became a commonplace. Repentance without the giving of alms, in some sources, is unimaginable.[19] There is no

15. In the Septuagint translation one finds a variant of the Greek word *lytrōsis*, which means "redemption" or "ransom price."

16. Note that the person here is not technically a slave according to the theology of Leviticus. But for our purposes, this fine point is not significant. On this problem, see the discussion of Jacob Milgrom, *Leviticus 23–27*, AB 3B (New York: Doubleday, 2000), 2212–41.

17. In Isa. 40:2 we read that Jerusalem can now be consoled because "her term of service (as a debt-slave) is over, her iniquity has been paid off" (AT). On the translation of this verse, see Anderson, "From Israel's Burden to Israel's Debt," 19–24. In Isa. 50:1 Israel is described not as being sold into slavery by God but as having sold itself through its iniquities: "To which of my creditors have I sold you? Behold, for your iniquities you were sold" (AT). The subject of Israel as a debt-slave in Isaiah has been discussed by K. Baltzer, "Liberation from Debt Slavery after the Exile in Second Isaiah and Nehemiah," in *Ancient Israelite Religion: Essays in Honor of Frank Moore Cross*, ed. P. D. Miller, P. D. Hanson, and S. D. McBride (Philadelphia: Fortress, 1987).

18. As James A. Montgomery notes, this startling formula has been a *locus classicus* between Catholic and Protestant interpreters over the centuries. He quotes a tart comment from Matthew Poole's *Synopsis Criticorum* (1694): "Pontificii ex hoc loco satisfactiones suas et merita colligunt." We can loosely translate: "The papists gather from this verse their notions of satisfaction and merits." See Montgomery, *A Critical and Exegetical Commentary on the Book of Daniel*, ICC 24 (Edinburgh: T&T Clark, 1927), 238. The wealth of textual material on this verse that the debates of the sixteenth century spawned is immeasurably vast and merits a study in its own right.

19. For many early Christian writers, almsgiving was the single most important means for taking care of sins that occurred after one's baptism. A classic exposition of the matter can be

question that somehow the act of giving goods to the poor allows one to raise a form of "spiritual currency" that will alleviate the debt of sin. There is a considerable paradox here: the act of giving away money allows one to turn a considerable profit. For the time being, we must suspend answering how this might work. There is another question that we must tackle first. How can it be that the term we have translated as "almsgiving" (Aramaic ṣidqâ, a cognate of Hebrew ṣədāqâ) once meant "righteousness"?

Justice, Judgment, and the Jubilee

It is, in fact, surprising that the word for righteousness would come to be the standard designation for almsgiving. Righteousness, after all, is a term that conveys the sense of a just and equitable distribution of goods. And justice is usually considered blind: it is not a respecter of persons, be they rich or poor. The Bible itself gives elegant testimony to this fact: "You shall not render an unjust judgment; you shall not be partial to the poor or defer to the great" (Lev. 19:15). So how could the term ṣədāqâ come to mark an act of gracious benevolence toward the poor?

To answer this conundrum, we must turn to the cultural world of the ancient Near East. As scholars have long noted, it was not uncommon for a Mesopotamian king to declare a period of "liberation" when he ascended the throne.[20] This proclamation of liberation entailed the lifting of the obligation to repay one's debts. The political purpose of such a move is simple to understand. By lifting the obligation to repay an onerous debt, the king sought to rectify extreme disparities that existed between the rich and the poor that would, in time, threaten the stability of the kingdom. This act of generosity on the part of the crown was termed "the establishment of release."[21]

And it cannot be accidental that the Akkadian term for release, durārum, has an almost exact Hebrew cognate, dərôr. For no doubt Israelite culture experienced a similar set of problems with disparities between the rich and the poor. In the Bible, however, it was not the human king who declared a year of release but God himself. Every forty-nine years, the Israelites were

---

found in Cyprian's *Works and Almsgiving*, written in the third century. For the text, see Roy J. Deferrari, ed. and trans., *Saint Cyprian: Treatises*, Fathers of the Church 36 (Washington, DC: Catholic University of America, 1958), 225–56. See also the discussion in Roman Garrison, *Redemptive Almsgiving in Early Christianity*, JSNTSup 77 (Sheffield: JSOT Press, 1993).

20. There is a vast literature on this subject, but the best discussion of it and its implications for the Bible remains that of Moshe Weinfeld, *Social Justice in Ancient Israel and the Ancient Near East* (Minneapolis: Fortress, 1995).

21. See "Andurāru," in *CAD* 1/2:115–17.

commanded to inaugurate a Jubilee year by means of a trumpet blast on the Day of Atonement.[22] On that day a "release" or dərôr (Lev. 25:10) was proclaimed and every Israelite who had lost his land due to personal debt was freed from the obligation to repay and allowed to return to his ancestral patrimony. Because God was the owner of all the land ("The land shall not be sold in perpetuity, for the land is mine; with me you are but aliens and tenants," Lev. 25:23), it was fully within his prerogative to redistribute it according to his will.

For our purposes, it is important to note that this edict of liberation—which was an extraordinary boon to the poor and underprivileged—was also termed in Akkadian "the establishment of *righteousness*" (*mîšaram šakānum*; compare the Hebrew cognate *mîšôr/mêšār*).[23] Righteousness does not mean a blind application of equity toward all, but rather the specific act of *redressing economic injustice*. For this reason Isa. 11:4, a text about the coming of an ideal Davidic ruler, links the justice of the king with his compassion for the poor: "But with righteousness (*bəṣedeq*) he shall judge the poor, and decide with equity (*bəmîšôr*) for the meek of the earth."

As Weinfeld documents at considerable length, it is difficult to understand the prophetic pleas that Israel's ruling elites act justly without recourse to this larger concern of restoring equity to the poor and marginalized. From this perspective, then, we can understand why the root *ṣədāqâ* acquired the secondary meaning of "acting charitably toward the poor." For just as a king might demonstrate his righteousness by releasing the poor from debt, so the ordinary citizen could do his part through more personal acts of benevolence. Such acts of "liberation" on the part of a private citizen were appropriately termed *ṣədāqâ*, "[deeds of] righteousness."

Giving to the Poor, Loaning to the Lord

For a long while, however, many interpreters were not convinced that *ṣidqâ* in Dan. 4:24 (4:27 Eng.) meant "almsgiving." Although there can be no question that the word developed this meaning in rabbinic literature, what proof is there that it already had this meaning in Daniel? One argument in its favor

22. On the Jubilee year and the early history of its interpretation, see John S. Bergsma, *The Jubilee from Leviticus to Qumran: A History of Interpretation*, VTSup 115 (Leiden: Brill, 2007).

23. In the Bible *mîšôr/mêšār* often stands in parallel to *ṣedeq/ṣədāqâ*. As an example, note Ps. 9:8–9: "[The Lord] judges the world with righteousness [*ṣedeq*], he judges the peoples with equity [*mêšārîm*]. The Lord is a stronghold for the oppressed, a stronghold in times of trouble." In these verses, righteousness and equity are singled out as divine qualities that have a special concern for the rights of the poor.

is the Greek translation of Daniel, which renders *ṣidqâ* with *eleēmosynē*, the normal Greek word for "almsgiving."[24] Indeed, as Jan Joosten has shown, the Septuagint was aware of the rabbinic meaning of both *ṣədāqâ* and *ḥesed* as acts of mercy toward the poor.[25] The Dead Sea Scrolls also provide confirmation that the root *ṣdq* could mean almsgiving in this period.[26] Yet one might still wish to claim that, though the possibility of rendering *ṣidqâ* as "almsgiving" was a very real one, the author of Daniel was innocent of such a usage. To rebut this position, let us turn to Franz Rosenthal's landmark article on the problem.[27] As he noted, the key to translating this verse properly is noting its parallel structure. The command to "redeem your sins through *ṣidqâ*" is balanced by the clause "and be generous to the poor." Given that *ṣidqâ* can mean almsgiving, the parallel structure would appear to require that sense here.

Let us pause for a moment on the phrase "be generous to the poor [*miḥan 'ănāyîn*]." Like *ṣədāqâ*, the root *ḥnn* originally has a quite general sense. It usually means "show favor" or "be generous," and is not regularly associated with a specific act of generosity to the poor. However, it struck Rosenthal as significant that twice in the Psalms we find this root used in exactly this sense:

> The wicked borrow, and do not pay back,
> but the righteous give generously [*ḥônēn wĕnôtēn*]. (Ps. 37:21)[28]

> [The righteous] are gracious [*ḥannûn*], merciful, and righteous;
> it is well with those who lend generously [*ḥônēn ûmalveh*]. (Ps. 112:4–5)

24. Indeed, it is a curious accident that the English word "alms" is nothing other than a corruption of the Greek term *eleēmosynē*.

25. Jan Joosten, "*Ḥesed* 'bienveillance' et *eleos* 'pitié': Reflexions sur une equivalence lexicale dans la Septante," in "*Car c'est l'amour qui me plait, non le sacrifice . . .*": *Recherches sur Osée 6:6 et son interprétation juive et chrétienne*, ed. Eberhard Bons, JSJSup 88 (Leiden: Brill, 2004), 25–42.

26. See the collection of proverbs known as 4Q424 or 4QWisd, of which frag. 3.7–10 reads: "A man of means is zealous for the law—he is a prosecutor of all those who shift boundaries. A merciful and gracious man gives alms [*ṣədāqâ*] to the poor—he is concerned about all who lack monetary capital." Though the original edition (prepared by S. Tanzer in *Qumran Cave 4; Cryptic Texts and Miscellanea Part 1*, DJD 36 [Oxford: Clarendon, 2000], 342) testifies to the reading *ṣədāqâ*, I am dependent on Elisha Qimron's new readings (*The Hebrew of the Dead Sea Scrolls*, HSS 29 [Atlanta: Scholars Press, 1986]) for the rest of the line. Also note that the word occurs in the Qumran fragments of the book of Tobit (4Q200, frag. 2 [= Tob. 4:9]: [*ba'ăś*]*ōtekā ṣədāq śîmâ ṭôbâ*, "through your giving of alms, there will be a good treasure"). For the text, see Florentino García Martínez and Eibert J. C. Tigchelaar, eds., *The Dead Sea Scrolls Study Edition* (Leiden: Brill, 1997–98), 396–97. For a discussion of these lines, see Joseph A. Fitzmyer, *Tobit*, Commentaries on Early Jewish Literature (Berlin: de Gruyter, 2003), 171.

27. Franz Rosenthal, "*Sedaka*, Charity," *HUCA* 23 (1950–51): 411–30.

28. The biblical texts from Psalms and Proverbs in this section and the next have been slightly altered from the NRSV for clarity.

In these two texts there can be no question that the verbal phrase *ḥônēn wĕ-nôtēn/ûmalveh* means "give/lend *generously*."[29] The most likely recipients of such largesse would be disadvantaged persons in need of charity.

Yet these two examples, as Avi Hurvitz has noted, are just the tip of the iceberg.[30] They indicate the development of a more limited and technical usage of the root *ḥnn* that varies from the conventional meaning of the term. Strikingly, this special meaning is limited to two wisdom psalms and four wisdom teachings in the book of Proverbs. Isac Seeligmann noted long ago Wisdom literature's concern about non-interest-bearing loans to the poor.[31] There are eight such texts, four each from Psalms and Proverbs. First, from Proverbs:

> Those who despise their neighbors are sinners,
>   but happy are those who *give generously* to the poor. (Prov. 14:21)

> Those who oppress the poor insult their Maker,
>   but those who are *generous* to the poor honor him. (Prov. 14:31)

> Whoever is *generous* to the poor [*ḥônēn dal*] lends to the LORD,
>   and will be repaid in full. (Prov. 19:17)

> One who augments wealth by exorbitant interest
>   gathers it for another who is *generous* to the poor. (Prov. 28:8)

In each of these texts, to "be generous to the poor" means to provide the poor with material goods. Proverbs 14:31 and 19:17 make the somewhat startling point that the poor person can be a direct conduit to God. In 14:31 giving

---

29. Seeligmann has astutely observed that the verb *nôtēn* frequently has the technical sense of "to issue a loan" (see Deut. 15:7–11, esp. the use of the verb *natān* in v. 10). In that case, the verse from Psalms would be telling us that the righteous are quick and generous in their loans to the poor—loans they may not be able to repay. See I. Seeligmann, "Darlehen, Bürgschaft und Zins in Recht und Gedankenwelt der hebräischen Bibel," in *Gesammelte Studien zur Hebräischen Bibel*, ed. I. Leo Seeligmann, R. Smend, and E. Blum, FAT 41 (Tübingen: Mohr Siebeck, 2004), 319–48.

30. Avi Hurvitz, "Reshitam Ha-Miqra'it shel Munahim Talmudiyyim—Le-Toledot Tsemihato shel Musag Ha-'Sedaqâh,'" in *Mehqarim be-Lashon* 2–3 (Jerusalem: Center for Jewish Studies, 1987), 155–60.

31. He writes ("Darlehen, Bürgschaft und Zins," 319): "Eine besondere Bedeutung für Einsichten in die gesellschaftlichen Verhältnisse in Israel kommt den volkstümlichen Sentenzen zu, die uns in den Proverbien erhalten sind. Dies gilt auch für einige Psalmen, insbesondere die Weisheitspsalmen." ("Special insight into social conditions in Israel can be found in the popular aphorisms handed on to us in Proverbs. This is true, too, with some psalms, especially the sapiential psalms.")

a gift to the poor is akin to honoring God.[32] Most striking is 19:17, which declares that a donation to the poor is like making a loan to God. In the fourth-century Babylonian Talmud, Rabbi Yohanan expresses his shock at its theological implications: "Had it not been written in scripture, it would have been impossible to say it! It is as though the borrower becomes a slave to the one who offers the loan (Prov. 22:7)."[33] The Peshitta, the third-century Syriac version of the Bible, does Rabbi Yohanan one better and drops the idea completely through an intentional mistranslation.[34]

In any event the point is clear: what one does toward the poor registers directly with God. It is as though the poor person was some sort of ancient ATM through which one could make a deposit directly to one's heavenly account. Just as an altar was a direct conduit of sacrifices to the heavenly realm, so also the hand of the impoverished soul seeking charity.

The texts from the book of Psalms strike a similar note. For instance, in Pss. 37:21 and 112:4–5, quoted above, *ḥnn* also refers to a gracious gift to the needy. We note two further examples:

> [The righteous] are *generous* lenders
>   and their children become a blessing. (Ps. 37:26)

> May there be no one to do him a kindness,
>   nor anyone to be *generous* to his orphaned children. (Ps. 109:12)

It is striking that in all eight of these texts, the object of generosity is not humankind in general but the poor, downtrodden, and orphans. This

---

32. In the Bible the act of honoring God is frequently conjoined with the delivery of some specific gift such as an oblation or sacrifice. "To honor" someone entailed some sort of external display. (For this, see Num. 22:17 [cf. v. 37], where the king Balak promises to honor Balaam for his services, by which he means that he will pay him handsomely.) It is altogether appropriate, then, that the act of honoring God in this proverb is fulfilled by being generous to the poor. A charitable gift stands in the place of a sacrificial offering.

33. See *Baba Batra* 10a, in *New Edition of the Babylonian Talmud*, vols. 13–14, ed. Michael L. Rodkinson (New York: New Amsterdam, 1896–1903).

34. The Syriac in Prov. 19:17 reads: "He who accompanies [*metlawwe*, same root as the Hebrew term for loaning but a different meaning] the Lord shows mercy on the poor, he will be repaid according to his deeds." But the concept of making a loan to God was not unknown in the Syriac tradition. This wisdom teaching from Proverbs, though slightly reworked, found its way into the Peshitta version of Sirach: "Give to God as he gives to you with a good eye and a large hand; for he who gives to the poor, lends to God; for who is a repayer if not he? For he is God who repays and he will repay you ten thousand times the thousand" (35:10–11). And strikingly, one Hebrew manuscript of Sirach includes similar wording in the same location in a marginal note. See Pancratius Beentjes, *The Book of Ben Sira in Hebrew: A Text Edition of All Extant Hebrew Manuscripts and a Synopsis of All Parallel Hebrew Ben Sira Texts*, VTSup 68 (Leiden: Brill, 1997), 61.

certainly proves that these texts are not talking about the display of a general congenial disposition; the matter on the table is providing material support for the poor.

Righteousness and Deliverance from Death

If it is the case that a select group of late wisdom psalms and the book of Proverbs uses the root *ḥnn* to mark specific acts of generosity to the poor, then we might wish to examine whether the same would be true for the root *ṣdq* in these texts. Our suspicions are confirmed. In both Ps. 37:21, 26 and Ps. 112:4–5, it is precisely the righteous one (*ṣaddîq*) who is described as being generous (*ḥônēn*) with his wealth toward the downtrodden. In these psalms, the root *ṣdq* is linked with *ḥnn* just as we saw in Daniel. And in the very same group of Proverbs the noun *ṣədāqâ* is used in parallel to expressions about financial capital, as though *ṣədāqâ* referred to a way of handling one's monetary resources. Consider, for example, these very similar maxims in the book of Proverbs:

> The treasuries of the wicked do not profit,
>   but *ṣədāqâ* delivers from death. (Prov. 10:2)

> Riches do not profit in the day of wrath,
>   but *ṣədāqâ* delivers from death. (Prov. 11:4)

Both of these sayings contrast the way in which the wicked acquire goods with the way of the righteous. The point here is that wealth, which is often accumulated as a hedge against the future, will have no value if it is improperly valued. Jesus depicted quite well the dangers this proverb has in mind:

> Then [Jesus] told them a parable. "The land of a rich man produced abundantly. And he thought to himself, 'What should I do, for I have no place to store my crops?' Then he said, 'I will do this: I will pull down my barns and build larger ones, and there I will store all my grain and my goods. And I will say to my soul, *Soul, you have ample goods laid up for many years; relax, eat, drink, be merry.*' But God said to him, 'You fool! This very night your life is being demanded of you. And the things you have prepared, whose will they be?' So it is with those who store up treasures for themselves but are not rich toward God." (Luke 12:16–21, emphasis added)

Jesus is not critical in the least of how this man has acquired his wealth. For all we know, he may have been the most moral farmer in town. The subject of his critique has to do with the man's confidence that such a treasury will deliver him in a day of distress (see in particular the man's assessment, italicized in the quotation above).

But what do Prov. 10:2 and 11:4 mean when they say that righteousness will save from death? It seems highly unlikely that they are referring to the general behavior of a person. Proverbs are not in the habit of trading in vague banalities. More likely is the supposition that our author wants to contrast a righteous attitude toward the accumulation of wealth with a wicked one. It would seem that wickedness is defined not so much by how one acquires the wealth as by what one expects from it. Why else would 10:2 use the term "treasuries"? This word choice suggests the activity of *hoarding* one's money. So whatever would be the opposite of hoarding is most likely the type of righteousness that delivers from death. One possibility is that righteousness refers to the proper distribution of wealth. As we shall see, this was the way most readers of the Second Temple period interpreted this verse.

Good Treasure against the Day of Necessity

At the conclusion of my discussion of Dan. 4, I asked how almsgiving could repay one's debt. To get a handle on this let us turn to the book of Tobit, a book that was a rough contemporary to that of Daniel.[35] In chap. 4, Tobit gives what he believes is his last address to his son prior to his imminent death. In this context, he boils down the large corpus of Torah instruction that would have been at his fingertips to three main categories: tending to one's parents, giving alms, and selecting a proper wife. In terms of the larger structure of the book, there can be no question that pride of place falls upon the command to give alms. And in regard to that theme, Tobit has this to say:

> Revere the Lord all your days, my son, and refuse to sin or to transgress his commandments. Live uprightly all the days of your life, and do not walk in the ways of wrongdoing; for those who act in accordance with truth will prosper in all their activities. To all those who practice righteousness give alms from your possessions, and do not let your eye begrudge the gift when you make it. Do not turn your face away from anyone who is poor, and the face of God will not be turned away from you. If you have many possessions, make your gift

35. This book is difficult to place in terms of date and provenance, but I incline toward the view of those who date it to the third century and place it in Mesopotamia. Since we have fragments of the book in both Hebrew and Aramaic from Qumran, we know it cannot be any younger than the mid-first century BCE.

from them in proportion; if few, do not be afraid to give according to the little
you have. So you will be laying up a good treasure for yourself against the day
of necessity. For almsgiving delivers from death and keeps you from going into
the Darkness. Indeed, almsgiving, for all who practice it, is an excellent offering
in the presence of the Most High. (4:5–11)

There are many important ideas about almsgiving in this text, but I am
focusing on the final three sentences (vv. 9–11). Having urged his son to give
alms in proportion to what wealth he has, Tobias declares that by doing so
he will be "laying up good treasure for [him]self against the day of necessity. For almsgiving delivers from death and keeps [one] from going into the
Darkness." Clearly the clause "almsgiving delivers from death" is a verbatim
citation of the second half of Prov. 10:2 and 11:4. But I would claim that
the reference to a "good treasure" in Tobit also derives from our two proverbs. Because the words for the wicked and the righteous are frequently set
in parallel in the Bible, one could expect that the treasuries of the wicked
would be counterbalanced by the treasuries of the righteous. And since it
is in the very nature of good poetry to be elliptical, an astute reader of the
Bible in the Second Temple period could gloss both of our proverbs in the
following manner:

> The treasuries of the wicked provide no benefit,
>> but the treasuries gained by almsgiving save from death. (Prov.
>> 10:2 AT)
>
> Financial capital provides no benefit on the day of wrath,
>> but the capital gained by almsgiving saves from death. (Prov.
>> 11:4 AT)

If we fill out the logic of our poetic couplet in this fashion, we arrive at our
text in Tobit. What the author of Tobit has done is to interweave these two
proverbs to get his own unique formulation: "One should store up a good
treasure [in heaven by giving alms] against a day of wrath. For [it is] almsgiving [that] delivers one from death [and not hoarding one's money]."

Let us step back for a second and see where all of this has led us. The book
of Tobit, I contend, provides us with an important puzzle piece for my larger
argument. In the book of Daniel we are told that King Nebuchadnezzar is
likened to a debt slave who must redeem himself. What we did not learn from
Daniel is why the money one gives to the poor can be used to pay down a
debt that has accrued in heaven. According to Tobit, one of the surprising
features of giving alms is that it directly funds a treasury in heaven. For Tobit,

this treasury will be needed to save the family from future trials. In the book of Daniel, the treasury is needed to clear King Nebuchadnezzar's account of the sins he has accrued.

Before closing this section of my argument, I would like to consider a few other texts that address the linkage between a gift to the poor and a treasury in heaven. In the Gospels one thinks of Jesus's teaching: "Do not store up for yourselves treasures on earth, where moth and rust consume and where thieves break in and steal; but store up for yourselves treasures in heaven" (Matt. 6:19–20). And there is also the story of the rich young man who desires eternal life. In response to the question of what he must do, Jesus advises him to give his riches to the poor so as to acquire a treasury in heaven (Matt. 19:16–30 and parallels). But Jesus's teaching on the security of a heavenly treasury was already anticipated by an earlier Jewish sage, Ben Sira, writing in the late second century BCE:

> Help a poor man for the commandment's sake,
>> and because of his need do not send him away empty.
> Lose your silver for the sake of a brother or a friend,
>> and do not let it rust under a stone and be lost.
> Lay up your treasure according to the commandments of the Most
>> High,
>> and it will profit you more than gold.
> Store up almsgiving in your treasury,
>> and it will rescue you from all affliction;
> more than a mighty shield and more than a heavy spear,
>> it will fight on your behalf against your enemy. (Sir. 29:9–13 RSV)

Ben Sira anticipates the teaching of Jesus by advising his pupils not to let their silver come to ruin; rather they should lay up a proper treasure in heaven. But Ben Sira also acknowledges the teaching of Tobit when he declares that such a treasury will rescue from affliction better than any weapon made for battle.

The instruction of both Jesus of Nazareth and Ben Sira implies that coins put in the hands of a poor person do double duty. They help to alleviate the pain of poverty but are also directly transferred to the heavenly realm to the benefit of the donor. This double benefit is neatly summed up in a rabbinic teaching of the fourth century CE.

Rabbi Ze'ira observed: Even the ordinary conversation of the people of the Land of Israel is a matter of Torah. How might this be? A [poor] person on occasion will say to his neighbor: "*zĕkî bî,*" or "*izdakkî bî,*" by which he means: "acquire a merit for yourself through me."[36]

This is a remarkable text for a couple of reasons. First, the act of giving alms to a needy person is considered tantamount to depositing money directly into a heavenly treasury. Mere mammon becomes a heavenly merit (*zəkût*; also recall Sir. 29:10–11: "Lose your silver for a friend . . . and lay up your treasure [in heaven]"). But second, the saying shows how deeply into the popular imagination this notion of heavenly merits has penetrated.[37] This is not simply a learned trope that circulated among the sages; it was the idiom of casual conversation on the streets of fourth-century Israel. And no doubt this colloquial expression—precisely because it was an accepted commonplace—must have been much older than its occurrence in this particular text. Indeed, I would argue that the same sort of logic that informed the semantic development of the verb *zākâ* also informed the logic of Daniel's advice to King Nebuchadnezzar. Almsgiving funds a treasury in heaven.

Alms and Sacrifice

One more line is worth attending to in Tobit's speech. At the very close of this unit, Tobit adds, "Almsgiving is a *good gift* in the sight of the Most High for all who give it" (Tob. 4:11 AT). To call almsgiving a *gift* in the sight of God calls to mind an offering or sacrifice that one might bring to the temple. Indeed, the Greek term *dōron* regularly translates the Hebrew term for a donation to the altar, *qōrbān*. And the reason one brings a *qōrbān*, according to the book of Leviticus, is to put it on the altar in the presence of God. In other words, Tobit is suggesting that placing coins in the hand of a beggar is like putting a sacrifice on the altar—for both the hand and the altar provide direct access to God.

Ben Sira sheds ample light on this. In one section of his work, he considers a theme that is dear to the wisdom tradition: the fear of, or perhaps better, reverence for, the Lord. Of course, one of the most exemplary ways of displaying such reverence is by means of a gift.

> With all your soul fear the Lord,
>   and honor his priests.

36. *Leviticus Rabbah* 34.7, in H. Freedman and Maurice Simon, eds., *Midrash Rabbah*, vol. 2 (London: Soncino, 1939).
37. So Shlomo Naeh of the Talmud department of Hebrew University in a private communication.

With all your might love your Maker,
    and do not forsake his ministers.
Fear the Lord and honor the priest,
    and give him his portion, as is commanded you:
the first fruits, the guilt offering, the gift of the shoulders,
    the sacrifice of sanctification, and the first fruits of the holy things.
Stretch forth your hand to the poor,
    so that your blessing may be complete.
Give graciously to all the living,
    and withhold not kindness from the dead.
Do not fail those who weep,
    but mourn with those who mourn.
Do not shrink from visiting a sick man,
    because for such deeds you will be loved.
In all you do, remember the end of your life,
    and then you will never sin. (Sir. 7:29–36 RSV)

This important text juxtaposes two different classes of people through which one can demonstrate one's reverence for God: the priests and the poor. Fearing the Lord means both honoring the priest—that is, providing the priest with the requisite temple donations—and stretching out one's hand to the poor. Only with priest and poor in view can one's blessing be complete.[38]

The comparison of almsgiving to a sacrificial offering is met frequently in Sirach. Clearly, it is rather basic to his religious worldview. For example in Sir. 35:1–2 it is stated that

He who keeps the law makes many offerings;
    he who heeds the commandments sacrifices a peace offering.[39]

38. This idea is also present in the book of Tobit if one attends carefully to its opening chapter. The book opens with a reference to the many acts of charity that Tobit performed over the course of his life (1:3). And as soon as he arrives in Mesopotamia, we see him acting on this principle (1:16). Sandwiched in between is an account of Tobit's religious fervor while he resides in the land of Israel. There he is distinguished by his alacrity and zeal to bring sacrifices to the temple (1:4–8). The point seems to be that almsgiving in the Diaspora replaces revenue for the temple in Israel. His acts of charity are done against the backdrop of a less than obedient set of Jewish peers. His neighbors mock him for tending to Israel's dead (2:8), and eventually his wife mocks his charity (2:14). His devotion to the temple also sets him apart from his neighbors ("I *alone* went often to Jerusalem for the festivals," 1:6). The point seems clear: what the sacrifices signified in the land of Israel has now been assumed by almsgiving and other acts of charity.

39. Strikingly this text has set in parallelism the act of keeping the commandments and the giving of alms. I shall return to this theme in a future article. For now, one may wish to note that the term *hammiṣwâ* in rabbinic Hebrew or *miṣwatâ'* in Aramaic normally means "the commandment." It can be a shorthand expression for "almsgiving." In other words, almsgiving is *the* commandment. And accordingly, Tosefta *Pe'ah* 4.19 will declare that the giving of alms

> He who returns a kindness offers fine flour,
>> and he who gives alms sacrifices a thank offering. (RSV)

It is worth noting that a thank offering is simply a special type of peace of-fering and that fine flour, because it is the least expensive of the sacrificial objects one can bring, is something that can be brought *many* times. Sirach's famous exhortation to honor father and mother concludes with these words,

> For kindness to a father will not be forgotten,
>> and against your sins it will be credited[40] to you;
> in the day of your affliction it will be remembered in your favor;
>> as frost in fair weather, your sins will melt away. (Sir. 3:14–15 RSV)

This text is very close to the theological world of Dan. 4, for here we learn that acting charitably toward one's father can serve in place of a sin offering. As in Tobit, this kindness will not be forgotten but will be remembered to one's favor on a day of affliction.

Redemptive Giving

I think we have arrived at one of the more important reasons that Daniel advises King Nebuchadnezzar to redeem his sins through almsgiving. In a world that viewed sin as a debt and the poor person as a direct conduit to heaven, what more logical way could be imagined to balance one's bank ac-count than to put a plentiful deposit in the hands of the needy? According to the logic of the texts that we have been tracing, the money deposited in heaven in this fashion could be used to pay down what one owed on one's sins. And it is certainly not the case that Daniel's advice to give alms is some sort of backwater in the history of Jewish and Christian thinking about the forgiveness of sins. Quite the opposite is the case. Almsgiving becomes the most important means of securing divine favor. Consider this ancient tradi-tion attributed to Rabbis Meir and Akiba (second century CE):

> It has been taught: R[abbi] Meir used to say: The critic [of Judaism] may bring against you the argument, "If your God loves the poor, why does he not support them?" If so, answer him, "So that through them we may be saved from the

---

is equal to all the other commandments in the Torah (see the translation by Roger Brooks in Jacob Neusner, *The Tosephta* [Peabody, MA: Hendrickson, 2002], 75).

40. The text of the Hebrew here is quite difficult, and one should not make too much of this translation, which too confidently conveys a monetary idiom.

punishment of Gehinnom." This question was actually put by Turnus Rufus (Roman Governor of Judea) to Rabbi Akiba: "If your God loves the poor, why does He not support them?" He replied, "So that we may be saved through them from the punishment of Gehinnom." (*Baba Batra* 10a)[41]

And we find a similar set of judgments being made by Christian writers of the time. For example in *2 Clement*, written in the mid-second century, we read:

> Almsgiving is therefore as good as repentance from sin. Fasting is better than prayer, but almsgiving is better than both. Love covers a multitude of sins but prayer from a good conscience rescues from death. Blessed is every man who is found full of these things for almsgiving lightens sin. (16.4)[42]

The *Didache*, which some date to the first half of the first century CE adds,

> Do not be one who stretches out his hands to receive, but shuts them when it comes to giving. Of whatever you have gained by your hands, you shall give the redemption-price for your sins. (4.5–6)[43]

For the author of *2 Clement*, almsgiving is better than prayer for the forgiveness of sin. In the *Didache* we find language that directly echoes that of Daniel: almsgiving provides the redemption funds for what one owes. We should note that the Greek term that is translated "redemption-price" is *lytrōsis*; the same root is used to translate the Aramaic term *praq*, "redeem." For the *Didache*, as in Daniel, almsgiving provides a sort of currency to cover one's sins.

The Problem of Self-Redemption (*Selbsterlösung*)

Yet there is something unsatisfactory about the matter-of-fact way in which I have framed the issue. Is the act of giving alms nothing more than a simple financial exchange? Can human beings buy their way out of their sinful state? If so, the critique of the Protestant Reformers would seem to apply: a person saves himself by his own good works. Roman Garrison has confronted this

41. Isidore Epstein, *Baba Bathra: Hebrew-English Edition of the Babylonian Talmud* (London: Soncino, 1976), 196.

42. For the text, see Bart D. Ehrman, ed. and trans., *The Apostolic Fathers*, LCL (Cambridge, MA: Harvard University Press, 2003).

43. For the text, see James A. Kleist, trans. and annot., *The Didache, The Epistle of Barnabas, the Epistles and Martyrdom of St. Polycarp, The Fragments of Papias, The Epistle to Diognetus*, ACW 5 (New York: Newman, 1948).

problem straight on.[44] In his view there is a dramatic difference between the process of salvation outlined by the anonymous author of the *Epistle to Diognetus* and that of Clement of Alexandria. In *Diognetus* we read:

> For what else but his righteousness could have covered our sins? In whom was it possible for us, the lawless and ungodly, to be justified, except in the Son of God alone? O the sweet exchange, O the incomprehensible work of God, O the unexpected blessings, that the sinfulness of many should be hidden in one righteous person, while the righteousness of one should justify many sinners! (9.3–5)[45]

Here the "sweet exchange" that our writer has in view is the atoning death of Christ. No other covering for sin is possible "except in the Son of God alone." The gracious decision of Christ to die on behalf of humankind was so inexpressible that proper response was simply to stand in awe of it.

When we turn to Clement of Alexandria, we find a similar sort of elevated rhetoric about an exchange—but the subject matter is completely different. Rather than putting the emphasis on the divine work of salvation having been achieved by Christ, Clement seems to reserve his praise for the human act of giving alms.

> O splendid trading! O divine business! You buy incorruption with money. You give the perishing things of the world and receive in exchange for them an eternal abode in heaven. Set sail, rich man, for this market, if you are wise. Compass the whole earth if need be. Spare not dangers or toils, that here you may buy a heavenly kingdom.[46]

For Garrison, these two texts provide quite a challenge for the theological reader. Clement's praise of a human work seems to share the same stage with that of *Diognetus*'s praise of the work of Christ.

This is why the exalted position of almsgiving in the early apostolic tradition of the church has bothered Protestants. As Martin Hengel put it: "The idea of merit, taken over from Judaism . . . may be seen as a theological regression but it was this that provided a strong motive for concrete social and philanthropic

44. See his discussion in *Redemptive Almsgiving*, 11. In relation to Clement and the *Epistle to Diognetus* he writes, "The early Christian belief that the death of Jesus is the unique atonement for sin seems to be incompatible with the doctrine of redemptive almsgiving."

45. The translation is that of Michael W. Holmes, ed. and trans., *The Apostolic Fathers: Greek Texts and English Translations*, 3rd ed. (Grand Rapids: Baker Academic, 2007), 711.

46. Clement of Alexandria, *Who Is the Rich Man That Would Be Saved?*, 32. Text in G. W. Butterworth, ed. and trans., *Clement of Alexandria: With an English Translation*, LCL (London: Heinemann, 1919).

action."[47] For T. F. Torrance, excessive claims such as Clement's suggest that the original gospel message had fallen from view.[48] But this assessment puts Torrance in a peculiar predicament. The importance of almsgiving for the purposes of reconciliation is nearly universal in the early church. To say that it represents a departure from the gospel implies that nearly every early Christian thinker got the matter wrong. That cannot be correct. Perhaps the problem is that we have not properly taken the measure of this important theological idea.

The Enricher of All Borrows from All

There is much to be said on this topic and space prevents me from following all the important angles that could be discussed. Let me restrict my examples to that of one important thinker from the Syriac world, Saint Ephrem. Ephrem is a valuable witness on this subject because as an Aramaic speaker it was altogether natural for him to refer to sins as debts. For Ephrem, one of the fundamental purposes of the incarnation is for Christ to void the bond of indebtedness that stands against us (see Col. 2:14). But closely related to this is Christ's surprising intention to become a debtor to us. In Ephrem's *Hymns on the Nativity*, he writes:

> On this feast of the Nativity the openings in the curtains
> are joyous, and the Holy One rejoices
> in the holy Temple, and a voice thunders
> in the mouth of babes, and the Messiah rejoices
> in His feast as Commander of the host.
>
> On the birth of the Son, the king was enrolling
> the people in the census,
> so that they would be indebted to him. To us the King came out
> to cancel our debts, and He wrote in His name
> another debt, so that He would be indebted to us. (5.11–12)[49]

Ephrem refers to the census reported in Luke's account of the nativity (see Luke 2:1–2). The emperor's motivation for the census was to facilitate taxation and conscription. By enrolling all citizens, Roman officials could make

47. Martin Hengel, *Property and Riches in the Early Church: Aspects of a Social History of Early Christianity* (Philadelphia: Fortress, 1974), 82.
48. T. F. Torrance, *The Doctrine of Grace in the Apostolic Fathers* (London: Oliver & Boyd, 1948).
49. The translation is from Kathleen E. McVey, *Ephrem the Syrian: Hymns*, CWS (Mahwah, NJ: Paulist Press, 1989), 107.

sure all were held accountable for their civic obligations. Ephrem, however, contrasts the interests of the state with the interests of heaven. Our king, the Messiah, Ephrem writes, "came out to cancel the debts we owed him." That is, by his death he abrogated the bond that was held against us.

But God's intention was not simply to annul a bond that hung over the head of humanity. What, in the end, would be accomplished by such a one-time declaration? As soon as the period of release was over—that is, after baptism—we would be back in the "market," ringing up debts on our spiritual charge cards. For this reason, Christ writes a new bond, the purpose of which is to repair our desperate state. Under the terms of this new bond, Christ will become obligated to us. But what is Ephrem referring to here? Elsewhere in these hymns he provides a clue:

> He Who is Lord of all, gives us all,
> And He Who is Enricher of all, borrows from all.
> He is Giver of all as one without needs.
> Yet He borrows back again as one deprived.
> He gave cattle and sheep as Creator,
> But on the other hand, He sought sacrifices as one deprived. (*Hymns on the Nativity* 4.203–5)[50]

Ephrem describes God as one who "borrows from all." By this he means that, in condescending to make a covenant with Israel, the Lord made promises that allowed and enabled Israel to serve him—even though he has no need of human service. In the Old Testament, this service took the form of offering sacrifices. At the altar the One who was "without needs" acted as "one deprived." But now, in the era of the new covenant, the "Enricher of All" has taken a new tack. Rather than request a donation of food, he seeks to borrow from our purse. The hand of the needy replaces the sacrificial hearth.[51]

For Ephrem, the religious life requires that God engage humanity at a personal level. Otherwise God would remain nothing more than the detached

---

50. Ibid., 103.

51. One should note that in the Gospel of Mark the story of the rich young man (10:17–31) occurs within Jesus's threefold prediction of his own death and resurrection (8:31–33; 9:31; 10:32–34). The Gospel imagines that the donation of all one's goods to the poor is equivalent to taking up one's cross. This reading is confirmed by the disciples' reaction: when Jesus says that he must die by crucifixion, this is simply unimaginable for them (8:32). They are similarly shocked by Jesus's demand that the rich young man give all he has to the poor (10:26). I would suggest that Ephrem also understood the crucifixion and the distribution of all one's wealth to the poor as homologous acts of self-donation. Almsgiving becomes part of the economy of salvation that Christ has graciously bequeathed to the church.

"unmoved mover" of Aristotle. This belief in God's gracious self-condescension is very evident in this hymn:

> Give thanks to him who brought the blessing
> and took from us the prayer.
> For he made the one worthy of worship descend
> And made our worship of him ascend.
> For he gave us divinity
> And we gave him humanity.
> He brought us a promise
> And we gave him the faith
> Of Abraham, his friend.
> For we have given him our alms on loan
> In turn, let us demand their repayment. (*Hymns on Faith* 5.17)[52]

Ephrem here praises the sort of commercial exchange that has been effected by the incarnation. In exchange for our prayer, God provides a blessing. In exchange for our humanity, he has given us divinity. He gave a promise, but we must have sufficient faith to rely on that promise. We give him a loan and in return can be assured that it will be repaid. For Ephrem, the one who makes a loan to God through almsgiving is not simply doing a human work—he is making a public testimony to his faith. On this view, alms are not so much a human work as they are an index of one's underlying faith.

The relationship between belief and the granting of a loan is well reflected in a number of languages. For example, in English, the one who issues a loan is called a "creditor" (from *credere*, to believe) while in German the term is "Gläubiger" (from *glauben*, to believe).[53] The widespread attestation of this semantic phenomenon makes it difficult to ascribe it to semantic borrowing. The connection between issuing a loan and having faith must be so basic to human culture that it can arise in any language on its own. A midrash captures the linkage between faith and issuing a loan to the poor quite poignantly.

---

52. Text in Edmund Beck, ed., *Des Heiligen Ephraem des Syrers: Hymnen de Fide*, CSCO 154–55 (Louvain: Imprimerie Orientaliste, 1955).

53. One should note that the same phenomenon can be found in Hungarian (the noun *hit* means "faith" while a *hitelező* is "one who issues a loan") and Akkadian (see the entry for the verb *qâpu/qiāpu* in *CAD* 13:93–97). One of its meanings is "to have faith, believe" ("As for the words that So and So said to you, you said thus: I do not believe it [*ul qīpāku*]"), while another meaning is "to issue a loan" ("A woman tavern keeper who made a *qīptu* loan of beer or barley cannot collect anything that she has loaned out [after the remission of debts announced by the king]").

A certain philosopher asked a question of Rabbi Gamliel. He said to him, "It is written in your Torah: '*Give to [your needy kinsman] readily and have no regrets when you do so* (Deut. 15:10).' And do you have such a man that can give away his property to others and his heart would not be grieved? Such a person would eventually need to be supported himself!"

He replied to him, "If a man comes to borrow from you, would you give him a loan?" He replied, "No!" "If he brought you a deposit, would you give him a loan?" He replied, "Yes!"

"If he brought you someone that was not quite fitting to stand as surety would you give him a loan?" He replied, "No." "If he brought you as surety the head of the province would you give him a loan?" He replied, "Yes."

"Well then, is this not a matter of *a fortiori* logic? If when an ordinary mortal will go surety for him, you will issue the loan, how much the more so when he who spoke and made the world goes surety for him. For Scripture says, '*Whoever is generous to the poor lends to the* LORD'" (Prov. 19:17).[54]

No one gives away their hard-earned money without some reasonable trust in the recipient. But if the recipient is God, Rabbi Gamliel concludes, then one should be supremely confident. Ephrem would concur completely. In the stanza we cited from his *Hymns on Faith*, there are four nicely balanced couplets from which we learn the expectations that govern the relationship between God and humanity:

> God brings a blessing
>   we offer a prayer;
> God provides one worthy of worship
>   we offer worship;
> God provides something of his Godhead
>   we offer our humanity;
> God provides a promise
>   we supply the faith.

There is a great asymmetry in these pairs. What God puts on offer far exceeds what human beings provide in exchange. In the enacting of any of these modalities of relationship one is taught the radical dependence of the creature upon the Creator. But Ephrem surprises us with his rhetorical flourish. His last two lines provide a commentary on how we might respond with faith to the promises God has made:

---

54. My translation (AT) from *Midrasch-Tannaïm zum Deuteronomium*, ed. David Hoffmann (Berlin: Itzkowski, 1908), 84.

For we have given him our alms on loan,
In turn, let us *demand* their repayment. (italics added)[55]

The boldness of these lines is surprising—can one really *demand* repayment from God? Yet for Ephrem, only one who truly believes in God as the ultimate guarantor of his loan to the poor would have the temerity to demand its repayment. Scripture, Ephrem reasons, has shown that it is precisely in the hands of the poor that God's promise of grace is to be found. Timidity about the reward for such a loan reveals nothing other than a lack of faith.[56] At this point, we are well beyond the standard contours of a debate about the merits of human works.

The reference to the saints providing God with loans is so ubiquitous in Ephrem that one wonders whether the idea had shaken loose from its original biblical mooring and become a standard poetic trope. Indeed, all the acts of religious virtue practiced by the saints become a sort of currency that one could loan to God. Ephrem says of Julian Saba, the fourth-century Syrian ascetic:

> [God] will open his treasury and make you a
> possessor of notes of indebtedness regarding all that you lent him.
> Your prayers are recorded in his books
> Your treasures are guarded in his treasury.
> Rise up O community of ours and give thanks
> before our Lord for Saba everyday. (*Hymns to Julian Saba* 6.14–16)[57]

Like Christ before him, Saba's religious fervor has made him into a creditor.[58] In his new financial standing he can "demand" that God repay what was lent to him. But the shocking boldness of making such a demand of God is nothing other than an index of the underlying faith (credo, "I believe") of the creditor who trusted God sufficiently to make the loan in the first place.

55. The reference to giving alms on loan must derive originally from Prov. 19:17 (though on the problem of this verse in the Syriac, see note 34 above).

56. Ephrem treats the treasuries of the reliquaries in Edessa in a similar fashion in *Carmina Nisibena* 42.4. These boxes, which contain the bones of the saints, are thought to house something of the inexhaustible power of resurrection itself since the bones were thought to participate proleptically in those very benefits. Ephrem argued that the spiritual treasures in the boxes will actually grow in size the more they are plundered by the faithful. These treasures did not follow the rules of a zero-sum economy. It is as though the natural world has apertures of grace that God has designated for the use of his faithful. One demonstrates faith in God by availing oneself of their riches.

57. The text is from E. Beck, *Des Heiligen Ephraem des Syrers: Hymnen auf Abraham Kidunaya und Julianos Saba*, CSCO 322–23 (Louvain: Imprimerie Orientaliste, 1955).

58. See my discussion of *Hymns on Fasting* 1.13 at the beginning of this chapter.

Ephrem returns to the theme of making a loan to God when he praises the merits of Saint Abraham Kidunaya.

> Two heroic commandments: to love one's neighbor and God. You
>   bore them like a yoke. Between man and God you sowed a beautiful
>   deposit.
> You listened in order to act. You acted in order to issue a loan.
> You issued the loan in order to believe. You believed so as to receive.
> You received so as to reign.
> Your alms and prayers are like loans; in every location they enrich
>   those who take them, while to you belongs the capital and interest.
>   What you offer as a loan returns to you.
> The alms of the giver are like a loan that the Just give. For it is in the
>   full possession of both the borrower and the loaner. For it returns
>   to him with interest. (*Hymns to Abraham Kidunaya* 1.5–8)

What is striking in this poem is the phenomenological description of the life of faith. One might expect that faith would come first and deeds would follow. For Ephrem, though, the order is reversed: first one hears the command to give a "loan" to the poor, then one puts it into action; then, after putting it into action, one comes to believe. Again, the close nexus between belief (*credere*) and action (a loan, becoming a creditor) does not allow us to parse the behavior of this saint in the standard axis of faith versus works. Through the "work" of giving alms one enacts his faith.

For most of us, language that implies that God owes us something appears to be an unnecessary exaggeration that does not properly honor the Godhead. But for Ephrem, the holy witnesses Julian Saba and Abraham Kidunaya were simply taking proper advantage of what God has promised in Scripture. They become creditors of God only because God has allowed himself to be approached this way in the economy of salvation. In being generous to the poor, Saba and Kidunaya are not saving themselves. Rather, they are trusting in the promises that God has freely and publicly made. In the Old Testament, God acted as though he were in need of food. In the new age he is short of currency. In the former one could feed him at the altar. In the latter he is served through the hands of those in need.

But this is not the only part of Ephrem's text that is worth noting. It is striking how Ephrem conceives of the type of economy that is on display here. The person who loans to the poor turns out to be extremely wise in business because of the way in which God has set up this system of exchange. No one gets cheated in this arrangement; from every angle the beneficence of God is on view. "In every location [your alms] enrich those who take them," Ephrem declares, "while to you belongs the capital and interest. What you offer as a loan returns to you." There can be no question that the theology of Prov. 19:17 undergirds this text. Because God himself is the ultimate recipient of this loan to the poor, a different sort of economic exchange comes into view. And it is perhaps no accident that rabbinic writers have a similar attitude toward the way alms work in the heavenly economy, for the Mishnah declares that the generous soul that gives alms will retain the principal and in addition gain interest.[59] The operative modality here seems to be the infinite goodness of God, who takes our small donations and multiplies them in heaven. This deeply Jewish notion of God's graciousness finds a classic expression in the Gospels when Jesus instructs the disciples that one who gives alms will receive back a hundredfold in this life and eternal life in the age to come.[60]

And perhaps at this point in my argument we will not be surprised to see that Augustine (d. 430)—the classic representative of the importance of grace over works—is in complete agreement with what our rabbinic and Syriac texts have articulated. In commenting on Ps. 37:26 ("the righteous are generous lenders"), Augustine notes that there is something odd about this verse: "If you have lent to someone—handed out money as a loan, I mean . . . you expect to get back from the other person more than you gave." But the only way to get back more is to charge interest, and that is an act that Scripture as a general rule says "deserves blame, not praise." So how is one to understand this verse that praises the otherwise forbidden practice of taking usury?

> Study the money-lender's methods. He wants to give modestly and get back with profit; you do the same. Give a little and receive on a grand scale. Look how your interest is mounting up! Give temporal wealth and claim eternal interest, give the earth and gain heaven. "Whom shall I give it to?" did you ask? The Lord himself comes forward to ask you for a loan, he who forbade you to be a usurer (see Matt. 25:34–36). Listen to the Scripture telling you how to make the Lord your debtor, "Anyone who gives alms to the poor is lending to the Lord."[61]

Scripture, Augustine concludes, is not condoning the taking of interest from another person. Rather, interest can be drawn only when one loans to God. This means that the treasure that one establishes in heaven works by a set of rules that is entirely different from conventional savings programs.

59. See Eliezer Diamond, *Holy Men and Hunger Artists: Fasting and Asceticism in Rabbinic Culture* (New York: Oxford University Press, 2004), esp. chap. 2.
60. See Mark 10:23–31 and parallels and the lengthy discussion of this text in my *Charity: The Place of the Poor in the Biblical Tradition* (New Haven: Yale University Press, 2013), 149–61.
61. Augustine, *Expositions of the Psalms 33–50*, trans. M. Boulding (Hyde Park, NY: New City, 2000), 133.

One would expect that the relationship between a donation and its accumulation would be that of simple arithmetic. For every dollar donated, a dollar is accumulated. This is precisely the way a zero-sum economy works. No earthly bank could provide its customers with a two-for-one sale where one's money grows out of proportion with the dictates of financial markets. But the heavenly treasuries know no such restrictions. It would be better to imagine the growth of one's investment in heaven as one of geometric expansion, not unlike a graph that shows how an investment will grow if its generous rate of return is compounded year after year. Buying into this savings plan is like acquiring Google at a dollar a share. The very little we pay out provides sufficient leverage to open the gates of immeasurable divine generosity (so Augustine: "Give a little and receive on a grand scale . . . give the earth and gain heaven"). If we understand Nebuchadnezzar's situation against this frame of reference then this human king is hardly repaying the full extent of what he owes for his sins. Rather, the little he gives is enough to prime the pump of a flood of divine generosity. In sum, when we enter the realm of the heavenly treasuries we are a long way from *Selbsterlösung*.

Interpretation in the Wake of the Reformation

If we return to our text in Daniel with the insights we have gleaned from Ephrem, we can read it in a quite different light. And in light of our new reading, I think that much of what became so divisive about this text in the wake of the Reformation can be set to rest. Let me summarize my argument in three points and add a fourth for further reflection.

1. The giving of alms need not be construed as a purely human work.[62] God has gamed the system, so to speak, in a way that allows our small donations to

---

62. One should note the fine essays by Michael Root, "Aquinas, Merit, and Reformation Theology after the Joint Declaration on the Doctrine of Justification," *Modern Theology* 20 (2004): 5–22; and Joseph Wawrykow, "John Calvin and Condign Merit," *Archive for Reformation History* 83 (1992): 73–90. Root argues that the Thomistic understanding of the relationship between human merit (that is, the result of doing good works) does not contradict in any essential way the Reformation emphasis on salvation by grace alone. Wawrykow goes even further and argues that on most essential points, Calvin and Aquinas are on the same page regarding the value of human merits in the scheme of human salvation. As these two scholars note, everything depends on how we understand the relationship between divine and human agency in the performance of a merit-worthy action. If the achievement of merits is the result of the infusion of the Holy Spirit, then many of the worries Protestants harbor about this topic dissipate rather quickly. For the most recent assessment of the issues, see Charles Raith II, "Calvin's Critique of Merit and Why Aquinas (Mostly) Agrees," *Pro Ecclesia* 20 (2011): 135–67.

count against the immeasurable debt of our sins.[63] As Anselm of Canterbury would say in the twelfth century, the doing of penance at one level makes no sense for there is nothing that a human can give God that could repay the debt that is owed.[64] Anything one would give God is already his in the first place. Yet that does not mean that the practice of penitential deeds should be dispensed with. The sinner is something like a child who wishes to purchase a present for his mother for Christmas. Given the fact that his mother has provided the child with the funds, what exactly does the child give to her? At one level, the child gives nothing; he simply returns to his mother what was once hers. But at another level, this gift allows the child to part with something in order to express his gratitude. The gift does not create the relationship—the child need not do anything in order to be loved by his mother—but the gift does in some sense enact the love that characterizes it. So it is for King Nebuchadnezzar. By giving alms he is giving nothing of his own. He is returning to God what is God's. God is paid back a debt with funds that he provided in the first place. Yet at the same time, the gift is the king's free choice and enables him to display publicly his gratitude toward his maker. By giving alms to the poor, Nebuchadnezzar is given the chance to enact a faith in the God he had once spurned (here it is worth recalling that one who gives a loan to the poor becomes a creditor in its etymological sense). In other words the merit he will generate by giving alms is at the same time a declaration of faith and trust in the God he would wish to serve. As Ephrem wisely noted, it is not possible to divide the work from the faith it enables and generates.

2. I have argued that if these alms are imagined as accruing in a heavenly treasury then a whole new set of rules takes effect as to how that treasure will accumulate. When doing business with God, either at the sacrificial hearth or through the medium of a poor man's hand, it is not a matter of a one-for-one exchange. The little that one gives to God is repaid a hundredfold, nay a thousandfold. Only a logic such as this can explain how the paltry alms of

63. At this point, the practice of almsgiving shows strong parallels with sacrifice. Early theorists of sacrifice had posited that the exchange made at the altar was a simple quid pro quo—one got back what one put in. But as I have already written, such an account "fails to account for the asymmetry of the sacrificial process. How is that the human being can give so little (a single animal) and receive so much (the promise of divine blessing in its many varied forms)? Here one is greatly aided by recent anthropological theories of gift giving: the gods establish their superiority by giving more than they receive. . . . It is in this way that reciprocity can coexist with hierarchy, and that the sacrificial exchange can represent the gods' superiority over men." See my "Sacrifices and Sacrificial Offerings (OT)," in *ABD* 5:871–72.
64. See his *Cur deus homo* 1.20. Text in Anselm, *Cur deus homo: To Which Is Added a Selection from His Letters*, Ancient and Modern Library of Theological Literature (Edinburgh: John Grant, 1909).

a sinner like Nebuchadnezzar could ever repay the unfathomable debt that he owed.

3. There is yet another level to the problem the Reformation has bequeathed us. As we noted, the designation of alms as an act of ṣədāqâ ("righteousness") recalls the ritual of the Jubilee year, when the divine king established righteousness among his earthly citizens by mandating the release of all those who had fallen into debt slavery. This act, whether done by the divine king in Israel or the human king in Mesopotamia, was an act of pure grace. Those who suffered from terrible financial hardship had done nothing to merit this act of largesse. The only fit response of these debtors would be the expression of utter gratitude. By giving alms as his penance, King Nebuchadnezzar was enacting in his own person this model of divine love.[65] Paradoxically, it was this imitation of divine grace that would secure his own release from sin. Perhaps Nebuchadnezzar was to infer his own standing in the eyes of God from the way in which the poor would view him. In both instances an individual was giving without any expectation of receiving something in return. Nebuchadnezzar was, of course, something of a debt slave himself. By his enactment of grace toward the poor, he secured the showering of grace upon himself.

4. The sensitive reader will recognize that the entire discussion of this paper is not too distant from another issue that created grave misunderstandings in the wake of the Reformation: indulgences. For the granting of an indulgence was nothing other than the pope authorizing the utilization of some portion of the "treasury of merits" that had been left to the church by the work of Christ and the saints. As one could infer, this idea is deeply rooted in Second Temple Judaism and has a clear parallel in the rabbinic notion of the zəkût 'abôt, or the "merits of the patriarchs" (see note 7 above). Though this idea could be subject to abuse (especially when the "treasury" was understood as the pope's personal bank account which he could tap as needed), it is deeply rooted in the notion that outstanding acts of charity create a font of grace

65. Thomas Aquinas noted a similar problem in his *Summa Theologiae*. There he poses the question: "Is almsgiving an act of charity?" He begins by providing four reasons why one would think not. The second reason claims that almsgiving cannot be an act of charity because it was appointed to Nebuchadnezzar as a means of *satisfaction*, that is, as repayment of what was owed. Almsgiving pertains to the virtue of justice not charity. Yet having subsequently established that Scripture understands almsgiving as an act of charity (in the *sed contra*), Thomas explains that almsgiving can both repay what is owed on a sin *and* be an act of charity. For insofar as the giver of alms directs his heart to God (and so gives alms with "pleasure and promptitude and everything else required for its proper exercise"), his act of serving the poor becomes an act of worshiping (*latria*) God. As such, the giving of alms is concerned not simply with satisfying a penalty but with loving God as he is found among the poor. See *Summa Theologiae*, 2/2.32.1, in *Summa Theologiae: Latin Text and English Translation*, Blackfriars English Translation (New York: McGraw-Hill, 1975), vol. 34.

from which others can borrow. Indeed, Anselm's entire notion of the atonement in *Cur deus homo* rests on the notion that Christ's sacrifice created an infinite store of merit that he had no need for. In his love for humanity Christ ceded these immeasurable riches to the church. With the merits of Christ, any sinner could find the resources to cover his debts.

I think that it is fair to say that the practice of issuing an indulgence is not as unbiblical as one might have imagined. Indeed as early as the book of Tobit we can see that the act of giving alms was seen as a deposit to such a treasury that could save one from death. The "merits of the fathers" in Judaism and the "treasury of merits" in the church go beyond what is described in Tobit by presuming that other members of the faith community can derive benefit from the deposits of others. But this fact, in and of itself, need not cause alarm for the Christian reader, for Paul argued that the church is nothing other than the body of Christ and that what the head (Christ) has achieved redounds to the benefit of all the members. The treasury of merits is nothing other than the boundless credit that Christ (and the saints by way of their imitation of and hence incorporation into the person of Christ) gained through his passion. To pray that one might benefit from the power of those merits should not, in and of itself, offend the theological sensibilities of a Protestant.[66] That the bishop of Rome might have some say in how those merits are distributed is, of course, a different matter. But that is a problem of ecclesiology rather than soteriology and stands outside the framework of this modest essay.

66. Indeed the early Luther is quite revealing on this matter. Notice numbers 42–45 of his Ninety-Five Theses:
  42. Christians are to be taught that the pope does not intend that the buying of indulgences should in any way be compared with works of mercy [read: charity toward the poor].
  43. Christians are to be taught that he who gives to the poor or lends to the needy does a better deed than he who buys indulgences [whose main purpose was to aid the rebuilding of St. Peter's Church in Rome].
  44. Because love grows by works of love, man thereby becomes better. Man does not, however, become better by means of indulgences but is merely freed from penalties.
  45. Christians are to be taught that he who sees a needy man and passes him by, yet gives his money for indulgences, does not buy papal indulgences but God's wrath.
    (K. Aland, ed., *Martin Luther's 95 Theses* [Saint Louis: Concordia, 1967], 54)
  What emerges from this discussion is the significance of traditional acts of charity as opposed to the act of buying indulgences to assist in the refurbishing of Saint Peter's. Luther's critique is not church dividing; he is, at this point in his career, a reformer within the bounds of Catholic thought.

10

Purgatory

Sanctification in This Life and the Next

The biblical case for purgatory is generally made on the basis of two texts: 1 Cor. 3:13–15 and 2 Macc. 12:45b.[1] Most scholars, both Roman Catholic and Protestant, agree about the inadequacy of the former text. The latter text, being from the deuterocanonical books, is a somewhat unstable foundation on which to build a major doctrine. In this chapter I follow the lead of the Protestant theologian Jerry Walls and begin by probing the nature of sanctification. If the goal of the Christian life is to be conformed to the person of Christ, then what happens to those individuals who fail to achieve this state before their natural death? If Walls is correct, properly grasping the character of this doctrine requires that we attend to its central subject matter. Once we have done that, a different set of biblical texts falls into place. To be sure, these texts do not provide definitive proof of the doctrine, but they do provide analogical support for what the church has proposed. Again, we see that a proper grasp of what the doctrine intends to teach is crucial for determining whether it has a biblical basis.

An Indulgence is a remission before God of the temporal punishments due to sins whose guilt has already been forgiven, which the faithful Christian who is duly disposed gains under certain prescribed conditions through the action of the Church which, as the minister of redemption, dispenses and applies with authority the treasury of the satisfactions of Christ and the saints.

Catechism of the Catholic Church, §1471

1. The verse numbering of the NAB/NABRE differs from the NRSV at this point. What is numbered 12:46 in the NAB/NABRE is identified as 12:45b in the NRSV.

(Leah) commanded from her sickbed close to death that all the revenue (of her trust) would go to assist marrying orphans or for clothing the poor and similar causes—these are commandments which elicit reward from God.

A Jewish will from medieval Spain[2]

The Methodist philosopher Jerry Walls has encouraged his fellow Protestants to reconsider their aversion to the doctrine of purgatory.[3] He begins his argument by describing a context with which everyone is familiar: listening to a homily at a funeral in which the pastor confidently asserts that a particular uncle is enjoying all the delights of heaven regardless of the type of life he might have lived on earth. On the one hand, it is easy to see the pastoral reasons that would generate such buoyant optimism about a family member who has died, but on the other hand one is saddened at how sentimental efforts like this trivialize what the Christian tradition has taught about the seriousness of the choices we make in this world.

On purely pastoral grounds, one can make a case for the doctrine of purgatory, for this teaching allows us to give voice to the deep and legitimate hopes that are shared by the family and friends of the deceased while at the same time acknowledging that the work of spiritual transformation does not come to closure at death. The task of being transformed into the image of Christ continues even after our departure from this life.

But a pastoral case should not be confused with a theological justification. For that, we need to look a little deeper. Most Protestants will concede, and many will vigorously insist, that there is an inextricable connection between "justification by faith" (God's declaration of our righteousness based on the merits of Christ) and "sanctification" (our growth in holiness of life).[4] Saving faith cannot be simply an intellectual assent, nor can it be limited to a

---

2. The second epigraph is from a will found in Judah D. Galinsky, "Jewish Charitable Bequests and the Hekdesh Trust in Thirteenth-Century Spain," *Journal of Interdisciplinary History* 35 (2005): 423–40, here 437.

3. The citations of Jerry Walls in this chapter come from his "Purgatory for Everyone," *First Things*, April 2002 (http://www.firstthings.com/article/2002/04/purgatory-for-everyone). One should also consult his book *Purgatory: The Logic of Total Transformation* (New York: Oxford University Press, 2012). A helpful treatment of recent Protestant engagements with the doctrine can be found in Neal Judisch, "Sanctification, Satisfaction, and the Purpose of Purgatory," *Faith and Philosophy* 26 (2009): 167–85. In particular, see the articles he lists at 168n1.

4. Catholics, however, do not distinguish "justification" and "sanctification" in quite the same way as many Protestants. According to the *Catechism of the Catholic Church*, "Justification is not only the remission of sins, but also the sanctification and renewal of the interior man" (§1989, quoting the Council of Trent). I would like to thank my doctoral student John Sehorn for helping me express the distinctiveness of the Catholic position on this question.

onetime decision. Somehow it must press forward to remake the entire person in the image of Christ.

This leads Walls to pose what he calls an indiscreet theological question: "If salvation essentially involves transformation—and, at the same time, we cannot be united with God unless we are holy—what becomes of those who plead the atonement of Christ for salvation but die before they have been thoroughly transformed?" Appealing to the forgiveness of sins alone "does nothing to address the fact that many Christians are imperfect lovers of God (and others) at the time of their death." What began as a *pastoral* problem has now become a *theological* challenge. Being forgiven—which occurs most prominently at baptism—is a profound moment of grace, but it does not transform *completely*. For this reason, the words of C. S. Lewis (a Protestant in good standing!) ring particularly true:

> Our souls *demand* purgatory, don't they? Would it not break the heart if God said to us, "It is true, my son, that your breath smells and your rags drip with mud and slime, but we are charitable here and no one will upbraid you with these things, nor draw away from you. Enter into the joy"? Should we not reply, "With submission, sir, and if there is no objection, I'd *rather* be cleansed first"? "It may hurt, you know."—"Even so, sir."[5]

At the heart of Walls's argument lies the deep Wesleyan conviction that those who are called in Christ are called to a journey toward sanctification. As he puts the matter: "Wesleyans insist that God not only forgives us but also changes us and actually makes us righteous. Only when we are entirely sanctified or fully perfected in this sense are we truly fit to enjoy the beatific vision of heaven." Though it is perhaps theoretically true that God could complete our sanctification at point of death with a snap of his fingers, Walls asserts that this would entail a complete trumping of our free will. And sanctification is achieved by the cooperation of the human agent with the power of the Holy Spirit; the person is not transformed against his will. If this is the manner in which God has chosen to heal us in this life, why would that process suddenly stop with our death? Indeed, if God is willing to dispense with our free will in the next life, "it is hard to see why He would not do so now, particularly in view of the high price of freedom in terms of evil and suffering." This logic constitutes a compelling argument for a period of purgation after death that allows the person to complete the transformation begun at baptism.

5. C. S. Lewis, *Letters to Malcolm: Chiefly on Prayer* (New York: Harcourt, Brace and World, 1964), 108–9 (italics in original).

And what then of the classic Reformation rebuttal that Scripture provides us with no clear-cut support for such an idea? In Walls's mind this is not sufficient to settle the matter. "The deeper issue," he argues, "is whether it is a reasonable inference from important truths that are clearly found [in Scripture]. If theology involves a degree of disciplined speculation and logical inference, then the doctrine of purgatory cannot simply be dismissed on the grounds that Scripture does not explicitly articulate it."

Walls has provided some very good arguments for why contemporary Christians might wish to rethink their wariness about purgatory. (And I use the term *Christian* rather than *Protestant* intentionally. For though the doctrine of purgatory remains an official teaching of the Catholic Church [*Catechism*, §§1030–32], it has almost fallen into desuetude among practicing Catholics.) What I would like to suggest is that the argument for this doctrine goes deeper than just "disciplined speculation" and "logical inference." It is my thesis that purgatory depends upon a robust understanding of sanctification and merit, an understanding that is deeply grounded in the biblical text.[6] The doctrine of purgatory is not as far from Scripture as is often thought.

King David Forgiven

In order to see its scriptural grounding we need to consider how the Bible understands the concept of forgiveness. There is a widespread assumption that forgiveness is a yes or no proposition. One is either forgiven or not, end of question. In certain Protestant circles this is often associated with what is known as the "forensic" theory of the atonement. On this view, forgiveness is likened to a judge declaring an accused party innocent. The legal declaration depends not on the spiritual constitution of the forgiven but on the authority

6. My approach will be different from conventional approaches that appeal to biblical proof-texts such as 2 Macc. 12:38–45 NRSV and 1 Cor. 3:11–15. On the text from Maccabees, which does support the case I wish to make, see the commentary of Daniel Schwartz, *2 Maccabees*, CEJL (Berlin: de Gruyter, 2008), 443–44. In his discussion of 12:45, he writes: "The sacrifice was offered due to the fear that, despite the prayer mentioned in v. 42, death was not enough to atone for the sins of the fallen and they were in need of yet more merit, supplied by the sacrifice. The assumption is that if their sin is not atoned they suffer even more, and might even be excluded from resurrection. This implies that sinners are punished after their death, an implication that easily begets the notion of a place where that happens—Gehenna/Purgatory." Schwartz refers to the important article of Elmer O'Brien, "Scriptural Proof for the Existence of Purgatory from 2 Maccabees—12:43–45," *Sciences Ecclésiastiques* 2 (1949): 80–108. On 1 Cor. 3, see the comments of Joseph Fitzmyer (*First Corinthians*, AB 32 [New Haven: Yale University Press, 2008], 201), who writes, "Verses 14–15 do not speak of a purification or refining fire [for removing sins after death], but rather of a testing of constancy and subsequent deliverance achieved only with great difficulty."

of the judge. This is, of course, at considerable variance from the process of sanctification that Walls has taken such care to outline. There forgiveness is not so much a forensic declaration as a process. It begins at baptism with the infusion of justifying grace but presses on toward the complete transformation ("sanctification") of the individual. It is not, in any sense of the word, a simple yes or no proposition; it is not the "cheap grace" that Dietrich Bonhoeffer worried about. Salvation entails shedding the old Adam in favor of the new.

But it is important to emphasize that this does not mean that God's grace is active solely at conversion and that afterward persons press forward on their own. The Catholic-cum-Wesleyan tradition has often been accused of this Pelagian tendency. Rather, God's grace is understood to have spurred the will of the individual at conversion and to have continued to enable the person to make those choices that lead to sanctification. To paraphrase Augustine: Command of me, O God, whatever you will, but give me the grace to pull it off.[7]

Perhaps the best place to see how this process works in the Bible is the story of David. As careful readers of the books of Samuel have long noted, God's choice of David as his anointed comes at the cost of the rejection of Saul. On the face of it, one might think that this choice was decidedly unfair because David does not seem to be a character worthy of the office God has bestowed upon him. Saul, to be sure, has his faults—he twice violates the ritual commands that the prophet Samuel gives him (1 Sam. 13 and 15)—but these sins seem minor compared with those of David. In the event that will define his tenure as king, David spies Bathsheba bathing outdoors, has her summoned to his quarters, and sleeps with her; then, when he learns she has become pregnant, he has her husband murdered to cover his tracks. An unhappy chain of events to say the least. How could God prefer David over Saul?

The only way to make sense of what the Bible is doing here is to attend not to the sins themselves but to how these two kings respond to the reprimands made by their respective prophets. In Saul's case, the chief concern is personal vanity. Though he has the good sense to admit straightaway that he has failed ("I have sinned; for I have transgressed the commandment of the LORD and your words"), he qualifies the nature of his fault by foisting blame on his soldiers ("I feared the people and obeyed their voice," 1 Sam. 15:24). He then begs Samuel to accompany him to the altar to worship the Lord. When Samuel refuses, Saul reaches out to pull him back but instead catches

---

7. The citation is from Augustine's *Confessions* 10.29.40. On the surprising similarities between Aquinas and Calvin on the subject of human merit, see Joseph Wawyrkow, "John Calvin and Condign Merit," *Archiv für Reformationsgeschichte* 83 (1992): 73–90; and Charles Raith II, "Calvin's Critique of Merit and Why Aquinas (Mostly) Agrees," *Pro Ecclesia* 20 (2011): 135–67.

his robe and tears a piece from it. The reader is taken aback by this sort of desperation. The story ends as abruptly as it began: "Samuel did not see Saul again until the day of his death," our narrator reports. "And the Lord was sorry that he had made Saul king over Israel" (v. 35).

When David is confronted by Nathan, he, too, is condemned for his deeds, and in far harsher terms. Speaking in God's voice, the prophet tells David that a host of evils shall now bedevil him the remainder of his days in the royal office: "I will raise up trouble against you from within your own house; and I will take your wives before your eyes, and give them to your neighbor, and he shall lie with your wives in the sight of this very sun. For you did it secretly; but I will do this thing before all Israel, and before the sun" (2 Sam. 12:11–12). David immediately confesses, as Saul did, and Nathan rescinds the penalty of death that was David's due. But the other consequences of David's misdeeds cannot be so easily dismissed. As the story continues to unfold, we learn that his tempestuous relationship with his son Absalom leads to a successful coup d'état. In order to solidify his reign, Absalom gathers all of David's women onto the roof of the royal palace in order to sleep with them in full view of those in the city. David, meanwhile, flees the city in fear for his life.

What is striking, however, is the attitude of David as he makes his way down from Mount Zion into the Kidron Valley and then ascends the Mount of Olives, from which he turns eastward toward the Jordan Valley. He does not begrudge his lot in any way, shape, or form. All that is unfolding, he realizes, is the consequence of his own shameful actions.

Two moments in particular are quite revealing as to the state of his soul. First, the priests who have been in the employ of David are naturally anxious about the loss of their sacerdotal responsibilities. Chief among them would be service of the ark of the covenant, the most sacred object within the tent of meeting. Zadok, the chief priest of that time, takes care to fetch the ark before the exodus from the city and brings it to David as he heads east out of the city. But David is not pleased by his efforts. "Carry the ark of God back into the city," he commands. "If I find favor in the eyes of the Lord, he will bring me back and let me see both it and the place where it stays. But if he says, 'I take no pleasure in you,' here I am, let him do to me what seems good to him" (2 Sam. 15:25–26). Scholars have long noted the parallels of these lines to those of Jesus in the Garden of Gethsemane. Each speaker is eager to do his Lord's bidding, even at the highest possible cost to his own person. And both submit themselves to God's providence while following identical paths out of the holy city. David is to be especially commended for the way in which he puts his entire future as Israel's king in the hands of his God; this was the sort of piety God had hoped for when he took the risk of appointing a king back in the opening chapters of 1 Samuel. It was not the sort of piety that Saul was capable of displaying.

The second moment comes when David makes his way over the summit of the Mount of Olives. There he is met by Shimei, an opponent of David's from the beginning of his royal rule. As David marches along with his able warriors on both his left and his right, Shimei lunges forward and curses David: "Out! Out! Murderer! Scoundrel! The LORD has avenged on all of you the blood of the house of Saul, in whose place you have reigned. . . . See, disaster has overtaken you; for you are a man of blood" (2 Sam. 16:7–8). Not satisfied with expressing his contempt in words alone, he throws stones and flings dirt at David and those gathered beside him. David's military advisers are understandably shocked at this rude behavior and, noticing the vulnerability of this fellow, seek David's permission to do him in. But David will hear none of it. "My own son seeks my life," David reasons, "how much more now may this Benjaminite! Let him alone, and let him curse; for the LORD has bidden him" (v. 11).

One stands in amazement at David's response. He is the bearer of an eternal promise of God (2 Sam. 7). He knows, in a way Saul never did, that his throne is invulnerable. Yet in spite of this (or precisely because of it?), David will not use his favor with God as a pretext for exempting himself from the humiliating consequences of his sins. David proves himself worthy of the high calling God has granted him by virtue of his indifference to the perquisites of that office.

But we can say more. Though Nathan has rescinded the penalty of death that threatened David, not all the consequences of his actions can be undone. The effects of sin endure long after its perpetration.[8] One can take consolation in being forgiven, but one should not confuse forgiveness with the *process* of spiritual repair. Though one could say that David has to pay the full price for his sin, it would be misleading to leave it at that, as though in enduring the punishment he is like a wayward adolescent taking his licks at the woodshed. For God's punishment is never solely punitive in effect. The pain that David must endure is nothing other than the logical consequence of what he has done, and by submitting to this terrible moment of humiliation, he allows himself to be refashioned in the image of the God he longs to serve. Fleeing the city and humiliated by his adversaries, David puts his

8. Yochanan Muffs, "Who Will Stand in the Breach? A Study in Prophetic Intercession," in *Love and Joy: Law, Language and Religion in Ancient Israel* (New York: Jewish Theological Seminary, 1992), 9–48.

future solely in the hands of God. "If I find favor in the eyes of the LORD," David confesses, "he will bring me back" (2 Sam. 15:25). Put simply: not my will, Lord, but thine.

For someone committed to a forensic understanding of the atonement, the story of David's penance will remain an enigma. For according to this theory, once Nathan pronounced the words of absolution, the matter should have been closed. God had acted; human deeds can make no material contribution to the process. But for those beholden to a robust doctrine of sanctification, every detail in this story about David can be pondered and savored. Salvation is not limited to the punctiliar experience of forgiveness or justification (being declared "innocent"); it involves gradual moral and spiritual transformation—something like purgatory for David, at least in this world.

Almsgiving and Sanctification

So far I have made two points. The doctrine of purgatory depends on a robust understanding of sanctification, and this doctrine of sanctification is deeply grounded in biblical narrative. Forgiveness is not merely forensic; it entails transformation of the self. Yet one of the shortcomings of the example I provided about David is that one might get the idea that sanctification is simply a process of coming to terms with the effects one's sins have had on oneself and others. David's role in the narrative we examined is in many respects passive—he must *patiently await* what Nathan has prophesied to come about in order to demonstrate his spiritual growth. But the Bible knows of another, more activist strategy—the giving of alms. In order to understand how this comes about, we need to consider how sins are understood in the later sections of the Old Testament.

As I have argued elsewhere, the Bible does not understand sin as a purely philosophical concept but always explains both its gravity and means of repair by way of metaphor.[9] At the close of the Old Testament period and on into the New, the predominant metaphor is that of a debt. So the famous words of the Our Father, "Forgive us our debts as we forgive our debtors," or the many stories that Jesus tells about forgiveness that involve debtors and creditors. On this understanding, when one sins, one incurs a debt to God, and forgiveness will involve the repayment of what is owed. The means of repayment will vary depending on the story that we consult, but one particularly esteemed means of paying down the debt can be through charity to the poor.

9. Gary A. Anderson, *Sin: A History* (New Haven: Yale University Press, 2009).

There are a number of reasons one could give for the high esteem that almsgiving has enjoyed in the Christian tradition. But, as we saw in our previous chapter, pride of place should go to the scriptural precedent of King Nebuchadnezzar. When this wayward monarch approaches the prophet Daniel in deep contrition over his errors, Daniel famously advises: "Pay off the debt you owe for your sins through charity toward the poor" (4:24 [4:27 Eng.]).[10] (Nebuchadnezzar, we might add, was the model penitent sinner in early Christian homiletic literature for obvious reasons: if this heinous sinner could be forgiven, then anyone could.)

The novelty of Daniel's advice should not escape us. This text, as we saw in our previous chapter, reflects a major revolution in how the Bible understands sin. Whereas David had to make amends for what he had done by graciously *enduring the consequences*, Nebuchadnezzar was given the option of *taking active steps* in the repair of his own soul. Forgiveness was no longer dependent on awaiting what the future might bring but could be achieved by putting into effect a set of spiritual disciplines revealed by God.

And so the revolution that the book of Daniel sets in motion. Whereas David has to *await* what the future will bring in order to complete the repair of his soul, Nebuchadnezzar can *initiate* that process on his own. This is why almsgiving became such a prestigious act in the spirituality of Judaism and Christianity. It allowed the individual to enact the miracle of God's grace in his own life and assume the role of an active participant in the repair of the world.

The Raising of Tabitha

The book of Daniel shows how almsgiving pays down the debt of sin. But the Bible teaches us another important lesson about the power of almsgiving—its ability to deliver one from death (Prov. 10:2). In the book of Tobit, as we saw in an earlier chapter, this was primarily understood as restoring vision to Tobit and allowing him to see his son return home safely and then sire numerous grandchildren. In the wake of the bodily resurrection of Jesus, this proverb assumed a different meaning. We see this in bold relief in the story of the raising of Tabitha:

> Now in Joppa there was a disciple whose name was Tabitha, which in Greek is Dorcas. She was *devoted to good works and acts of charity*. At that time she

10. The slightly periphrastic translation of Dan. 4:27 (4:24 MT) is my own. For further information about the figure of Nebuchadnezzar in early Christian thought, see David Satran, *Biblical Prophets in Byzantine Palestine: Reassessing the Lives of the Prophets*, Studies in Veteris Testamenti Pseudepigrapha 11 (Leiden: Brill, 1995).

became ill and died. When they had washed her, they laid her in a room upstairs. Since Lydda was near Joppa, the disciples, who heard that Peter was there, sent two men to him with the request, "Please come to us without delay." So Peter got up and went with them; and when he arrived, they took him to the room upstairs. *All the widows stood beside him, weeping and showing tunics and other clothing that Dorcas had made while she was with them.* Peter put all of them outside, and then he knelt down and prayed. He turned to the body and said, "Tabitha, get up." Then she opened her eyes, and seeing Peter, she sat up. (Acts 9:36–40, emphasis added)

Most New Testament scholars ignore the references to Tabitha's generosity that I have put in italics and focus their attention solely on the power of Peter, acting in *imitatio Christi*, to raise someone from the dead.[11] But this ignores an important dimension of how the story has been told. She was not just a woman of faith, but as the author of Acts emphasizes, "She was devoted to good works and acts of charity." Furthermore, when Peter comes to her dead body, the biblical author takes care to place the recipients of her charity alongside the apostle: "All the widows stood beside him, weeping and showing tunics and other clothing that [Tabitha] had made while she was with them." To whom were they showing their tunics? Certainly Peter, but it is not hard to imagine that God was also being urged to take notice. That almsgifts could intercede on one's behalf was well known in contemporary Judaism and confirmed just a few verses later when in a different episode an angel tells the centurion Cornelius that both "your prayers and your alms have ascended as a *memorial* before God" (10:4).

Artists were also careful to draw our attention to the role of almsgiving in facilitating Peter's command that she rise from her bed, as a mosaic from the Palatine Chapel in Palermo so graphically shows.[12] In this image Peter stands at the left, his right foot striding toward the viewer while his left points in the direction of Tabitha. He raises his right hand in blessing while his left grabs Tabitha's wrist and pulls her forward. Behind the figure of Tabitha a garment is draped over the back of what appears to be a piece of furniture with spindles (perhaps a stand to display a piece of clothing?). That the garment belongs to Tabitha is clear from the fact that it wraps around her waist. But that it also belongs to the widows is obvious from the way it has been placed directly in front of them. That the intercession of the garment is at least as important as the prayers of the widows themselves is evident from the fact

11. Cf. Luke 7:11–17 (the widow's son at Nain) and 8:41–42, 49–56 (the daughter of Jairus).
12. The interested reader can find the image from the Palatine Chapel at http://www.christian iconography.info/sicily/peterTabithaPalatineChapel.html.

that it dwarfs the widows. One gets the impression that the garment has been cast as an independent actor into the scene; besides praying with the widows, it appears to lift Tabitha up from her temporary repose.

Cyprian, the bishop of Carthage (third century), was also very sensitive to the important role charity plays in our story. He begins his discussion by citing the words of Raphael in the book of Tobit about the power of almsgiving. It is superior to prayer and fasting because it not only can garner the attention of God but also can redeem from the power of death. He then turns to the story of Tabitha as a concrete example of Raphael's teaching. His retelling of the story takes care to put special emphasis on the intercessory character of the garments that Tabitha had woven: "When, in keeping with his apostolic kindness, [Peter] had come quickly, the widows stood about him weeping and beseeching, showing the cloaks and tunics and all those garments which they had earlier received, *and interceding for the dead woman not with their voices but with her corporal works of mercy.*"[13] Peter, for his part, Cyprian concludes, is aware of the power that these almsdeeds possess. Cyprian continues: "Peter judged that what was asked for in this fashion could be obtained, and that Christ would not fail to grant the widows' intercession, since He Himself had been clothed in the person of the widows" (see Matt. 25:40). Cyprian concludes his retelling of Tabitha's resurrection by bringing his readers back to the principal point—the miraculous powers of charity: "Such was the miracle wrought by the merits of mercy, such was the power of just works. She, who had bestowed on suffering widows the means of life, merited to be recalled to life by the entreaty of the widows." In Cyprian's mind one must not divorce the generosity of Tabitha from the reward it generated—her being raised from the dead. To be sure, Peter had acted in imitation of Christ, and it was through Christ's grace that she rose to new life. But Tabitha was no passive agent; her deeds literally spoke for themselves. Almsgiving rendered her ripe for resurrection.

The picture that I have been painting is just about complete. As the example of King David has shown, forgiveness in the Bible is far more than just being declared innocent; it requires a *process* of spiritual transformation. For David this meant dealing with the consequences of what he had done wrong as they slowly surfaced over his lifetime. Punishment was nothing more than a means to the larger goal of being fashioned anew. At the end of the biblical period the prophet Daniel shows us that this process can be accelerated through the act of almsgiving. Finally, Tabitha's example teaches us that charity allows

13. The translation is from Edward Rebenack, *De Opera et Eleemosynis* (Washington, DC: Catholic University of America Press, 1962), 65–67 (emphasis added).

one to amass a treasury of merit that can provide deliverance even from the bonds of death. But one essential element has not been explicitly addressed in the Bible: What happens to the person who dies before being able to amend fully his or her life as David was privileged to do? Here the church has had to use the hints provided in Scripture to extend the scope of its witness. We can see the results of such a reasoning process in the *Apostolic Constitutions*, a text from the fourth century that provided a number of theological answers to issues about which the Bible had not spoken clearly. In regard to the rites to be observed for the dead we read: "Let the third day of the departed be celebrated with psalms, lessons, and prayers on account of Him [Jesus] who arose within the space of three days. . . . And let alms be given to the poor out of his [the deceased's] goods *for a memorial* of him" (7.4.42, *ANF* 7:498). Like Tabitha's gifts to the poor widows in the book of Acts, alms given on behalf of the deceased function as prayers that continue to have their effect after death. No wonder that Henry VIII, even though he rejected the power of the Mass to deliver one from purgatory, made sure his will included instructions for substantial postmortem almsgiving.[14]

Almsgiving as Suffrage

We now have enough of the puzzle pieces in hand to tackle a larger theological problem that dogs anyone who wishes to understand purgatory. The Reformers rejected this doctrine because it implied that salvation could be purchased. But the Catholic Church does not make this claim.

Traditionally, the church has taught that there were three possible destinations for the deceased: (1) heaven, for the few who had achieved what John

14. Stephen Greenblatt notes that Henry VII, the father of Henry VIII, funded many charitable institutions as well as thousands of masses to be said in his name. Henry VIII's suppression of the monasteries where those masses were to be said was, in Greenblatt's words, "a son's violent repudiation of his father's attempts to ease his soul's torments" (*Hamlet in Purgatory* [Princeton: Princeton University Press, 2001], 23). But Henry VIII did not reject all of what the Catholic Church taught, as reflected in the words of his last will and testament: "We will and charge our Executors that they dispose and give in alms to the most poor and needy people that may be found (common beggars as much as may be avoided) in as short space as possibly they may after our departure out of this transitory life, *one thousand marks* of lawful money of England, part in the same place and thereabouts, where it shall please Almighty God to call us to his Mercy, part by the way, and part in the same place of our burial after their discretions, and to move the poor people that shall have our alms to pray heartily unto God for remission of our offenses and the wealth of our soul" (italics Greenblatt's). Henry VIII, Greenblatt concludes, "does not want to linger in the fires of Purgatory. Thousands of masses will not be sung to haste him toward Heaven, but a thousand marks could purchase the prayer of many poor people. In the unlikely event that he did not go straight to Hell, he would certainly have needed all of them."

Wesley would call Christian perfection; (2) purgatory, where most would go and await the moment of their completed sanctification; and (3) hell, where there was no chance of redemption. One could assist those in purgatory because, like King David, through repentance they had benefited from the grace of Christ and had received the promised salvation. What they awaited in the interim was their full sanctification.

But we must say even more than this. Purgatory has also been criticized as providing a mechanical model for understanding the process of sanctification. Günther Bornkamm, the highly esteemed New Testament scholar of an earlier generation, condemned Judaism and Catholicism on this ground, claiming that in this system the reward ceases to follow from the grace of God but rather "becomes a form of financial capital which individual observers of the law acquire for themselves in heaven and whose payout they can await with certainty."[15] In Bornkamm's mind, the problem with a concept like purgatory is that it allows the religiously minded person to think his good deeds have forced God to reward human works.

In order to respond to the worries of Bornkamm, one must note two things. On the one hand, it is true that for Catholics and Jews obedience to the divine law yields a "merit" that God has promised to reward. But this hardly compromises the freedom of God, for the rewards are based on a choice God has already made regarding the order of salvation. Even Calvin is willing to say that Tabitha was raised by virtue of her good works, as long as one bears in mind that those works were the result of a faith in God and the promises he has made. God has ordered the way of salvation in such a manner that human beings participate in the grace he has to offer. Acts of charity to the poor are a privileged way of participating in the love of God and thus constitute a claim to a future reward. On the other hand, things are quite different when we begin to speak about the transfer of merits from the agent who earned them to a second party. Here Bornkamm's worries are weighty and in need of clarification. The Dominican preacher Johann Tetzel (b. 1465) set the framework for Martin Luther's posting of his famous Ninety-Five Theses by proclaiming that "as soon as the coin [you offer] in the coffer rings, the soul from purgatory springs." By this witty saying, Tetzel implied that one could assure the release of a loved one from purgatory by a simple financial transfer. Yet as scholars have long noted, the rhetorical excesses of preachers like Tetzel did not fully represent the teaching of the Catholic Church in the sixteenth century. Performing

15. Günther Bornkamm, *Der Lohngedanke im Neuen Testament* (Lüneburg: Heliand-Verlag, 1947), 12.

an indulged action on behalf of another does not mechanically generate an intended reward.

When undertaken to benefit souls in purgatory, the giving of alms on behalf of the dead was identified as a suffrage, that is, as an *appeal* for mercy. The indulged charitable deed was simply a prayer manifested in human action. Consider the words of Bonaventure on the relationship of indulgences to the treasury of merits. Though he concedes the power of the pope (as holder of the "keys" of the kingdom [cf. Matt. 16]) over the distribution of goods from the divine treasuries, the pope's power does have limits. "Because the dead are outside the forum of the Church and of ecclesiastical judges," he writes, "it seems that absolution [of the temporal punishment due to one's sins] is not possible for them, except as a prayer for pardon; and so, to speak properly, indulgence is not granted to them." He goes on to say that if an indulgence can be called a "dispensation of the goods of the Church," one must concede that some concrete good has been extended to the intended party, but the church does not act as a "judge" (over the state of the deceased—that being solely the domain of God) but as a "supplicant."[16]

What we see here is a standard worry in the Bible about protecting the freedom of God. There is a reason why the captain of the ship on which Jonah had taken refuge exhorts Jonah to pray, saying, "Get up, call on your god! *Perhaps* [your] god will spare us a thought so that we do not perish" (Jon. 1:6). And the king of Nineveh similarly orders his citizens to fast, saying: "*Who knows?* God *may* relent and change his mind . . ." (3:9). Prayer and fasting certainly raise the odds of deliverance—they are merit-worthy actions—but they provide no hard and fast guarantee. And so for the giving of alms. In biblical terms they are meant to establish a memorial in heaven that God *may* be pleased to consult.[17] As with the widows who gathered around the bier of Tabitha, alms can become living prayers to God but never rigid financial instruments that compel his action. Though the notion of giving alms to fund a treasury in heaven is built on a metaphor of accounting, it cannot be reduced to purely monetary terms. When it works, it is because

16. Bonaventure, *Commentaria* 4.20.2.5 (4:538). For the translation, see Robert Shaffern, "The Medieval Theology of Indulgences," in *Promissory Notes on the Treasury of Merits: Indulgences in Late Medieval Europe*, ed. R. Swanson, Brill's Companions to the Christian Tradition 5 (Leiden: Brill, 2006), 35.

17. It is important to note that the Catholic Church puts special emphasis on the suffrage side of any indulged act of charity when it is done on behalf of the deceased. One cannot be fully certain that it will be of assistance; one can only pray on the deceased's behalf. But indulged acts performed by and applied to the faithful are more than simple appeals. They become merit-worthy when carried out through the assistance of divine grace. In those cases, God has promised to bestow a reward and can be trusted to fulfill his word.

of God's gracious decision to honor the merits of his saints; when it does not, it remains a testimony to God's unfathomable freedom: "[I] will show mercy on whom I will show mercy" (Exod. 33:19). A divine treasury does not compromise God's freedom; rather, it grounds that freedom in a manner that makes human supplication on behalf of the dead intelligible. A Protestant who ponders carefully what Bonaventure says should have no principled reason to reject prayers and alms for the dead *tout court*.

Purgatory in Judaism

So where does all this leave us? Is purgatory a retrievable notion for Christians in the twenty-first century? The answer to that question will surely be a matter of personal taste and ecclesial affiliation. But perhaps the joint declaration on the subject of justification by Catholics and Lutherans will lead more Protestants to reopen this door.[18] As a goad to that end, let me return to the evidence of Judaism. Over the course of the past decade or so, there have been a number of studies that have highlighted the surprising interdependence of Jews and Catholics on this doctrine. Judah Galinsky, for example, an Israeli scholar of rabbinic culture, has shown that in the mid-thirteenth to fourteenth centuries Jewish communities in Spain began to imitate the Christian practice of leaving sizable charitable bequests in their estate "for the benefit of their souls" after death.[19] The language used in these wills is so patently close to the words found in their Christian counterparts that it cannot be doubted from which direction the influence has come. Similarly, Stephen Greenblatt and Leon Wieseltier have noted that the traditional Jewish practice of having the son pray on behalf of a dead parent for eleven months after the parent's death ("kaddish") appears at roughly the same time that the doctrine of purgatory was gaining tremendous momentum.[20]

In the Jewish folklore that arises in the wake of this practice, it becomes clear that the father's safe arrival in the world to come is dependent on his son saying these words in synagogue. In Wieseltier's moving account of the year in which he said kaddish for his own father, he spends a good portion of his narrative exploring a tale that probably emerged in the early Middle Ages and was disseminated in an extraordinary number of copies and elaborated

18. See the epochal document *Joint Declaration on the Doctrine of Justification* (Grand Rapids: Eerdmans, 2000), coauthored by the Lutheran World Federation and the Roman Catholic Church.
19. Galinsky, "Jewish Charitable Bequests."
20. Leon Wieseltier, *Kaddish* (New York: Knopf, 1998); and Greenblatt, *Hamlet in Purgatory*.

in many variants. In the version from an eleventh-century prayer book known as the *Mahzor Vitry*, Rabbi Akiba is walking in a cemetery when he meets a naked man, black as coal, carrying a large amount of wood on his head. The rabbi stops him and asks why he is working so hard, offering to buy him from his master if he is a slave. The man answers, "The man whom you are addressing is a dead man. Every day they send me out to collect wood and use it to burn me." Why such a terrible fate? The man explains, "I was a tax collector and I would favor the rich and kill the poor."

"Have your superiors told you nothing about how you might relieve your condition?" Rabbi Akiba asks, and the man begs the rabbi not to detain him, because that will anger his tormentors.

> For such a man [as I], there can be no relief. Though I did hear them say something—but no, it is impossible. They said: If this poor man had a son, and his son were to stand before the congregation and recite [the prayer] "Bless the Lord who is blessed!" and the congregation were to answer amen, and the son were also to say "May the Great Name be blessed!" [a sentence from the kaddish], they would release him from his punishment. But this man never had a son. He left his wife pregnant and he did not know whether the child was a boy. And if she gave birth to a boy, who would teach the boy Torah? For this man does not have a friend in the world.

Deeply troubled by this, the rabbi traveled to the man's hometown and found that he had a son, but that the people of the town had not circumcised him. Rabbi Akiba promptly circumcised him and tried to teach him Torah, but he refused to learn. Rabbi Akiba fasted for forty days. A heavenly voice asked him, "For this you mortify yourself?" and the rabbi replied, "But Lord of the Universe, it is for You that I am preparing him." The Lord opened the boy's heart. Rabbi Akiba taught him Torah and the prayers and presented the boy to the congregation. When the boy recited the prayer "Bless the Lord who is blessed!" his father was released from his punishment.

The man then appeared to Rabbi Akiba in a dream and said: "May it be the will of the Lord that your soul find delight in the Garden of Eden, for you have saved me from the sentence of Gehenna." Rabbi Akiba responded: "Your Name, O Lord, endures forever, and the memory of You through all the generations!"[21]

The major theme of the story is evident to even the casual reader: "That the dead are in need of spiritual rescue; and that the agent of spiritual rescue is the

---

21. Wieseltier, *Kaddish*, 126–27.

son; and that the instrument of spiritual rescue is prayer, notably the kaddish."[22] So important was the practice that if a father lacked sons, or worried that his son might not fulfill the obligation of saying the appropriate prayers, he would leave money in his will to have someone else say the prayers. In some circles, the firstborn son of a Jewish family was referred to as his "kaddish." Should a man die childless, one could say he left this world without a kaddish.[23] This practice sounds a lot like the Catholic custom of having masses said in one's name, an ancient Christian practice that Augustine already alludes to when he speaks of his mother's death in book 9 of his *Confessions*.

Yet the key point, as both Galinsky and Wieseltier observe, is not the observation of the interreligious borrowing but the nature of Jewish mourning practices that made this borrowing possible. After all, there are many Christian practices that Judaism showed no interest in whatsoever. Why practices that one associates with the doctrine of purgatory? As it turns out, there is evidence stretching back to talmudic times that almsgiving was thought to benefit the journey of the deceased after his death. Mar Uqba, for example, was queried as to why he had designated such a high percentage of his money for the poor in his will. "My provisions are scanty," he replied, "but the road is long."[24]

Even more illuminating is the *responsum* of Rabbi Sherira Ha-Gaon, a leading authority of the Jewish community in Babylon during the tenth century CE. (A *responsum* is an authoritative rabbinic figure's response to a question formally submitted to him.) He said that alms given in the name of a particular deceased man could provide benefit. "If a Holy Man seeks mercy for the deceased whether with alms for the poor or without [that is, by prayer]," Rabbi Sherira writes,

> it is *possible* that the Holy One (Blessed be He!) will lighten his punishment in recognition of that meritorious person's merit. But if no [such person is available], we take the poor [who received alms on his behalf] to [his grave] to petition that he be granted mercy. If one of them has [sufficient] merits . . . they may *possibly* help him; but there is *no presumption* that it will help: May it be God's will that He accede to their petition.[25]

22. Ibid., 127.

23. Greenblatt, *Hamlet in Purgatory*, 7

24. The story of Mar Uqba can be found in the Babylonian Talmud, *Ketubbot* 67b. The subject of the journey of the dead to their heavenly repose and the role that mourning rites, prayer, and almsgiving play in rabbinic Judaism is a subject that warrants further study. For now, see the article of Saul Lieberman, "Some Aspects of Afterlife in Early Rabbinic Literature," in *Harry Austryn Wolfson Jubilee Volume on the Occasion of His Seventy-Fifth Birthday*, 2 vols. (Jerusalem: American Academy for Jewish Research, 1965), 2:495–532.

25. My translation (AT). For the original, see B. M. Lewin, *Otzar ha-Geonim*, vol. 4, *Tractate Jom-Tow, Chagiga and Maschkin* (Jerusalem: Hebrew University Press Association, 1931), 27–28.

What comes out clearly in this *responsum* is that rabbinic Judaism clearly imagines that the state of the person is not always settled at the time of death and that there is a period of time during which further purgation from sin is possible. Judaism, like early Christianity, imagines that specific human actions like prayer and the offering of alms *could* have an effect.

Once again we see some of the crucial elements of the doctrine of purgatory: sins require not just forgiveness but transformation, a process that can extend beyond the confines of a finite human life. That transformation, in turn, can be abetted by acts of mercy toward the poor (alms), deeds that generate merits that can deliver one from death. The final move is one in which these merits are potentially transferrable to another person. That final move goes beyond the explicit teaching of the Bible. Christians have the example of Christ to draw upon. The merits won by his passion and death apply to us. But it is striking that Jews come to a similar conclusion about the way merit can be communicated from one person to another. The fact that both faiths drew out such a similar implication argues strongly in favor of its roots in the common scriptural inheritance that Jews and Christians share.

The Enduring Appeal of Purgatory

I have tried to suggest that the practice of giving alms on behalf of the deceased is an ancient practice built on biblical texts such as Dan. 4:24 (4:27 Eng.) and Prov. 10:2. The terrible detritus left in the wake of one's sins can be redeemed by showing mercy to the poor, and charity provides the basis for the promise of resurrection. Such practices need not ruffle the feathers of anyone committed to a high doctrine of salvation *sola gratia*. Almsgiving was meant to participate at the human level in what has been done for us through Christ at the divine level. Certainly this is one of the main reasons why artistic depictions of purgatory in the Middle Ages paired the sacrifice of the Mass with the charity shown toward the poor: both actions are about showing mercy to the undeserving.

And finally, there do remain the pastoral considerations. It is striking that Stephen Greenblatt, a nonobservant, secular Jew, was drawn back to the ancient Jewish ritual of saying kaddish for his deceased father in light of what he learned from his study of purgatory. At the close of his prologue he writes: "This practice, then, which with a lightly ironic piety I, who scarcely know how to pray, undertook for my own father, is the starting point for what follows."[26] Later on in his narrative, when addressing the deeper human reasons for the development of such practices within the church, he writes,

> Anyone who has experienced the death of a close friend or relative knows the feeling; not only the pain of sudden, irrevocable loss but also the strange, irrational expectation of recovery. . . . These are not merely modern feelings; in fact it is startling that we continue to have them so vividly, since everything in the contemporary world works to suppress them. They were not suppressed in the past. The brilliance of Purgatory . . . lay in its institutional control over ineradicable folk beliefs and in its engagement with intimate, private feelings. . . . The notion of suffrages—masses, almsgiving, fasts, and prayers—gave mourners something constructive to do with their feelings of grief and confirmed those feelings of reciprocity that survived, at least for a limited time, the shock of death.[27]

Greenblatt's reflections bring us back to the profoundly pastoral dimension in the doctrine of purgatory. Who among us does not desire to show some sign of love for our friends and family whom we mourn at the graveside? Both Judaism and Christianity have long held that the prayers and alms of the faithful can be a benefit for our beloved dead. Salvation, after all, is both individual *and* communal in nature, and the doctrine of purgatory reminds us that our lives are not ours alone. We are linked in a great chain of being (one body, many members, to invoke the Pauline metaphor) to all of our beloved ancestors. We do not have to pretend that all are saved and by so doing make a mockery of our moral choices, but neither must we consign our beloved to eternal suffering.

Purgatory makes Christ's atoning sacrifice come alive in our religious practices. C. S. Lewis put the matter just about perfectly when he wrote:

> Of course I pray for the dead. The action is so spontaneous, so all but inevitable, that only the most compulsive theological case against it would deter me. And I hardly know how the rest of my prayers would survive if those for the dead were forbidden. At our age, the majority of those we love best are dead. What sort of intercourse with God could I have if what I love best were unmentionable to Him?[28]

Yes, spontaneous, perhaps inevitable—but also biblical.

26. Greenblatt, *Hamlet in Purgatory*, 9.
27. Ibid., 102–3.
28. C. S. Lewis, *Letters to Malcolm*, 107.

EPILOGUE

In bringing this book to a close, I would like to survey three themes that have coursed their way through many of the chapters. First, there is no one-size-fits-all model for defining the relationship of Scripture to doctrine. Second, one of the biggest impediments for the exegetical grounding of Christian doctrine has been the ignorance of biblical scholars as to what these specific doctrines actually wish to affirm. Finally, I have tried to underscore the importance of the Old Testament (as well as Jewish interpretation of the same) as a source for Christian doctrine. I will discuss them in this order.

Let me begin by attending to David Downs's criticism of my work on the subject of charity and purgatory.[1] He claims that the arguments found in my book on charity are nothing more than an apologetic for Roman Catholic thinking on the subject. In the guild of biblical scholars it is hard to imagine a more stinging rebuke than this! Truth be told, if my argument had been cast as an attempt to show why the doctrine of purgatory *ought* to be adopted by every contemporary reader of the Bible, then this broadside against my contribution would have merit. As Peter Brown's work has confirmed, praying for the dead is something that evolves over the first several centuries of the Christian church.[2] If it is to be located already in the Bible, as some have argued, it would be more in the form of hints and allusions rather than a clear and compelling teaching. What I have tried to show is that the way this

---

1. David Downs, *Alms: Charity, Reward, and Atonement in Early Christianity* (Waco: Baylor University Press, 2016). See esp. his very critical assessment of the central thesis of my book on charity (282–83n24).

2. Peter Brown, *The Ransom of the Soul: Afterlife and Wealth in Early Western Christianity* (Cambridge, MA: Harvard University Press, 2015).

doctrine evolved in the early church is grounded *analogically* in the data that Scripture has bequeathed to us.

I pointed, in particular, to two important themes: first, the notion that the forgiveness of sins and personal sanctification (what the Orthodox call theosis) are intimately related. Forgiveness is not simply God waving his hand and magically erasing whatever wrongs have been committed (the so-called forensic approach). Forgiveness is, at its core, a process of *transformation*, the ongoing task of being brought into conformity with the person of Christ. This was already the line of argument used by C. S. Lewis and Jerry Walls, two very respectable Protestant thinkers. Secondly, attention must be paid to the role that charitable deeds play in the development of the notion of personal "merit" in early Judaism and Christianity and how this idea is inextricably linked to spiritual transformation. Showing mercy toward the poor becomes a privileged means of rectifying the consequences of sin and configuring oneself to the figure of Christ, who was mercy incarnate. Indeed the standard word for mercy in the Greek Bible—*eleēmosynē*—is also a word that could, oddly enough, occasionally be translated "merit"!

Peter Brown's work has underscored how these two themes, deeply embedded in Second Temple Judaism and early Christianity, shaped the way late antique and early medieval Christianity thought through these issues. With those two building blocks in place, the development of the doctrine of purgatory can be seen as a natural outgrowth of scriptural modes of thinking. My claim has not been that the doctrine of purgatory is *explicitly* sanctioned in Scripture; the claim is rather that all the building blocks for that doctrine derive from biblical sources. I think that Walls gets the matter just right when he argues that the absence of an unambiguous scriptural prooftext is something of a red herring. "The deeper issue," he contends, "is whether it is a reasonable inference from important truths that are clearly found [in Scripture]. If theology involves a degree of disciplined speculation and logical inference, then the doctrine of purgatory cannot simply be dismissed on the grounds that Scripture does not explicitly articulate it."[3]

Other doctrines that we have examined, however, have a clear and more compelling scriptural grounding. One of those would be original sin. Here the primary problem was that most discussions take the perspective of Saint Paul as wholly determinative, and when his interpretation fails to meet the bar of what the original authors of the book of Genesis intended, then the doctrine loses its claim to a biblical foundation. On this score, Karl Barth

3. Jerry L. Walls, "Purgatory for Everyone," *First Things*, April 2002. http://www.firstthings.com/article/2002/04/purgatory-for-everyone.

has considerable utility, having noted what Jewish commentators had long observed: when exploring the question of human fallenness, the place to turn is the story of the golden calf.[4] As Barth puts it, and my discussion would certainly corroborate this, the move to locate the Fall in the garden of Eden was christologically driven. It gave to the stories of what I have labeled "immediate sin" the prestige of origins (to use a phrase coined by the great historian of religion Mircea Eliade). Readers of the Christian Bible need not reject the exegesis of the apostle Paul; rather they can appreciate it by being aware of its analogical origins. If one wishes, we could say Paul is simply grounding a basic biblical conviction about theological anthropology in a "midrashic" fashion.

The second theme concerns the *definition* of the doctrines themselves. Frequently biblical scholars will claim a doctrine has no scriptural basis because they do not understand what is truly at stake in the doctrine itself. The most obvious example of this would be that of impassibility. Anyone who is familiar with the landmark essay of Yochanan Muffs on intercessory prayer is aware of how deeply the portrayal of the deity as an *impassioned* figure is enfolded into the Bible. The notion of a detached, emotionless deity seems to be more of a Greek philosophical ideal than a biblical reality. But the concept of impassibility, in its Christian inflection, is not devoid of an emotional register. It is important to bear in mind that Cyril of Alexandria, the man most closely tied to the origin of this concept, spoke specifically of a Christ who *suffered* impassibly. What was crucial about this notion as Cyril developed it was the insight that one could say God suffered during the passion as long as one also affirmed that God remained unchangeable. Impassibility in this construal is more concerned with the integrity of God's providential guidance of human history than a description of various emotive states. Muffs noticed the same sort of concern in rabbinic reflections on the figure of Moses. In chap. 2 I argued that reading Moses's act of intercession in conjunction with the story of Jonah showed that biblical writers were familiar with the problem and had their own canonical solution to the theological issues at stake.

Biblical scholars face a similar challenge regarding the doctrine of *creatio ex nihilo*. Most scholars have presumed that the doctrine stands or falls on a proper grammatical parsing of Gen. 1:1. If that is the case, the doctrine rests on shaky grounds. Our investigation, however, showed that the doctrine's chief intent is to define the relation of God to the world, how divine immanence is

---

4. On the place of this narrative in rabbinic theology, see Joel Kaminsky, "Paradise Regained: Rabbinic Reflections on Israel at Sinai," in *Jews, Christians, and the Theology of the Hebrew Scriptures*, ed. A. O. Bellis and J. S. Kaminsky, Semeia Studies 8 (Atlanta: Society of Biblical Literature, 2000), 15–43.

related to transcendence and how that, in turn, provides a means of resolving the apparent contradiction between God's providential guidance of human history and human freedom. When viewed this way, the problem of how to understand the first verse of Genesis is relativized and the interpreter is directed elsewhere in the Bible to establish the truth of the doctrine.

Last, but not least, this book has dealt extensively with the relation of the Old Testament to the New. This has been a very troubled area in the field of biblical studies for a variety of reasons. One of the hallmarks of the modern approach to the Bible has been its sensitivity to human authorship and the historical contingencies that inform the production of the various documents in the Bible. To interpret properly any biblical text requires that one develop the requisite understanding of the historical conditions of the age in which it was written and be careful not to read later developments back into earlier texts where they do not belong. In the study of Mary this has meant attending to the distinctive treatment of her person in each of the Gospels and attending to the slow yet methodical expansion of her person in the early church. An outstanding example of this is the volume edited by Raymond Brown, *Mary in the New Testament: A Collaborative Assessment by Protestant and Roman Catholic Scholars.*

There is much to commend in an effort such as this. But the narrative of historical development that follows from such investigations cannot do justice to the way the fathers of the church approached the problem. For them, the act of plumbing the mystery of Mary's person was not limited to teasing out what could be learned from the references to her person found in the New Testament. Because the fathers believed that God had dwelled in both the temple in Jerusalem and Mary's womb, a typological link was drawn between the two. The reverence that developed toward the person of Mary cannot be understood without recourse to the reverence that belonged to the temple within the world of ancient Israel. Strikingly, even modern evangelicals have not been sensitive to this dimension of biblical piety and as a result limit their appreciation of Mary to the nature of her obedience and discipleship.[5] What I have argued is that the reverence toward the person of Mary that grows over the first few centuries is inextricably linked to the growing awareness of the unspeakable mystery of what it would mean to hold the second person of the Trinity in one's womb. This staggering thought is often absent in modern treatments of the development of her cult.

I might add, as a final addendum to this same issue, the role that Jewish exegetical tradition has played in several chapters of this book. In an important

5. See Timothy George, "The Blessed Virgin Mary in Evangelical Perspective," in *Mary, Mother of God*, ed. C. Braaten and R. Jenson (Grand Rapids: Eerdmans, 2004).

essay on this subject, Jon Levenson observed that Jews and Christians meet as equals in their study of the Bible only because they have bracketed their religious commitments in the pursuit of historical-critical rigor. Modern scholars tend to see only the benefits that historical criticism provides for ecumenical collaboration and ignore the cost those same efforts impose on the respective communities themselves. Though Jewish and Christian scholars can sit side by side in a modern department of religious studies, they accomplish this by bracketing the distinctive religious predilections that brought them to the Bible in the first place. In the concluding paragraph of his essay, however, Levenson suggests that all is not lost. If these historical critics can learn to interact with the broader senses of the scriptural text, then there may be the possibility that Jewish and Christian collaborative efforts can be fruitful for the adherents of each tradition.[6] In the course of this book we have seen numerous examples of where the Christian exegete can profit from attending to what the Jewish tradition has seen in the biblical text through the lens of rabbinic tradition. Perhaps no better example of that can be found than what I treated in chap. 9. Though rabbinic writings and the church fathers say different things about the value of charity and its relationship to an individual's religious life, the overall trajectory of development from their respective biblical origins is strikingly similar. The fact that these similarities exist between rabbinic and patristic commentators should compel the reader of the biblical text to return to the sources in order to discern what it is about them that generated these remarkably similar results.

6. Jon D. Levenson, *The Hebrew Bible, The Old Testament, and Historical Criticism: Jews and Christians in Biblical Studies* (Louisville: Westminster John Knox, 1993), 105.

SCRIPTURE AND OTHER ANCIENT WRITINGS INDEX

AUTHOR INDEX

Achenbach, Reinhard 13n30,
14n32, 15n38
Aland, K. 184n66
Anatolios, Khaled 52, 52n28,
57
Anderson, Gary A. 4n5, 54n32,
84n15, 87n21, 130n18,
137n3, 145n14, 153n2,
154n3, 159n17, 180n60,
182n63, 192n9
Anselm of Canterbury 182,
182n64, 184
Athanasius 116–17, 117n47
Auerbach, Eric 131, 131n20
Augustine *xviii*, 55–57, 57n39,
180–81, 189n7, 201

Baentsch, Bruno 12n24
Balthasar, Hans Urs von
36n20, 89, 89n25
Baltzer, K. 159n17
Barclay, John *xviii*, *xviii*n6,
50–51, 52, 52n26
Barr, James 59n1
Barth, Karl *xvi*, 37n21, 50–51,
73, 73n30, 206–7
Bauckham, Richard 114n41
Beck, Edmund 156n10,
176n52, 178n57
Beentjes, Pancratius 164n34
Berger, Klaus 99–100, 100n10
Bergsma, John S. 161n22
Bibb, Bryan 20n50

Bieble, Franz 123n5
Blenkinsopp, Joseph 61n4,
63n8, 70, 70n26, 71n27
Bloom, Harold 28, 28n9
Blum, Erhard 10n18
Bodner, Keith 4n5
Bonaventure 198–99
Bonhoeffer, Dietrich 189
Bornkamm, Günther 197,
197n15
Brecht, Martin 20n51
Brooks, Roger 171n39
Brown, Peter 53, 54n31, 153,
153n1, 205–6
Brown, Raymond 100–102,
102n14, 132n21, 208
Butterworth, G. W. 173n46

Calvin, John 81n10
Caquot, André 5, 5n6
Childs, Brevard *xii*, *xii*n1, *xv*–
xvi, 43, 43n9, 61n2, 61n5,
96, 101, 101n12, 135n1
Clement of Alexandria 173–74
Congar, Yves 113n40
Copan, Paul 42n5
Craig, William L. 42n5
Cross, Frank Moore 14n32,
14n33, 105, 105n21
Cyprian 160n19, 195
Cyril of Alexandria *xiv*

Daley, Brian 127, 127n12,
127n13, 128n14, 133
Damrosch, David 14n34,
67n19, 68n22
Davis, Ellen 24n3
Deferrari, Roy J. 160n19
Denis (Pseudo-Dionysius) *xiv*,
17n44, 19–20, 119–20
Derrida, Jacques 17, 17n44,
19–20
Diamond, Eliezer 180n59
Dillman, August 104, 104n20
Dionysius (Pseudo-Diony-
sius). *See* Denis
Di Vito, R. 60n1
Dolle, Dom René 125n10
Douglas, Mary 20n51
Downs, David *xviii*, *xviii*n7,
205, 205n1

Ehrman, Bart D. 172n42
Eire, Carlos 122n3
Enemali, Mark 4n5
Ephrem the Syrian 156,
174–82
Epstein, Isidore 172n41
Evans, Craig 101n13

Fishbane, Michael 3, 21n53
Fitzmyer, Joseph A. 136n2,
162n26, 188n6
Freeman, H. 155n7
Frevel, Christian 7, 8n12, 15n39

SUBJECT INDEX

Abraham 26, 30, 50–51, 57, 75, 77–82, 142, 155n7
  election of 77–81
Adam. *See also* sin: of Adam and Eve
  in the thought of Paul 59–60, 71–73
agency 57, 66. *See also* free will; God: freedom of
  relation of divine and human *xvi–xvii*
Akedah 77–78, 83–84, 155n7
  cost of election and 80–81
alms/almsgiving 54–56, 137, 141, 143, 158–60, 162, 166–69, 170n38, 172–74, 175n51, 179–84, 201–2. *See also* charity
  and deliverance from death 165–66, 193–96
  as gift or sacrifice 169
  redemptive 171–72
  and sanctification 192–93
  as suffrage 196–99
Ambrose 96
Antiochenes 123–25
apophatic theology / apophasis *xiii, xix*, 17, 19, 21–22
  versus kataphatic revelation 19, 21
  transcendence of God and 19
Apostolic Constitutions 196
Arius 95, 116
ark of the covenant 4–7
  divine presence and 7, 21, 103–9, 112

Athanasius 52, 116–18, 123, 125
atonement 15, 67n18, 173n44, 184, 187
  Day of 13, 66n14, 67, 161
  rite of 65
  theory of in relation to sanctification 188, 192
Augustine *xviii*, 55–57, 96, 129–30, 144n11, 180–81, 189, 201

Calvin, John 81, 129, 181n62, 189n7, 197
Catechism of the Catholic Church 56n38, 185, 186n4, 188
Chalcedon 99–100, 128–29, 133
chaos/*Chaoskampf* 44–46
charity *xviii*, 53–55, 58, 137, 141, 143, 170n38, 197, 202, 205, 209. *See also* alms/almsgiving
  loans to the poor and 161–65
  righteousness and 161–66
Christology *xii, xvi–xvii*, 31n13, 99–120
  of Antiochene fathers 123–25
  communication of properties and 116, 126
  figural relation to firstborn sons of Israel and 76–77
  impassibility and doctrine of 23–24, 38

representation and 23–24, 31–32, 36–38, 145–49
  tabernacle and 95, 99–102, 113–20
  Tobit and 135–36
Clement of Alexandria 173–74
creation
  and Bible's final canonical form 48
  ex nihilo xvi, xix, 41–58, 207–8
    central systematic-theological concerns of 48–53
    historical-critical interpretation and 41, 48
    versus pre-existent, eternal, and/or unformed matter 42–43, 45, 49–50
  human participation in work of 63–64
  without opposition 44–45
  sacrifice and 64
  stories of 60–61
  tabernacle/temple/sanctuary and 17, 63–65
Cyprian 195
Cyril of Alexandria *xiv*, 125, 126n10, 207

David 6, 68–69, 104n19, 105–7, 136, 147n18, 161
  sanctification and 188–92, 195–97
Day of Atonement. *See* atonement: Day of

218